CW01203780

DELVE, PIVOT, PROPEL

350 Writing Secrets to Elevate Your Storytelling and Transform Your Novel

FICTION KEY SERIES VOL. 1

STEVEN JAMES

OUTLIERS PRESS • SUSPENSE PUBLISHING

Delve, Pivot, Propel:
350 Writing Secrets to Elevate Your Storytelling
and Transform Your Novel
by
Steven James

PAPERBACK EDITION
* * * * *
PUBLISHED BY:
Outliers Press • Suspense Publishing

COPYRIGHT
2024 Steven James

PUBLISHING HISTORY:
Outliers Press • Suspense Publishing, Paperback and Digital Copy, December 2024

Cover Design: Shannon Raab
Cover Photographer: Shutterstock AI/Shutterstock.com
Cover Photographer: Shutterstock AI/Shutterstock.com
Cover Photographer: Chinch/Shutterstock.com
Cover Photographer: ASolo/Shutterstock.com

ISBN: 979-8-218-55026-4

All rights reserved. Without limiting the rights under copyright reserved above, no part of this publication may be reproduced, stored in or introduced into a retrieval system, or transmitted, in any form, or by any means (electronic, mechanical, photocopying, recording, or otherwise) without the prior written permission of both the copyright owner and the above publisher of this book.

All dialogue, descriptions, action, and characters in this book are fictitious. Names, characters, places, brands, media, and incidents are either the product of the author's imagination or are used fictitiously. The author acknowledges the trademarked status and trademark owners of various products referenced in this work of fiction, which have been used without permission. The publication/use of these trademarks is not authorized, associated with, or sponsored by the trademark owners.

BOOKS BY STEVEN JAMES

The Patrick Bowers Series
Opening Moves
The Pawn
The Rook
The Knight
The Bishop
The Queen
The King
Checkmate
Every Crooked Path
Every Deadly Kiss
Every Wicked Man

The Jevin Banks Series
Placebo
Singularity

The Blur Trilogy
Blur
Fury
Curse

Other Books
Synapse
Broker of Lies
Fatal Domain
Rift
Story Trumps Structure (Fiction Key Series Vol. 2)
Troubleshooting Your Novel (Fiction Key Series Vol. 3)
The Art of the Tale (with Tom Morrisey)

To my mom, who has always encouraged me to have an overactive imagination.

ACKNOWLEDGMENTS

*To Kath, Doug, John, and Shannon
for believing in telling worthy stories*

PRAISE

"Steven James has a knack for asking the right questions about what really drives a compelling story. Better still, he has the answers—for writers at all levels. Keep your highlighter handy: **Delve, Pivot, Propel** is a resource you'll turn to again and again."
—JESSICA STRAWSER, *Writer's Digest* Editor-at-Large and *USA Today* bestselling author of *The Last Caretaker*

"Steven James reliably teaches me things I didn't already know. As a testament not just to his humility and intellectual honesty but his seemingly inexhaustible curiosity, James continues to ask probing questions about how stories work, despite a 25-year career with over fifty books to his credit, including two on the craft of fiction. He keeps coming up with answers that break new ground, and his latest, **Delve, Pivot, Propel**, is no exception. Writers will especially benefit from his detailed examination of what he calls the "pivot," that part of the story that leads the characters into unexpected and yet inevitable directions. Writers at every level of accomplishment will find much to admire and take to heart in this brilliant new writing guide."
—DAVID CORBETT, award-winning author of *The Art of Character*

"Steven is both a deep thinker about story and someone who can make amorphous concepts as easy to understand as an Aesop fable."
—DONALD MAASS, renowned literary agent and fiction instructor

"Steven James is the best teacher I've ever worked with."
—ROBERT DUGONI, *New York Times* bestselling author of *My Sister's Grave*

"Steven is one of the best writing teachers I know. In 2014, when we

started Master CraftFest, which involves a day of extensive training with a small group of students at ThrillerFest each year, Steven was our first choice to be an instructor."
—STEVE BERRY, *New York Times* and
#1 international bestselling author

"Steven James is both a master storyteller and master teacher. Relatable, insightful, and down-to-earth with decades of experience, Steven's teaching is a boon for any writer wanting to improve their craft, lots of fun, and wonderful encouragement. I can't recommend the experience of learning from him highly enough."
—TOSCA LEE, *New York Times* bestselling author of
A Single Light

"The well-told story is often the turning point of the well-delivered speech, but it is also the element that mystifies many speakers. *The Art of the Tale* rectifies that deficit; it is like a master class in the oral storytelling tradition."
—Brian Jenner, Founder, U.K. Speechwriters' Guild

"[*Story Trumps Structure* is] the best book on writing you'll ever read. It's worth a thousand times its cover price to would-be authors."
—ERIC WILSON, *New York Times* bestselling author

"Steven is not only a deft craftsman of compelling fiction, but he's also a gifted communicator audiences love to hear and learn from."
—JERRY B. JENKINS, #1 international bestselling author

"Steven James is a master of the writing craft, as well as gifted teacher. He's both engaging and insightful. It's no secret that these qualities make him a Writer's Digest Conference attendee favorite. He knows what he's talking about and he knows how to effectively share his insights with others. Our post-conference attendee surveys confirm, beyond a shadow of a doubt, that he is one of the best. Certainly, we welcome his return."
—PHIL SEXTON, former publisher at *Writer's Digest*

DELVE, PIVOT, PROPEL

350 Writing Secrets to Elevate Your Storytelling and Transform Your Novel

FICTION KEY SERIES VOL. 1

STEVEN JAMES

PREFACE

I used to think I knew what a story was.

And I had pretty good reasons to: I had a master's degree in storytelling, I'd written over fifty books—including two on the craft of writing—and spent nearly twenty-five years teaching writing and storytelling around the world. So, when I began to question what I'd learned and what I'd been teaching in regard to story, let's just say it was more than a little unsettling.

But the thing is, I'd suspected for a while that I was missing something vital, that the typical paradigms were lacking, and that I needed a new approach to understanding story if I was going to grow as a storyteller.

So, what was the issue?

Well, ever since Aristotle wrote *Poetics*, people have been looking at story through a temporal lens: beginning, middle, end; first act, second act, third act; inciting incident, rising action, denouement.

And, while there's nothing necessarily wrong with that approach, I didn't love it because it gives the impression that stories are about a progression of events and not a collision of desires.

Stories are much more pursuits than they are reports.

So, the secret is not to ask, "What happens?" but "What is pursued?"

I wondered if there was a different conceptual framework that I could use to understand story, rather than just the traditional one of temporal progression.

From what I could tell, the existing story theories were missing something essential to great stories, a moment in the narrative that I've come to refer to as the Pivot.

I'll elaborate more on Pivots in the pages of this book, but for now, let me just say that three years ago as I was wrestling with all of this, I had an epiphany that transformed how I look at story and it led me to the idea of the Story Cube.

I believe that there are six elements to all great stories, and that we, as writers, can learn from them and can improve our writing dramatically if we begin to include them in each and every scene of our novels, no matter what genre we write.

I should mention that the concepts in this book are not just simply esoteric or theoretical ideas, but lessons gleaned from tens of thousands of hours of writing, editing, and rewriting a career's worth of novels.

In the following pages you'll learn to delve into a character's pursuit, Pivot into unexpected yet inevitable directions, and propel your story forward through unmet desire toward a riveting and unforgettable conclusion.

Take the journey with me and let's delve, Pivot, and propel our way into better stories, together.

—Steven James
Tennessee, 2024

CONTENTS

INTRODUCTION *16*
I: STORY PROGRESSION AND CHARACTERIZATION *20*
II: OPENINGS AND PROMISES *58*
III: ORGANIC WRITING AND CONTINGENCY *77*
IV: DIMENSIONALITY AND TENSION *97*
V: SCENES AND STRUGGLES *125*
VI: SETTINGS, TRANSFORMATIONS, AND DILEMMAS *167*
VII: STATUS, TENSION, AND BELIEVABILITY *194*
VIII: DIALOGUE AND DESCRIPTION *228*
IX: PIVOTS, CLOSURE, AND NARRATION. *259*
X: EDITING, REVISIONS, AND THE WRITING LIFE . . . *279*
APPENDIX A: THE STORY CUBE *303*
APPENDIX B: 100-POINT NOVEL WRITING CHECKLIST. *309*

INTRODUCTION

Let me guess.

Ideas distract you and scratch away at your attention so much that sometimes it's tough to be present, *really* present, when you're with other people.

Maybe it happens when you're at your son's baseball game, or your daughter's piano recital, or your wife's birthday party. You notice the sunlight dance across the batter's helmet, hear an off-key chord that takes you back to your own childhood, catch a snippet of dialogue that sounds *just right*, and you hastily scrounge for a scrap of paper and a pen, or whisper a transcribed note into your cellphone.

"*What are you doing, dear?*"

"*Nothing. Just had an idea.*"

"*Pay attention to the movie.*"

"*I will.*"

And you do.

Until another idea comes along. And you don't.

You're someplace else. Somewhere in your head. The people you're with will notice this, of course, and might think that you're either rude or aloof. So there's that. But there are also times when you *are* present, listening to your friends in a way that others don't—grasping the soft emotion and hard truth of grief and love and passion and pain hidden beneath their words.

So people don't know what to make of you.

You're a writer.

You believe in once upon a time. Angels and fairies won't leave you alone. Thoughts of the bogeyman still frighten you in the long moments just after dusk.

Ideas awaken you in the middle of the night and will not rest in the cage of your mind until you set them free.

And so, you scribble in notebooks at midnight.

Just as your predecessors did before you.

You get lost wandering among the musty shelves of used bookstores. You lurk in the corners of coffee shops. Eavesdropping is your secret addiction.

For you, tragedy is fodder. Sorrow, your muse. Pain, your barbed blessing.

You are a writer.

And this obsession devours your time—and since time is life, that means it's consuming huge, unrecoverable chunks of your precious, momentary, miraculous life. But for some reason, that doesn't bother you. It inspires you. And compels you to write even more.

You spend hundreds—thousands—of hours every year in voluntary solitary confinement, threading ideas through the needle-eye of your imagination until you see where they might lead. But it isn't *exactly* solitary. Because when you're alone with your story, you're never really alone. The characters keep you company. The story gets the best of you, and time races by.

Insight. Epiphany. Jolt.

Eureka!

From inside your car, you see raindrops easing down the window and realize that the drops are refracting the outside world to you upside down. And a story about magical rain rises within you. Where did it come from? Where do *any* ideas come from? You don't know, and you don't care because it's there now, and that's what matters, and you'll never look at a raindrop, or the world, the same way again. And that matters, too.

You care about the right word, the *only* word that'll make the sentence before you ring true. And so you wrestle with a phrase for half a day. Not because it makes any practical sense. Not because it'll pay off in bigger royalties. But because you can't help it.

Ah, yes. That's it! That's the way it should be. That's the way it should sound.

You force yourself to craft and edit and rewrite again and again until your story takes your breath away. And you question for a minute if there's something wrong with you.

And there is.

But there's something right with you, too.

You listen. You see. Yes, you do. And you find that you can't help but marvel at the searing pain and glorious grace and breathtaking mystery of life. At times, you find yourself wondering how anyone can make it through the day without either weeping at the horrors of our world or falling to their knees in awe at the glory of it all.

And so, you write.

Keeping stories trapped inside of you drives you nearly mad. It isn't something you can turn off. When people ask if you have trouble coming up with ideas, you don't know what to tell them because your problem isn't *coming* up with ideas; it's *keeping* up with them.

You put up with the long hours, the emotional turmoil, the constant self-criticism, and the bouts of heart-wrenching disappointment because there's a fledgling story there, and you feel compelled to set it free.

And so, yes, you write.

To set it free.

To set yourself free.

To set us all just a little bit more free.

You feel compelled to rip away the soothing, crippling lies about success that society likes to spin and to offer people a gift in their stead—laughter in the face of sorrow, a fist raised against the tyranny of the mundane, and a chance to *actually believe* the things we already know: that compassion is more important than possessions, that love is always worth the risk, and that no one dies wishing he'd spent more time in the cubicle and less time telling his daughter bedtime stories.

The blood-drenched passion you offer the world somehow scars you and heals you at the same time. Characters speak to you—those phantom artifices that share the truth through the lies you spin. You live with both eyes open, and you are consumed by the insatiable, unquenchable, uncompromising desire to get others to open their eyes as well.

This writing life of yours is risk and adventure and imagination. It is living on the razor-edged trill of a dream.

It's a wild life and perilous, and you're almost certain to fail. What will you do? You can't give up, so you must go on.

This book is written for you. This book is dedicated to you.

Write on, my friend. I'll show you how.

SECTION I

STORY PROGRESSION AND CHARACTERIZATION

1. "WHAT IS A STORY?"

Story is pursuit.

Simply put, stories result from characters desiring something that's out of reach and taking logical steps to get it, ideally in ways that are unexpected and yet inevitable.

If the characters don't want it, they won't reach for it and you have no story. If the object of desire is already within reach, they won't face any obstacles in acquiring it and you don't have a story then either—you only have the *premise* of a story. Throughout the story, characters will reach out for what they want in different ways and then readjust how they're striving to obtain it in response to the setbacks they face.

Stories aren't just about action but about desire-infused pursuit. They don't just include conflict (which holds the seed of tension but must be wedded with desire) for tension to result; they contain struggles that lead toward transformation (either of a character, a relationship, or a situation).

If nothing is pursued, your story never begins. So, with each scene, focus not so much on what the character is *doing* but on what he's *pursuing*.

2. "WHAT WILL THIS PURSUIT CONSIST OF?"

The movement of a story is inextricably tied to unmet desire. For instance, desire of something tangible (the fabled amulet), a new identity (confidence/self-assurance), an ideal (justice), or an individual (a lover).

Unmet desire both creates tension and initiates pursuit. Because of this, it is the engine of every story. Without unmet desire, your character would have no motivation to act, no intentionality to her choices, and no reason to pursue anything.

Characters will often desire (and therefore pursue) something that they perceive to be necessary in their quest to find happiness or fulfillment. Or, they might be trying to avoid something that will disrupt their current situation and (they believe) decrease their contentment or joy.

In either case, remember that the pursuit will be for something that's desired, out of reach, and—in the character's eyes at that point in the story—worth pursuing.

Your story will move through the journey of promise to plight to predicament to payoff: "At first…but then…and so…until at last…therefore…so from then on…"

3. "IF STORY IS PURSUIT, THEN WHAT IS PLOT?"

Plot is simply the journey that the *character* takes through the *setting* during his *pursuit* to overcome his *struggle*. Those four elements occur within all stories: character, setting, pursuit, and struggle. If you eliminate any one of them you cease to have a story. Taken alone, they don't guarantee that you'll tell a *great* story, but with all four, at least you'll be able to shape a story that holds together.

To elevate your story, you'll also include a *pivot* that moves the story in an unexpected and yet logical direction, and a *payoff* that carries deeper meaning, that makes the story worth reading, and that will touch your readers' lives and make them glad that they read your book.

Great stories include all six elements: character, setting, pursuit, struggle, pivot, and payoff.

4. "CAN YOU ELABORATE ON THAT?"

Think of a cube. Each side of the cube represents one element of a well-told story. Throughout the book we'll be examining each of these in depth. (Appendix A "The Story Cube" also includes detailed explanations and reflection questions for exploring each of the sides of the cube.)

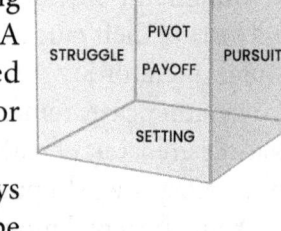

As you read through this book, always be on the lookout for how you can shape every scene in your story—and the story as a whole—to contain all six elements.

5. "HOW IMPORTANT IS PLOT?"

Not nearly as important as pursuit.

The character's journey through the story will either reveal deeper characterization or lead her toward transformation. That pathway includes action with intention and desire with consequences.

Rather than trying to "plot out" or outline your story, focus instead on following the progression of the characters along the natural route they take in pursuit of what they desire most. Plot is the by-product of pursuit, not its precursor. It is the result of pursuit, not the other way around.

As Ray Bradbury noted, "Remember: *Plot* is no more than footprints left in the snow *after* your characters have run by on their way to incredible destinations. *Plot* is observed after the fact rather than before. It cannot precede action. It is the chart that remains when an action is through."

Desire drives story. Plot is the smoke that's left in its wake.

6. "IS THIS PATHWAY OF PURSUIT THE SAME FOR EVERY GENRE?"

The pathway may look different, but those six elements will remain. As your characters pursue their desires, they'll take believable and natural steps to achieve their goals and then—as they face increasingly more devastating setbacks—make meaningful choices that they believe will take them closer to their objective.

Eventually, they'll come to a place in which all seems lost, but then solve their problem in a way that's at the same time unexpected and also logical (typically through cleverness or perseverance), and will find themselves or their situation altered at the end of the story.

This is how things play out in most genres: love stories, coming-of-age stories, horror, fantasy, thrillers, even literary novels. Some experimental stories try to leave out one of the elements, but readers can tell, and the story inevitably fails to connect with them.

Since stories are about journeys of desire rather than simply lists of sequential events, they're more centered on pursuit than plot and driven forward more by desire than by activity. So, pinpointing unmet desire is more vital than "making things happen" or even "making things go wrong."

7. "HOW CAN I FIGURE OUT WHAT MY CHARACTER'S PURSUIT OR JOURNEY OF DESIRE IS?"

The character's pursuit isn't necessarily a physical journey. It might involve any type of pursuit of unmet internal or interpersonal desires—the hope of forgiveness, the quest for adventure, the search for security, freedom, or love; it might also involve escape from shame or the quest for intimacy or companionship, the search for significance and meaning or for truth or hope. The pursuit of any universal human desire can be the impetus that moves the story forward.

Ask yourself, "What does this character want? What does she lack? Where does she hurt? What is she seeking?"

As you work on your story, this mental shift in focus from plot to pursuit will inevitably affect the shape and progression of the story and the questions you ask regarding it:

PLOT-BASED QUESTIONS	PURSUIT-BASED QUESTIONS
"What should happen?"	"What does the character desire?"
"What should come next?"	"Where does his desire lead?"
"What choices does he need to make?"	"What choices would he naturally make?"
"What does the ending require?"	"What does the moment require?"

When a character is engaged in meaningful, intention-infused pursuit, he is creating story. Rather than trying to dictate where the pathway of your character's pursuit "should" lead him (that is, predetermining the plot), stay responsive to his desires as you develop the story (that is, tracking his pursuit).

8. "WHO IS THE STORY'S PROTAGONIST?"

Your protagonist is the character whom readers will want the most to succeed, and the antagonist is the one they'll want the most to fail. They're cheering for the protagonist (*pro*=for) and against the antagonist (*anti*=against).

Most often, the protagonist is someone readers will identify with, admire, or aspire to be like while the antagonist will be someone they will identify with, fear, or desire to avoid becoming. Protagonists will be characters we care about. We'll be on their side, want them to succeed, and want to spend time with them.

(Note that not all stories have an antagonist or villain, but they do all have forces of antagonism that work against the protagonist in the pursuit of his unmet desires. We'll explore this principle more in-depth later.)

The forces of antagonism will be the primary obstacles for the protagonist to overcome. They're the setbacks stopping him from immediate success and thus necessitate his pursuit and will serve to test, reveal, or, if appropriate, change him as he navigates past them on his way through the story.

9. "HOW WILL MY PROTAGONIST RESPOND TO THE STRUGGLES AND SETBACKS THAT COME HIS WAY?"

He may (1) avoid them for as long as possible, (2) attempt to redirect his course around them, or (3) fight his way past them. His response will be determined by his character traits, the nature of his pursuit, and the type of setbacks he faces.

For instance, he might have recently retired from the CIA and just want to be left alone to fly fish in the mountains. Then, when he's called back for one last mission, he might initially resist but will be drawn inexorably into the story because he believes in something greater than his own placid existence—stopping terrorists, saving innocent lives, rescuing the oppressed, and so on.

Storytelling is always about tension. It's not about explaining or simply recapping what happened. That's court reporting. Readers want to know more than simply what a character is doing; they want to see who she is becoming.

Simply having things go wrong doesn't create tension—unless story characters desire them to go in a different direction and consequently make choices to see that happen.

10. "BUT DOES MY STORY REALLY NEED TENSION?"

Even though we might shy away from tension in real life, it's essential in fiction. Readers come to fiction to read about characters that they care about who are facing situations they would never wish the people that they care about in real life to experience.

There are, of course, different types of tension and different kinds of stakes. The tension doesn't need to be life-threatening, but it will threaten *something*, whether that's the character's dream, the status quo, a relationship, success (however she might define that), and so on.

Desire, obstacle, intentionality, and stakes are all vital within a story.

For instance, if the desire isn't clear to your readers, they won't know what the scene is about or why the character is choosing to act as he does. If there's nothing stopping him getting what he wants, there won't be any tension. If he acts in inexplicable ways, readers will be confused. And, if nothing is at stake, there's little reason for readers to care about the outcome of the scene.

The more imposing the threat and the more readers care about the outcome, the better the potential for tension.

11. "WHAT ROLE DOES ACTION PLAY IN THE PROGRESSION OF MY STORY?"

Not as big of a role as promises do. While action in real life might be the same as activity, in fiction, it's more than that. To reiterate: within a story, action is movement with intention, with events occurring during the pursuit of an objective.

Stories are more about revelations than events. Stop thinking of your story in regard to what happens, and start thinking of it in regard to what is revealed or transformed *because* of what happens. What makes a story interesting isn't so much the things that occur but the things that are chosen because of them.

If events happen for no discernible reason, or if readers can't figure out what's going on, they'll be confused and the story will stall out—no matter how much action is occurring on the page.

Instead, include action that is (1) logical, (2) revelatory, and (3) escalatory.

> 1. It's *logical* because it makes sense (both for the character and to the reader) for the character to take this specific step or make this specific choice at this specific time in the story.
>
> 2. It's *revelatory* because, by showing what a character is able to do (or who she's capable of becoming), action reveals traits or characteristics that readers might not have been aware of previously.
>
> 3. Finally, it's *escalatory* because tension will continue to

increase as the stakes increase while the story builds toward its climax.

12. "HOW IMPORTANT ARE MY CHARACTER'S CHOICES IN THIS PROCESS?"

In fiction, people act. They don't just mull over their problems or ignore them into oblivion. They make meaningful choices and react to the stimulus, and then have to face (and respond to) the consequences of what they've chosen to do. Your character's choices are the driving force in this process.

Action can be *rendered* (in scenes that add meaningfully to the progression of the story) or *summarized* (in scenes that do not).

Action without intention is the nail in the coffin of a story's escalation.

If things happen for no reason, or for reasons that readers simply cannot understand or discern, they'll disengage from the story and, eventually, set it aside.

PROBLEM	READER RESPONSE	SOLUTION
Action without intention	"Why is *this* happening?"	Specify/reveal intention
Intention without pursuit	"Why isn't *that* happening?"	Let the character take natural, logical steps toward his goal
Lack of escalation	"Nothing's going wrong!"	Ratchet up the tension and stakes

The most important decision the character will make happens

at the climax and often requires the greatest cleverness, courage, willpower, or sacrifice of the story. The climax is not the moment when everything is summarized; it's the most vital moment in the book for everything to be rendered.

So, at the climax, you will let your protagonist decide and act. He'll accomplish something. Let the scene play out, moment by moment on the page. If there's a fight, don't skip over it or just tell readers "they fought." Let it play out, blow by blow by blow.

The climax forces the character into a corner, requiring him to rise to the occasion, and results in a decision he might not have been able (or willing) to make at the story's beginning. It subsequently shifts his priorities, identity, awareness, or relationships into a new direction.

13. "BUT DOES THE CHARACTER NEED TO RESPOND TO THE STIMULI? WHY CAN'T HE JUST IGNORE THEM?"

He cannot help but respond—even stifling laughter, or refraining from arguing, or holding back from punching someone are all responses. He must respond because, in real life, we all must respond. Life is a series of responses to stimuli. His response, whatever it might be, will be immediate and the natural result of his beliefs or priorities.

Whatever he does must grow from the true nature of who he is and sustain the believability of the scene. If a character isn't responding as expected (or when expected), make sure it's because *he* wants something else to happen, not because *you* want something else to happen.

14. "MY PROTAGONIST DOESN'T SEEM LIKABLE

ENOUGH. WHAT ARE SOME WAYS I CAN MAKE HER MORE RELATABLE TO READERS?"

Give her a secret she must keep, a burden she must carry, a loss she must recover from, or a wound we all share (for instance, grief, guilt, regret, shame, or embarrassment).

Take away something from the character that readers (and the character) value. It might be something physical, but most often it's something more abstract—love, freedom, hope, justice, mental balance, contentment, relational stability, and so on. The story's pursuit will then revolve around the character trying to once again obtain her object of desire.

Let her suffer in a way that your readers will be able to identify with. For example, the teenage girl is emotionally wounded by the mean girls at school, the business professional loses his job, or the divorced single mom longs to find love again. Make sure your character is a problem-haver rather than an answer-giver. Readers will identify more with the person who needs to hear the advice than the one who offers it.

Note that the main character won't always do things that are *agreeable* to your readers, but rather that are *logical* to them. Avoid having her complain about things your readers believe in. Don't have her fuss or grumble about something readers don't think is important, beg for things to go her way, or use sarcasm that actually hurts someone else's feelings. All of these actions will distance readers from your character and make her less likable.

15. "HOW CAN I *SHOW* RATHER THAN *TELL* READERS WHAT MY CHARACTER IS LIKE?"

Give him a chance to act.

Include a scene early in the story that reveals a meaningful characteristic about the main character while something significant is at stake:

- A father shows his commitment to his children. (His dedication is revealed.)

- A CEO negotiates her way into a profitable deal. (Her talent is on display.)

- A spy escapes from imprisonment through her cunning. (Her tradecraft is portrayed.)

- A detective reveals his attention to detail. (His observational skills are evident.)

You can accomplish a lot by placing your character in situations that will:

- test her resolve,
- stretch her abilities,
- crystallize her priorities,
- reveal her noble convictions.
- force her to make tough decisions,
- offer her opportunities to sacrifice for others.

16. "HOW DO I FLESH OUT MY CHARACTERS?"

The phrase "flesh out your characters" is a good one since readers don't often fall in love with a skeleton.

Here are eight steps to create deeper characters. Not all of the techniques will be necessary for every character; in fact, applying all of them to every character would be overwhelming and, in the end, counterproductive. Rather, use these ideas as a springboard to lead you to develop your own approaches for fleshing out your characters.

1. Sharpen her interpersonal desire (the yearning for deeper or new relationships) or her internal yearnings (the pursuit of wonder, hope, answers, or transcendence).

2. Weave in moral dilemmas. A dilemma isn't the choice between the lesser of two evils (since if one isn't so bad, the choice wouldn't be difficult and wouldn't be a dilemma). Both options should be undesirable or, in some respect, unthinkable. Remember, dilemmas require deep belief. Without any convictions, there won't be any dilemma. So, give the character strong convictions and then hold him over a barrel. Make him choose between them.

3. Vary his status by giving him situations where he has different levels of submission or dominance. This isn't necessarily social dominance (being in charge or the person with the most clout). Rather, you'll be managing degrees of confidence, contentment, and compassion in various social contexts, all of which affect his substantive status in a scene.

4. Add quirks or hobbies that make her unique. Maybe she's obsessively neat, or has a ceramic turtle collection, or never goes running on cloudy days. If you can come up with something that's a little bit unique—and yet still believable or endearing—you can make the character memorable. And if you can make readers smile, you'll know you've got a winner.

5. Show your character's attitude about other characters, the story's pursuit, or the story's setting.

6. Remove characteristics from the protagonist that turn readers off. For instance, whining or being judgy, self-possessed, or arrogant. Readers won't be on the side of bullies, but they love to cheer for the underdog. Use that to your advantage.

7. Have your character pursue goals that readers consider virtuous or morally admirable, express traits or perspectives they find unique and intriguing, or work toward causes they believe in.

8. Let your character respond naturally to the actions of other characters. By showing how she reacts in difficult situations to a variety of different people, you'll reveal what she's really like, what she truly desires, or how she ultimately seeks (or defines) happiness.

17. "I NEED WAYS TO DEVELOP MORE DIMENSIONALITY IN MY CHARACTERS. HOW CAN I ACCOMPLISH THAT?"

Dimensionality grows from (1) personalizing the character's desire-infused choices, (2) building identification between readers and the character, and (3) creating idiosyncrasies that show the character's uniqueness.

Let's take those one at a time.

1. *Personalizing desire-infused choices:* Here, you'll take into account the context, the setting, and the relationship that your character has to the other characters he's interacting with. Allow her to respond to situations and challenges in ways that are in concert with who she is and that reveal what she values most.

2. *Building identification:* Give your characters desires that your readers share. This commonality will engender empathy, which will draw readers more deeply into the story. If readers feel that they understand the character's situation or can picture what it would be like to be facing a

similar difficulty, they'll identify with the character and her pursuit. So give her a universally shared quest. For instance, to love and be loved or to find independence, happiness, acceptance, companionship, or identity. To create more tension for characters, accentuate empathy, peril, desire, and stakes.

3. *Creating idiosyncrasies:* If you sense that your character is too cliché, then work at making her more distinctive by adding unique habits, mannerisms, interests, or linguistic markers.

18. "I DON'T KNOW WHAT MY MAIN CHARACTER WANTS THE MOST. HOW IMPORTANT IS IT FOR ME TO FIGURE THAT OUT?"

Knowing what your protagonist desires is vital. If you don't know what she wants (or thinks she wants), then you won't know what your story is actually about.

However, it's not essential to know all of this before you start to write or even as you work on early drafts of your story. As you spend more time with the character, you'll naturally begin to understand more clearly what she's hoping to accomplish, avoid, or overcome.

As you write, your story is in flux. It's fluid. You can always go back and revise what you've previously worked on as the character's desire becomes clearer to you, so don't stress about clarity too much too early on. Instead, keep your ears attuned to the story and your pen ready to make edits to what you've already written.

19. "I DON'T HAVE A VILLAIN IN MY STORY.

HOW CAN I STILL MAKE THE PLOT WORK?"

The forces of antagonism include whatever's opposing or oppressing the protagonist—and that might or might not be another person.

It could be the weather (in a survival story), his own views (in a spiritual awakening story), or any non-human obstacles that force him into a corner (in a supernatural horror story).

Even if the forces of antagonism have no will, they will often appear to act in a way that is contrary to and hinders the protagonist's pursuit: the storm might be personified to "rage against" someone, or the character might be in a "battle" against cancer.

These obstructions in his pursuit stop him from immediate success and help to reveal or develop his characterization. The forces of antagonism will have an effect on him. What they take from him or force him to do will matter in determining who readers understand him to be.

20. "IF I INCLUDE A VILLAIN, WHAT WILL HE THINK ABOUT HIMSELF AND HIS ACTIONS?"

As soon as an antagonist believes himself to be evil or to be pursuing evil, he stops being frightening. He's only scary as long as he is, in his own mind, doing what's necessary for the greater good.

He won't think that he's doing anything wrong, or if he knows the act is immoral, he'll have a higher ideal in mind that allows him to convince himself that the ends justify the means.

Often, he's trying to do what he believes to be a good thing (and that may very well be one), but he's going about it in the wrong way.

To reiterate, he won't act in a way that, in his eyes, is wicked. So, the radical Jihadist wouldn't see himself as a terrorist but as a freedom fighter. The hacker considers corporate corruption or environmental crimes to be far worse than his own, and so on.

The villain won't view himself as the villain. As has been pointed out by other authors over the years: From the villain's point of view, he's the hero. Your goal includes not just making that rationalization believable to him but also to your readers.

21. "WHAT ARE SOME WAYS FOR HIM TO JUSTIFY WHAT HE DOES?"

Think carefully about this. What does he tell himself about his actions or pursuit? How can you bring readers to the place where, even if they don't agree with the villain, they nod their heads and say, "Yeah, you know what—he's got a point there."

How would the following characters rationalize their choices?

An executioner: How does he draw the line between what he does and what "killers" do?

A traitor: What higher ideal does he appeal to?

A serial killer: What does he tell himself when he goes out to hunt for his victims?

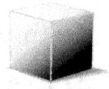

22. "ARE THERE ANY OTHER SECRETS TO CREATING MEMORABLE VILLAINS?"

The more committed the villain is to his plan, the scarier he is. The more impressed he is with his plan, the more comical he becomes.

CHARACTERISTICS OF A FORMIDABLE VILLAIN	
Astute	Nothing gets past him.

Complex	A criminal mastermind is often more frightening than a mindless killer.
Believable	He takes steps that make sense on his way to his goal.
Frightening	He shows us the dark side of human nature.
Reasonable	When we meet him, he's logical. The way he reasons out his actions makes sense.
Unpredictable / unbalanced	We can never quite guess just how far he'll go in the pursuit of his goal, and that makes us uneasy.
Morally justified	He's able to rationalize his actions in his own mind and, to some extent, to readers as well.
Unswervingly committed to his cause	He will not be easily deterred from his goal and will sacrifice to make the necessary progress.
Must overcome setbacks	Formidable foes often have the odds stacked against them.
Bigger than life	He can't be easily profiled, tracked down, or arrested; he's on a whole different level.
Ruthless rather than sadistic	He doesn't have to see others suffer to be satisfied. He's not needy in that way.

Rather than trying to come up with something devious for the villain to do, unfetter him, open the door, and let him walk out of the confining prison of your expectations. The story events will unveil themselves to you as he takes natural and believable steps in pursuit of his goal.

23. "LOTS OF VILLAINS DON'T SEEM ALL THAT SCARY, BUT MORE SILLY THAN ANYTHING ELSE. HOW CAN I AVOID THAT?"

Let him take actions your readers look up to and express traits or values your readers will want to emulate. Give him a worthy challenge, an admirable quality, or a meaningful vulnerability. Allow him to show confidence even when the odds are stacked against him. Expose a vulnerability that readers will identify with. He will have:

> 1. *Total commitment.* He'll show the same perseverance or dedication to his cause that the hero shows without the constraints of compassion reining him in.
>
> 2. *Moral complexity.* A penchant for or a weakness toward evil is often more frightening than an incapacity for good. Give your villain some redeeming qualities, not to make evil attractive to readers, but to make the villain relatable to them.
>
> 3. *Objectification of others.* She objectifies people and acts without remorse. Evil exhibits itself through callousness toward human misery even more than through taking joy in someone else's distress. Often this objectification begins by dehumanizing the victim. For instance, the enemy combatants become "targets." It's much easier to squeeze the trigger when you're trying to "neutralize a threat" than to kill a fellow human being.
>
> 4. *Justification for his actions.* As we've covered, he has

convinced himself that he isn't doing anything wrong. He doesn't intend evil, only the greater good.

Stick him in a situation that increases your readers' empathy toward him. For instance, he takes in stray dogs, defends the poor or the powerless, or gives a meaningful gift to someone who can never repay him.

Show how he's one step ahead of the police—but isn't self-congratulatory, impressed with himself, or out to prove anything to anyone. Smug is not scary or inspiring. The more he chortles, the more we yawn.

Look for ways to show how heartless or unbalanced he is. Readers will be frightened by someone who they know is capable of great harm. They'll also be unsettled when they're unsure how an unstable a character will react.

24. "WHAT ARE SOME EXAMPLES OF THE 'GREATER GOOD' THAT ANTAGONISTS MIGHT PURSUE?"

Here are four:

1. Vengeance or "balancing the scales." For instance, the vigilante feels compelled to take justice into his own hands when the criminal justice system fails to do so.

2. Protecting the environment. Perhaps a radical environmental group seeks to make a statement or disrupt the work of an oil company through domestic terrorism.

3. Stopping a war. An assassin justifies his actions of taking out potential dictators or the oppressive elite in order to stop a greater evil—war between two countries.

4. Caring for the poor. The antagonist justifies stealing

from the rich and giving to the poor. This might be through forced wealth redistribution or Robin Hood-esque adventures.

5. Though he's doing the wrong thing, he believes that, in this instance, it's the right thing.

To come up with more of your own ideas, brainstorm causes that your readers will believe in and then find a way for your villain to appeal to those ideals in his justification for the plan of action he has put into play.

25. "WHAT DO READERS EXPECT FROM A VILLAIN IN A HIGH-CONCEPT BOOK, SUCH AS A THRILLER?"

He won't be your run-of-the-mill bad guy. He'll be remarkably clever, cunning, or cold-blooded. He won't be intimidated and cannot be bribed, extorted, or deterred from this course of action. He has a plan and will take out anyone or anything that gets in his way as he seeks to carry it out.

As we examined earlier, apathy toward human suffering is more frightening than sadistic "Mua-ha-ha!" villainy. He's able to commit a perfect crime or series of crimes and evade capture. He's someone who the hero has to take seriously.

He usually has a special ability (perhaps great intelligence, martial arts expertise, or hacking skills). Also, he'll have complexity, depth, and resolve. Often, villains who are completely evil aren't as intriguing as those who have some desirable traits or redeeming qualities. To make the devil believable and frightening, don't try to make him scary; instead, make him reasonable.

26. "SHOULD MY READERS LIKE THE VILLAIN?"

Maybe, maybe not. They might be repulsed by him, but they will not feel indifferent toward him. Bad guys can be, and often are, likable. Remember, even psychopaths can be charming, engaging, and fun to be around. They can listen and affirm and tell you what you want to hear. They're good at making promises and reassuring others.

To better delve into the villain's characteristics, ask yourself:

- Why should my readers fear this person? They won't fear cartoonish imbeciles. Remember, clever antagonists will have a good reason for what they do, flexibility in dealing with setbacks, and a backup plan in case things go sideways.

- Why did he start his crime spree at this time? Does that make any difference to the story? Will readers look for that psychological trigger or stimulus? If I don't give it to them, will they be disappointed?

- If the antagonist were to write a letter to the protagonist, how would he describe his own actions? How would he frame/explain hers?

Just as your protagonist will show what she's capable of while something tangible or meaningful is at stake, the antagonist needs a chance to do the same.

Incidentally, stories often include moments during which the protagonist's and antagonist's lives intersect throughout the story rather than encountering each other only at the climax. Perhaps there's a chase scene, a phone call, a text, or an email exchange between them earlier in the story. Whatever you choose, it needs to come across not as a cliché but as something genuine, natural, and contextually appropriate.

27. "MY BAD GUY SEEMS MORE INTERESTING THAN MY HERO. WHAT CAN I DO ABOUT THAT?"

This isn't an uncommon problem.

We're intrigued by evil. All of us have evil inclinations at times. We're curious about what it's like to pull the veil aside and see what lies on the other side. Villains let us do that with our own hearts and motives.

But what do you do if your villain becomes more memorable and intriguing than your protagonist? Here are five steps to take:

1. Allow your main character to face moral struggles that will test his mettle and call forth more courage or resolve.

2. Make sure your hero never comes across as whiny, judgy, or cowardly.

3. Let the protagonist act in a self-sacrificing way toward someone who can't return the favor.

4. Don't let the hero make a choice that ends up resulting in the villain looking more admirable than he is.

5. Show your villain taking advantage of your hero's (and, in a sense, your readers') values, turning them against him so that they become vulnerabilities. For instance, she might severely wound someone and force the hero to choose between saving the person's life or following her as she flees. Does the cop pursue the killer (to protect other potential victims) or help the dying person in front of him? The choice to stay with the victim will elevate your hero's status in the eyes of your readers.

28. "SHOULD I RELY ON ARCHETYPES TO CREATE MY CHARACTERS?"

Sometimes characters play the role of mentor or villain or gatekeeper. Those are archetypical roles in traditional or mythic stories.

Modern archetypes include the jock, the flirt, the slacker, the class clown, the final girl, the drama queen, the yuppie, the nerd, the bully, the wallflower, the black sheep, the tree hugger, the redneck, the lovable rogue, the haunted detective, the rebellious teen, etc.

Many sitcoms are built almost entirely on archetypes: the office bitch, the yes man, the geek, the clueless boss, the overachiever, and so on.

To avoid creating stereotypical or cliché characters, merge two types together to create a new category altogether. What about the nerd who's a bully? Or the redneck tree hugger? Or the kickboxing librarian? Just as with anything, it's possible to get carried away, but give it a shot and see what sort of believable character emerges.

You'll be tempted to create characters who fit into the mold of others in the genre in which you write. Avoid that. Strive to create memorable, entertaining, and poignant protagonists with fresh qualities and memorable characteristics that your readers haven't seen before.

29. "WHAT IF MY STORY HAS MULTIPLE PROTAGONISTS? HOW CAN I MAKE SURE THEY DON'T END UP ALL SOUNDING OR ACTING THE SAME?"

While it's theoretically possible to have multiple protagonists, most likely your story has one who is primary.

However, let's assume you have two characters who are equally vital to the story's movement or conclusion. Make sure their storylines are intertwined and that the success or revelation of each one will affect the outcome of the story for the other.

As far as making characters unique, show the contrast in how they would each uniquely pursue what they want (even if it's the same objective). Since their background will inevitably influence how they sound and how they act, create different backstory that affects how they respond in the present. Give them a different wound, different aspiration, or different perspective.

30. "I HAVE A LOT OF PRIMARY CHARACTERS. HOW CAN I TELL WHO THE PROTAGONIST IS?"

Look for the character readers are meant to worry about the most. You'll want readers to be on her side. Ask yourself:

1. Who is the first one introduced or the last one standing when the book concludes?

2. Who has the most intimate or most meaningful transformation or revelation?

3. Who makes the greatest sacrifice?

4. Whose unmet desire drives the story forward?

5. Whose questions beg the most pressing answers?

6. Who rises from the dead (in a physical or—most likely—metaphorical sense) at the end of the story?

Keep in mind that the protagonist is the one fighting for something readers believe in, even if he himself isn't aware of the nobility of his pursuit.

If the character in question has all the answers, she might be a mentor or part of the supporting cast, but won't likely be the protagonist who—rather than having or giving answers—will often be plagued by unresolved issues or overwhelming questions.

Crafting a story requires creating instances in which the protagonist can grow, reveal his inner strength, or sacrifice himself for the good of others. Most of the time, your protagonist will be (or learn to become) heroic in some sense.

31. "OKAY, SO NOW THAT I KNOW WHO MY PROTAGONIST IS, WHAT TRAITS OR QUALITIES SHOULD I GIVE HER?"

Readers won't worry about a character they don't care about. Despite how flawed she might be, she needs to be intriguing enough for readers to want to spend time with her. She might be idiosyncratic or powerful or empathetic or courageous—anything that draws readers in.

She won't have all of the qualities listed below, but you can evaluate how attractive she'll be to readers by consulting the following chart.

IN REAL LIFE, ATTRACTIVE PEOPLE ARE...		
passionate	but not	obsessed
dedicated	but not	workaholics
confident	but not	cocky
hopeful	but not	unrealistic
honest	but not	argumentative

forgiving	but not	dredging up the past
good listeners	but not	nitpickers
adventurous	but not	dangerous
emotional	but not	clingy
spontaneous	but not	impulsive
witty	but not	self-possessed
cool under pressure	but not	cold and unfeeling
self-respecting	but not	selfish
courageous	but not	demanding
roguish	but not	a buffoon
rough around the edges	but not	demeaning
mysterious	but not	beguiling
flirty	but not	a tease
generous	but not	enabling

(Notice how closely related each of the pairings are. There's only a thin line separating them, but a huge difference in terms of how the traits come across to readers.)

Even if your protagonist isn't always vibrant and scintillating in conversation, he'll be trustworthy and dedicated. And he won't be lukewarm or wishy-washy. He might bellyache about how things are going, but he won't whimper.

Readers want heroes who are nonconformists, characters they can believe in, who have a moral grounding, a unique way of looking at the world, and an infectious attitude.

Readers find it attractive when characters show compassion

for the less fortunate, sacrifice for or protect others, express thanksgiving, and celebrate the natural world.

32. "DOES MY PROTAGONIST NEED TO BE LIKABLE?"

Shoot for someone who's irresistible, not simply likable.

Whether the protagonist is admirable or not, readers have to be on his side. Our goal: create a character that readers are interested in enough to worry about and to want to spend the next two hours, or ten, or twenty hours of their lives alone with. If they don't care whether or not he succeeds, they won't care about the story, and they won't recommend the book to others—if they even finish it themselves.

Readers need to desire the protagonist's ultimate happiness or success, even if that might not always come in the way the character anticipates or the readers expect.

A spunky, quick-witted, or idiosyncratic character will keep readers enthralled longer than a likable one will, so rather than trying so hard to make her likable, focus on making her irresistible. Sometimes, the most engaging characters aren't all that likable, but they have intriguing traits. They're three-dimensional and compelling. Readers want to spend time with them. That's the key—is this character engaging? Interesting? Enchanting? Disquieting?

The best protagonists will have VALUE. They will be:

- V - Vulnerable but not fragile.
- A - Admirable but not perfect.
- L - Layered but not contradictory.
- U - Unforgettable but not annoying.
- E - Entertaining but not distracting.

Too many novels contain protagonists who are recalcitrant or gloomy or simply annoying. Readers don't want weak-willed, snooty, begrudging, or glum protagonists.

So why do so many writers portray protagonists in this way? Perhaps it's because they've been taught that the character needs to change as a result of facing the struggle of the story (that is, she needs a "character arc"), and since they want their characters to end in a good place, they start them in a bad one.

Though that's a valid goal, if readers put the book down because they can't stand the main character, they'll never see the change and the arc won't ultimately matter. So, make the protagonist someone readers will want to hang out with throughout the story.

When you evaluate how your character acts, consider if you would be drawn toward a real person who was acting this way. If not, readers won't likely want to spend time with that character either.

33. "ARE YOU SAYING THAT I SHOULDN'T INCLUDE A CHARACTER ARC?"

When people talk about the "character arc" or "story arc," they're referring to the amount of change to the character or to his situation in the narrative.

However, not all characters change as a result of navigating through a series of struggles. Some characters are static and remain fundamentally the same at the story's conclusion. In that case, you don't have a character arc but a "reader arc" as the reader's perception of the character is altered.

Ask yourself what changes the most in this story—the character or the readers' perception of him.

34. "WAIT—I'VE ALWAYS HEARD THAT A CHARACTER MUST CHANGE IN A STORY. ARE YOU SAYING THAT'S NOT THE CASE?"

Some story theorists believe that the story's struggles *reveal* the courage, fortitude, and so on that was already there, buried or hidden within the protagonist. Others point out that some stories serve to *test* characters. Still, others believe that the story's challenges *alter* the character in a fundamental way.

Think through whether your story is showing your character's true colors or changing them. Does she rise to meet the challenge, or does the challenge simply bring out facets of her characterization that weren't recognizable to her (or to readers) when the story began?

Many genres simply do not have a character arc. There isn't one in many ongoing television shows, sitcoms, or in many series characters in fiction (especially in the spy, military, thriller, and master detective genres). Readers don't come to these stories because the main character is fundamentally altered in every book or episode, but for the very opposite reason—because she remains fundamentally the same. They want to see her revealed, not transformed.

35. "HOW DO I DECIDE HOW MUCH CHANGE TO INCLUDE?"

Really take a moment to think through your views.

Does the challenge that requires courage change the character into a coward or show him to be the coward that he already is? What is your viewpoint: do we become cowardly (or heroic) when we're faced with a difficult or frightening situation, or do we already have those traits or characteristics within us, and that dangerous or challenging circumstance serves to reveal the truth about us? What do you think?

Do you become or do you emerge? In other words, do you change as a result of what happens to you, or does the real you finally come to the surface?

Consider this: Do sports build character, or do they reveal it? When you miss that easy putt, does it build your character or does your response reveal what you're really like, who you truly are?

When you're squeezed, what comes out? Something that wasn't there before, or something that just needed that pressure in order to be released?

Ask yourself, "How can I put this character under the pressure that'll reveal her true nature and priorities? How can I forge (or shape) her convictions in the fire of trials?" Then, explore what the struggles draw out of the character, require him to do or to sacrifice, lead him to become, or show him to be.

36. "HOW DOES THIS UNDERSTANDING OF CHARACTER DEVELOPMENT AFFECT HOW I SHAPE MY STORY?"

Since stories are not static events but rather dynamic progressions that move characters into and through struggles, readers instinctively look for change, either in the situation that the characters face or within the characters themselves.

If you believe that our personalities are intact from birth and that life simply reveals who we are, you'll likely shape stories that reflect that view and write characters who are fixed and stable. However, if you believe that people are dynamic and that the difficulties we face do more than draw us out of our shells but actually affect who we are becoming, you'll probably write more fluid, mutable characters.

Often, readers don't just want to see what the character can do; they also want to see who the circumstances are forcing him to become. What does the quest for justice require of your protagonist? Does your hero need to become evil to do good? How does that affect him from then on?

As you write, think about ways that the struggles might shape who your character is developing into, but also how those struggles might reveal who your character truly is.

Ask how facing this struggle would (1) alter her perspective; (2) harden or soften her resolve; (3) reveal what she's really like; (4) affect her understanding of herself, justice, or human nature; or (5) shape the direction of her life from that point on.

37. "HOW CAN I TELL IF MY STORY CHANGES WHO THE PROTAGONIST IS OR SIMPLY REVEALS WHAT HE'S REALLY LIKE?"

Readers expect to see transformation in the realm of the story's greatest or most intimate struggle. If the story is centered on internal struggles (realizations, questions, doubts, and so on), readers will expect that the transformation will occur *internally*. In that case, the character's nature or self-awareness will be transformed (for instance, in coming-of-age stories).

It's the same with external struggles—readers will expect to see the *situation* altered (action, thrillers, mysteries, etc.). And with interpersonal struggles (for example, romance stories), they'll anticipate that the *relationship* will be affected.

REALM OF THE PRIMARY STRUGGLE	WHAT WILL BE CHANGED	WHAT READERS WILL EXPECT

Internal	The main character's attitude, personality, or perspective	A moment of revelation or insight
External	The situation	A valiant choice that solves a significant, pressing problem
Interpersonal	The relationship	A hint that the relational problems have been resolved or that they will be

The deeper the struggle, the bigger the promise of a profound transformation in that realm.

In real life, when we face difficulties, we learn from them. We mature. We grow. Because of this, if the character remains completely unaffected after facing a tragedy or difficult dilemma, it'll strain the story's credulity.

As a result of facing the story's struggles, your protagonist might have become more aware of her resources (psychological, spiritual, intellectual, relational, etc.) or acquired more skills, insight, or acumen that will better equip her to face her next challenge.

In some cases, stories change the outcome of the character; in some cases, the character changes the outcome of the story. Often, both occur.

Keep in mind that in most standalone books, the main character will have a transformative moment. In most series books, the main character will learn a lesson as a result of facing the conflict but will remain essentially (at a core level) the same throughout the series.

38. "WILL STRUGGLES IN EACH OF THE THREE REALMS BE ALTERED AT THE END OF THE STORY?"

Not always, but the primary realm of struggle will have a satisfactory resolution. Since stories contain transformations, the situation or condition of the protagonist will typically be different at the end of the story than it was at the beginning.

Sometimes, there's a change for the better (in stories with a happy ending). But that's not always the case. Here's a simple way of remembering that stories are about changed opportunities and circumstances:

BEFORE THE STORY…	AT THE END…
He didn't have.	He has.
He wasn't.	He is.
He couldn't.	He can.
She had.	She doesn't have.
She was.	She isn't.
She could.	She can't.

39. "ARE THERE EASY WAYS TO MAKE MY HERO MORE HEROIC AND MY VILLAIN MORE VILLAINOUS?"

Let your hero take actions that readers will look up to or express traits or values they'll want to emulate. (In other words, write about a protagonist that they will *admire* or *aspire* to be like.) Valor comes from self-sacrifice, humility, and compassion; it'll make any character more heroic. Your hero might stand up for the oppressed and be called forth to do more than he thought he could do or that he was able to do when the story began.

(By the way, anti-heroes often just want to be left alone but are drawn into the story because of a deeper desire—often for justice or revenge. Anti-villains don't want to be villains, but their convictions lead them to make choices that they know they might live to regret.)

Being unconcerned about the suffering of others will make any character more cruel and show traits of psychopathy. Let your villain frighten readers by reminding them of their own dark side. In a sense, the villain serves as (1) a reminder of what we are capable of, (2) a mirror of who we are, (3) a warning of what we need to avoid.

Give your villain an honorable goal or a code of ethics, and then show him acting in a cold-hearted, calculating way to achieve his objective.

40. "SOMEONE OTHER THAN MY PROTAGONIST SEEMS LIKE THE HERO. HOW CAN I FIX THAT?"

The protagonist might not always be the hero. Sometimes, she's the one telling the hero's story, or she's the one who's saved at the end when the hero gives up his life to rescue her.

It might not be a bad thing to have your protagonist and the hero remain separate characters, but if you wish to elevate your protagonist:

1. Allow her to make a greater sacrifice at the climax.

2. Let her turn the other cheek.

3. Give her opportunities to hold back from exhibiting

her power. The one who has the ability to resort to violence and doesn't do so shows her self-control and raises her substantive status.

41. "CAN MY PROTAGONIST REFUSE THE CALL TO ADVENTURE?"

Yes, but she cannot choose to avoid the struggle, or if she tries to do so, it's going to catch up with her anyway and tug her into the heart of the story.

Some authors get very concerned about including a "refusal of the call to adventure" and insert it even though it might not fit organically into their story.

For example, the detective is called in, and the captain says, "I want you to catch this serial killer." "Naw," the guy says. "I'd rather not. But thanks for asking." That's ludicrous. Of course, he won't refuse the professional call to adventure. He'll immediately embrace it. The refusal of the call has become so common that it's now a cliché in certain genres—specifically, myth, science fiction, and fantasy.

Instead, get the story rolling. Make the protagonist face the struggle that he's going to be involved in during the story and forge ahead.

Though the goal will be clear, the path won't be easy. After all, if there's an easier route forward—a way to resolve things quickly, perhaps through a discussion, negotiation, or compromise—why wouldn't the protagonist just do that?

No. In your story, the central struggle cannot be resolved quickly. No compromise is possible. No amount of discussion will solve this. It needs to be tackled with action (and often sacrifice)—and that action, those choices, need to be done by the protagonist, not by others on his behalf.

Stories move forward, and every moment within them is a point of no return.

42. "HOW MANY CENTRAL STRUGGLES DOES MY PROTAGONIST NEED?"

At least one, and it will be clearly defined in her mind. Characters might have a multiplicity of relationships to navigate or challenges to overcome—and within each of these is the potential for some type of struggle.

While thinking in terms of her pursuit, focus on sharpening the desire and setbacks in the central areas where she's struggling—don't just pile on more random bad things happening. Make sure that the setbacks deepen each specific struggle rather than making them more and more diffuse.

43. "HOW DO YOU KNOW WHICH IS THE CHARACTER'S MOST SIGNIFICANT STRUGGLE?"

Look at the stakes, the promises made, the amount of the story dedicated to that struggle, the number of setbacks in that realm, the cost to the character, and the degree of change or revelation that the struggle results in.

The most significant struggle will typically be the last one that's resolved, otherwise, the story's tension will de-escalate as things fizzle out at the end.

44. "HOW IMPORTANT ARE MY READERS' FIRST IMPRESSIONS OF THE CHARACTERS?"

Just as in real life, first impressions are lasting impressions. Even if we're not aware that we're doing it, we tend to make certain assumptions and, over time, subconsciously look for ways to confirm those initial impressions. We sometimes view others through the lens of our first impressions for years afterward.

Because of that, make sure you really refine the first impression that your character makes so that it's both true to the character and helpful to readers. Pay close attention to how your character comes across the first time he's introduced.

For instance, don't let him seem judgy (against any demographic), impatient, or prejudiced. All of those things will turn readers off. Take care. Most of the time, confidence is attractive, but haughtiness is not.

As we covered earlier, many traits are closely related: exceptionalism and perfectionism, humility and doormat-ism, optimism and naivety. Evaluate which ones you'll want your character to portray, and let the first impression reflect attributes that will be attractive to your readers.

SECTION II

OPENINGS AND PROMISES

45. "WHAT NEEDS TO HAPPEN AT THE BEGINNING OF MY STORY?"

Your story's opening will (1) feature a character who matters, (2) orient readers to the setting, (3) introduce a meaningful pursuit, (4) set the mood, (5) establish the narrator's voice, and (6) hook readers' attention—hopefully making it difficult for them to put the book down.

Strive to create openings that engender concern for the protagonist, that both surprise and satisfy readers, that help them visualize what's happening in the scene, and that lock their expectations in to the type of story this is.

Introduce a character whom readers will either (1) empathize with, (2) care about, (3) aspire to be like, or (4) fear. Also, readers want to believe. When they stop believing, they stop caring, and when they stop caring, they stop reading. So, establish the world of your story, and then keep it believable as you move forward.

Don't stall the story out by dumping in too much background information. Instead, press forward right off the bat, make big promises, and leave your readers hungry for more.

46. "FOR AN OPENING SCENE, CAN I INCLUDE AN INTRIGUING HOOK TO START MY STORY AND THEN DROP BACK IN TIME FOR CHAPTER TWO?"

Only if your readers would want that—and that's rarely the case.

Here's how that usually plays out: You stick a character in a precarious or deadly situation—and then chapter two starts with a time stamp: *Three weeks earlier.*

No reader is thinking, *Man, that's awesome! I have to wait four hundred pages before I find out what happened here! Brilliant!*

If you use this gimmick, you'll turn off many readers right away as you de-escalate, rather than escalate, the tension. Don't start off by shooting yourself in the foot. Give your readers more of what they want and less of what they don't.

47. "CAN I START MY BOOK WITH THE CHARACTER IN THE OPENING SCENE GETTING KILLED OFF?"

You could, but why would you want to start with a cliché?

The "point of view character getting killed in the first chapter" routine doesn't satisfy readers anymore because it's so overused. It's simply too predictable (especially in thrillers, mysteries, and horror stories).

Often, you'll want readers to both feel sympathy for the person in the first scene and also want him to succeed.

For example, if your opening scene begins with an arsonist setting a building on fire, you'll want to craft it in such a way that readers will want him to get out of there alive while also wanting him to be successful in what he's doing.

After all, if the character is simply entirely evil, readers won't care if he dies—and you want them to start off caring deeply about the character, as well as his pursuit.

Tricky? Absolutely. But it's better than writing a trite opening or one that's become a cliché for your genre. Break from the norm and give readers something more riveting or surprising than they're expecting.

48. "CAN I USE DIALOGUE TO INTRODUCE A STRUGGLE IN MY OPENING LINE?"

Yes. The opening line can be used to develop urgency, mystery, concern, or intrigue.

Perhaps the characters are currently in pursuit of something vital (urgency) or are trying to figure out who is (mystery), or they're being pursued or endangered themselves (concern), or they're deciphering a puzzle about something that needs to be solved in order to avoid devastating consequences (intrigue).

The opening line would differ based on which of those four results you're shooting for:

- *Option #1* – Urgency: "Do I cut the red wire or the green one?"

- *Option #2* – Mystery: "Who do you think might have placed the bomb?"

- *Option #3* – Concern: "How much time do we have left before this thing goes off?"

- *Option #4* – Intrigue: "What if the traitor is actually one of us?"

49. "HOW DO I KNOW IF MY PREMISE IS INTRIGUING ENOUGH?"

Compare it to other books or films. You'll want a unique situation that allows for fascinating character development or a moral dilemma that has no clear-cut solution. While there's nothing new under the sun, there are certainly new ways of sharing old ideas.

Look for a fresh angle, something you haven't seen before, a new slant on a mythic, genre-specific, or traditional motif.

Honestly evaluate your premise. If it's too out-there, it'll seem gimmicky or perhaps abstruse to readers, but if it's too run-of-the-mill, it won't attract them either. Strive to be original rather than derivative in your storytelling.

50. "HOW MUCH OF MY STORY DO I NEED TO KNOW BEFORE I START WRITING IT? HOW FAR INTO IT SHOULD I GO WITHOUT KNOWING HOW IT WILL END?"

You don't need to know the ending before you start a story. If you understand what lies at the heart of story (orientation, disruption, pursuit, escalation, and transformation), the ending will become evident as the story develops.

Many writers start with only a premise, a fascinating character, an interesting phrase, an intriguing opening line, or a moral dilemma and begin their story there.

Trust the process. Keep asking questions to uncover the story and stay sensitive to the direction it's nudging you to go. To many authors, writing is like having a conversation with someone when you don't know how it will end or what you'll say next. A conversation is an act of faith. So is writing a novel.

That doesn't mean that when you sit down to write, you'll know precisely *what* you will write, but you trust *that* you will write.

51. "HOW CAN I MAKE THE STORY WORK IF I DON'T KNOW THE ENDING?"

Stay responsive to the narrative as it progresses. Some writers feel more confident starting a story when they have an ending in mind. Others like to see the end emerge as the characters progress along their pursuits.

The choice isn't so much between "plotting" or "writing by the seat of your pants" (often called "pantsing"), it's between presumption and receptivity.

Don't assume that you know where the story will go. Instead, take note of where it's logically heading based on the characters' choices and pursuits. Do your best to listen to the story rather than telling it what to do. Avoid deciding beforehand what your story is about; focus on discovering it instead.

Am I trying to dictate or to discover the story events and the character development?

Am I forcing the characters to do what I want them to do, or am I letting them respond naturally to their choices and dilemmas?

Am I the puppet master, the god of the tale, or do my characters have free will in determining their actions?

52. "WHAT'S THE KEY TO A GOOD OPENING?"

While it's certainly important to hook readers' interest early in the story, some authors make the mistake of including a gripping opening and then dumping in backstory to give their hook context. This creates de-escalation and waning reader interest.

Remember, setting isn't just a location in space but also in time. Setting is when you are where you are. It's important that readers realize (1) when the story is happening, (2) where it's happening, (3) what the characters want, and (4) why that matters—not just to the characters but also to them. To reiterate: Readers need to believe, see, feel, and care. It's your job to help them do so.

53. "WHAT SHOULD I AVOID IN THE OPENING LINE OF MY STORY?"

Here are a few overused openings that you'll want to steer clear of:

1. The character who's dead and is narrating the story from beyond the grave: "The day I died was an ordinary day."

2. The person who's waking up: "Her eyes flew open. What was that sound in the living room? Was there someone in the house? She decided she needed to find out!"

3. The convoluted sentence that's trying too hard: "It was on old Highway 9 on a torpid summer day when Jasper 'Rascal' Taylor—who was on his way to Albuquerque—found the dead body by the side of the road and realized he knew her since he'd slept with her the night before, four hundred miles away." If it's a sentence that people have to reread to keep everything straight, it's too long.

Instead, when opening your story, consider starting with someone we'll empathize with, admire, or fear. For your protagonist, introduce us to a character we'll care about, be intrigued by, and want to spend time with. Show them making a significant decision or sacrifice while something that matters is at stake.

54. "WHO SHOULD I INTRODUCE FIRST IN MY STORY?"

Stories typically start with readers meeting the villain, the victor, or the victim.

Villain: This character is often introduced first in thrillers and suspense stories.

Victor: Here, you start with the hero.

Victim: In detective and horror stories, you might find that a character is killed off in the first scene (although this is so common, you'll probably want to avoid it).

Since that's usually how stories start, that's what readers will be expecting. They'll think, *Gotcha. This is the bad guy.* Or, *Okay, it looks like this is the main character here.* Or, *Let me guess, this person gets offed in the first chapter.*

So, to include a plot pivot, you might choose to start your story with another character and then shift, in the second chapter, to the story's main character. If you do this, remember that readers will begin with the expectation that your story began with the villain, victor, or victim, and you'll need to make sure you don't let them down or leave them confused as they read on.

Once you introduce your main character, let readers get to know him for a while. Be careful not to jump around too much into other characters' points of view.

If you start a story with a narrator writing in the first-person point of view, that'll clue readers in that this is most likely the main character.

55. "HOW QUICKLY SHOULD I INTRODUCE OTHER CHARACTERS AT THE START OF THE

STORY?"

Readers know that you need to introduce your vital characters, so, at the beginning of the book, they'll give you grace as you bring those characters onstage. Don't rush too much at the start, but be sure to include the main players early on.

Many authors introduce too many characters in their stories all at once. Allow readers to meet and care about the characters that appear, and don't bring them in so quickly that readers have a hard time keeping them all straight.

By the way, set your protagonist's sex, age, and any defining physical characteristics early on so readers can better picture who he is. It's usually wise to let readers begin to understand this character's perspective and way of looking at the world early in the story as well.

56. "WHAT ROLE WILL THE SUPPORTING CHARACTERS PLAY?"

Supporting characters might help to unearth the story's moral dilemma or ask its central question. Often, they will serve one of the following five roles in regard to their relationship with the main character. (To remember these, remember the acronym CHAIR.):

- C – Challenge: to bring out the best in the protagonist.
- H – Help: to assist in her pursuit.
- A – Antagonize: to fight against her.
- I – Impede: to hinder her quest.
- R – Reveal: to show who she really is, at the core.

57. "WHAT DOES MY OPENING NEED TO ACCOMPLISH?"

It needs to focus reader expectations in the right direction, and it'll do so by making narrative promises that are in line with the story's movement and that the story's ending will fulfill.

Narrative promises refer to what readers will expect in terms of genre, mood, tone, characterization, and the protagonist's central struggle.

Often, the seed for the ending will appear in the opening, but you might not know what that is until you've finished writing your book. That's okay. Hold the opening loosely in your hand and be ready to revise it if the story nudges you in different, more intriguing, direction.

Lock in the genre and the constraints of this fictional world early on. Readers will willingly suspend their disbelief on page one. Don't ask them to start doing so selectively, starting on page three hundred.

Assure readers that they're in good hands. When they open your book, they want it to be compelling and entertaining. They really do. Don't disappoint them on this first page. Draw them in. Include absorbing, striking prose right off the bat. Earn their trust by keeping your promises.

Once the curtain opens, let the play begin. Who's onstage? What are they doing when the scene starts? Your goal: let this become clear to readers by rendering rather than summarizing. Also, you'll do so in a way that creates a sense of concern, empathy, or admiration for the protagonist without disorienting readers.

58. "SHOULD I START BY SHOWING THE NORMAL WORLD OF THE MAIN CHARACTER AT THE OPENING OF MY STORY?"

It's certainly possible to show a stable life at the start of the story, leaving readers to understand this as a promise that things are about to go terribly wrong, but if you dwell too long in the "normal world" without tension or pursuit, you run the risk of boring your readers.

Usually, starting with tension is a good idea. Ask if your current opening provides:

- an impetus for escalation,
- an occasion for revelation about the character,
- an opportunity for transformation of a situation, inner struggle, or relationship,
- an orientation to the setting,
- clear promises regarding the genre.

After you introduce the main character, keep her present long enough for readers to empathize with her, worry about her, or start cheering for her.

59. "WHAT IF MY CHARACTERS ALREADY HAVE A HISTORY WITH EACH OTHER WHEN THE STORY OPENS?"

The beginning of your story isn't necessarily the beginning of the characters' relationships. That means there'll likely be unanswered questions between the characters, a backstory that includes both good memories and old wounds, the residue of misunderstandings, and so on.

For instance, a childhood insult could have followed her into adulthood, a past flame might be reignited, or emotional baggage might be weighing her down.

Allow these past experiences to affect the current story, but don't feel the need to explain all of that history to readers right away. Only tap into what's relevant to this story.

Identify a scene in your story (or in the backstory preceding the first chapter) in which there's the potential for misunderstanding. How can you accentuate this and produce a sense of longing in your reader's mind for things to be resolved?

60. "WHAT ELSE SHOULD I REMEMBER ABOUT STORY OPENINGS?"

Your story actually begins where another one ends. For example, if there's a murder at the start of your book, it was planned, it was committed, it was covered up by someone and that previous story culminated in this story's beginning.

The end of that story initiates this current one, which might involve the search for the killer, the mourning of the surviving family members, and so on.

Many authors make the mistake of trying to explain the reasons behind the first scene of their book (often in the second chapter, where they dump in pace-killing backstory). Trust your readers to fill in the blanks.

Readers accept that this current story must start somewhere, so it's not necessary to delve into the previous story. It's much more important to orient readers to the character and the pursuit of this story than to try to explain all that led up to its initiation.

Remember, the beginning of your story includes not just the first in a series of events but the originating event, the one that sets into motion all that will follow.

Also, since readers know that a story needs to include tension, as yours opens, they'll expect that things are either about to go wrong or about to get worse. Meet those expectations. This is one way of making and keeping narrative promises.

61. "YOU'VE MENTIONED NARRATIVE PROMISES SEVERAL TIMES. WHAT EXACTLY ARE YOU REFERRING TO?"

The driving force of a story is tension, but a story is built on and bookended by promises and fulfillment. No matter how many acts your story has, it's over when the narrative promises (both stated and implied) that you've made to readers have been fulfilled.

- A stated promise: "I'm going to get that knife from you. And then I'm going to kill you with it."
- An implied promise: "That's a really cool cobra you have there. Does it ever get out of its terrarium?"

In the first case, if the character never goes after the knife, readers will be left unfulfilled. In the second case, if the cobra has nothing to do with the story—especially if it never escapes from the terrarium—readers will be left wondering, *Okay, so why did they make such a big deal about the cobra?*

Your stated and implied promises will affect your readers' expectations about the progression and outcome of the story. The promises also give readers something to worry about and to be intrigued about.

As you develop promises, consider what lies ahead for your character: mishaps, setbacks, postponements, obstacles, separation, passion in the wrong direction, anxiety, failure, or rejection.

62. "HOW CAN I DO A BETTER JOB OF KEEPING

PROMISES?"

Novelists draw attention to things through specificity and elaboration.

We magnify what's important, just like a filmmaker might do by having the shot linger on a canteen that ends up being the clue to everything later on or the fire extinguisher that the hero will use to blast in the face of the monster that comes after him. Novelists do that, not with longer camera shots but with evocative detail and subtle foreshadowing.

Promises are fulfilled when there's proportionality in relationship to significance.

What exactly does that mean?

Very often, promises are broken when something is built up to be important and then never really turns out to be all that significant to the story's progression. For instance, when you introduce a character's special ability, traits, or assets, you're promising that those aspects will play a meaningful role in the story. Narrative promises might include:

1. *Pursuit*: The unmet desire of the main character will matter to the story's direction.

2. *Setting*: The more unusual and intriguing the setting, the more significant it should be to the story.

3. *Significance*: The uniqueness of or memorability of the character should be congruent with her importance to the story.

4. *Choices*: Each struggle is a promise. Show the trajectory that the character's choices send him on.

Readers will be patient with you if you draw attention to what's vital to the story, but if you continually ask them to stare at or care about things that have nothing to do with the character's pursuit, they'll eventually put your book aside.

You're breaking a promise when you build something up as

significant but then don't have it play an important role in your story.

63. "CAN I MAKE PROMISES BY HAVING CHARACTERS REVEAL THEIR PLANS?"

Absolutely. And the more precise those plans are, the more effective they'll be as far as locking in your readers' expectations. Instead of having a character say, "I guess I'll see you tomorrow," try, "I'll swing by your office tomorrow morning at ten."

Think about having one character share his PLANs with another:

- P – Purpose: What he's there to accomplish. This is a way of stating or reaffirming his intention. "I'm looking forward to the concert tomorrow night."

- L – Longing: What stirs the character deeply. Reveal the ultimate goal he wishes to achieve. "I want to learn to play the cello."

- A – Apprehension: What makes him uneasy. This'll be a promise that he's going to face that situation later in the story. "I'm terrified of closed spaces."

- N – Needs: What he requires for his pursuit. When needs are stated, they become implied promises to what's going to happen later in the story. "I need to find my son by suppertime, or I'm going to call the police."

64. "CAN RESOLUTION EARLY IN A STORY BE A PROMISE OF MORE COMPLICATIONS TO COME LATER?"

Yes. If your hero captures the villain on page 250 of a 450-page novel, readers will anticipate that the bad guy will escape, that he'll get released, that he wanted to be arrested as part of his master plan, or that he's really innocent after all. Use early resolution to set things up for tension to come.

65. "THERE'S TOO MUCH HAPPENING IN MY STORY, AND IT'S TOO CONFUSING. WHAT SHOULD I DO?"

Cut back on the events that are occurring. You're not shooting for many things *happening* but many things *mattering*. So weed out what doesn't. Readers will remain engaged as long as the movement of the story is reasonable and logical, as long as the main characters are people they can cheer for, and as long as the tension continues to escalate.

Think in terms of causality, characterization, and progression. The events that happen in a story will cause ripples to flow out in a variety of directions, and those rippling results will consequently cause results of their own.

For instance, your character divorces her husband. Who else will be impacted? Well, any children that they have, their friends, the in-laws, neighbors, and so on. It's not your job to tell the story of all the ripples that the choice results in, but rather to use discernment and include only the ones that matter to this story. Then take those events and their results to their logical conclusions.

Ferret out which implications of the characters' choices are important here and now and focus on those.

66. "ARE THERE WAYS TO SIMPLIFY MY STORY WITHOUT LOSING THE MAIN STORYLINE?"

A story might become too convoluted for any number of reasons.

Here are a few secrets to working through them and improving your story.

PROBLEM	TO ADDRESS THE ISSUE
Things are too confusing.	Make sure your scenes are vital to the main storyline and that they're concise.
Too many plates in the air.	Eliminate extraneous storylines or threads or promises of struggle and desire.
Readers can't tell which characters are important.	Clarify which characters are the most significant by showing the intimacy or immediacy of their struggles, by creating more reader empathy and identification, or by specifying the character's goals and the negative consequences if they fail to achieve their goals.
Too many characters in general throughout the story.	Conflate characters so you don't have so many of them playing the same role.
Too much action.	Action without escalation soon leads to boredom, so make sure your story's tension is escalating.

Too many scenes.	You'll want scenes that have something vital at stake in order to reveal what matters to the character or to show what he's capable of achieving. So, verify that you've trimmed out scenes during which nothing is at stake (but that you've included just to show how a character might act).
The flow is choppy.	Pause between action scenes to allow the characters to regroup and make a plan that leads to the next scene.

There very well might be too much happening in your story, and it might be confusing. Strive to keep readers oriented as the story moves forward. That orientation will involve keeping them locked in to the central characters' pursuits in each scene, the consequences that their choices have, and the subsequent decisions that result because of those choices.

Do this even if it makes the story a little longer. For the most part, readers are more interested in things making sense than in unnecessary brevity. Readers won't complain that the story makes too much sense or that there are too many promises being kept, even if the story ends up being a little bit longer.

67. "WHAT IS A SUBPLOT, ANYWAY?"

A story will chart the primary pursuit of the main character—what he's trying to accomplish, obtain, overcome, avoid, withstand, or avenge. It focuses on his objective. His goal.

For instance, maybe he's trying to stop the alien invasion, or she's seeking the man of her dreams, or he's hoping to locate the sunken treasure, or she's training to become a bartender to pay off her college loans. That's the main plot (or main pursuit). A subplot is *also* a pursuit, but one that's not as vital to the character.

Romance, revenge, or family issues could all be subplots for the primary pursuits listed above.

68. "ONE OF MY SUBPLOTS IS TAKING OVER THE STORY. HOW CAN I FIX THAT?"

You might need to reevaluate what your story is essentially about. Perhaps you've been wrong about what the main storyline is up until now.

The more words you pour into any secondary storyline (that is, subplot), the bigger the promise you're making to readers that it'll be significant to the outcome of the story or to the development or revelation of the main character. And once again, remember: You must keep your promises.

Examine the desires and relationships of the main character. Every dynamic relationship she has with other characters can add dimensionality to the story. Consider staggering the resolution of different storylines so tension remains present throughout the story. Evaluate what each character desires most and what steps he takes to get it, then layer those in across the story's landscape.

69. "HOW MANY SUBPLOTS SHOULD I INCLUDE?"

Rather than getting hung up trying to delineate and differentiate your plot and subplots, round out your story by asking, "What else matters to this character?" "How will the other characters' intentions affect the main character?" "Where can I add depth by layering in more longing?"

A subplot isn't a separate plot; it's integral to the main plot. In fact, if it's not essential for either story development or entertainment value, it can probably be cut. Introducing storylines usually means introducing more characters or at least taking readers deeper into the psyche or viewpoint of the characters currently in the story. Ask yourself if that's necessary in this story.

In a well-told story, all of the storylines will meet and inform the resolution of each other.

Viewing the layers of the story as "subplots" can create an artificial differentiation between the characters' relationships with each other and the multiple, interwoven desires and struggles each character has. Stop thinking in terms of subplots, and start thinking in terms of story dimensionality.

70. "HOW WILL I KNOW IF I HAVE ENOUGH STORYLINES TO REVEAL MY PROTAGONIST?"

Some writing instructors teach that everything that happens in a story is meant to reveal the main character more or to develop his progression toward his eventual transformation. According to this viewpoint, every relationship he has is simply there to uncover or develop an aspect of his life.

In truth, however, every character isn't in a book just to reveal attributes of the protagonist. It's simply not the case. There are too many exceptions to this to claim that it's a rule, let alone the norm.

Introducing a character doesn't necessarily introduce a new storyline, but it does introduce the *opportunity* for one. Bringing in a character with an unmet desire will often add depth to the storytelling that you're engaged with—whether it's a new storyline altogether or one that deepens the story's main narrative thread.

SECTION III

ORGANIC WRITING AND CONTINGENCY

71. "I'VE BEEN TOLD TO START WITH AN OUTLINE. WHAT ARE YOUR THOUGHTS?"

While, to a certain degree, using an outline is a matter of personal taste, it's imperative to stay flexible and receptive to the unfolding story—whether you plan it out in advance or allow it to evolve as you write it.

Many writers see outlines as constricting, intimidating, frustrating, and tedious to come up with. They find that organic writing suits them better. If you think, *How could I write something that I haven't planned out?* you'll probably lean toward outlining. If you think, *How can I outline something that doesn't exist yet?* you'll likely thrive more as an organic writer.

72. "CAN YOU ELABORATE ON THE DIFFERENCE

BETWEEN THE APPROACHES?"

Organic writers learn what the story is about as they write it, not before. They can't necessarily tell you early on how the story will end because they don't yet know what happens beforehand to leap up to the climax. Outliners can usually tell you how their story is going to conclude. Often, they work backward from the ending to find the beginning.

Whatever your approach, it's vital to remain open and amenable to the characters as they reveal themselves to you, as you feel a tug to take the story in a different direction, or as new ideas unfold before you.

Stay nimble and responsive. Be open to the possibility that you've included some scenes you don't need or maybe missed out on some essential ones that you'll have to add. Outlines often short-circuit this flexibility and handcuff stories to presuppositions rather than setting them free.

The more you understand the forces that affect the movement of a story—believability, escalation, causality, tension, and so on—the less likely you'll need to outline it.

Staying receptive to discovery is a vital aspect of the creative process. Don't shy away from it, even though it might be a little intimidating to you. Rather than writing with the end in mind, write with the moment in mind, allowing context to shape every scene, every sentence, every word.

73. "I USUALLY PICTURE SEVERAL PLOT SIGNPOSTS TO GUIDE ME ALONG THE WAY— IS THAT WRONG?"

Not wrong, per se, but perhaps not wise.

Let's say that in real life, you're driving from Los Angeles to New York City. You start with a destination in mind, and you choose a number of significant places you're planning to stop at during your trip.

But what if something unexpected happens? A relative of yours dies? Your interests evolve? You hear about Orlando and how beautiful it is there? Maybe that's where you should go. Why plow on unquestioningly to New York City after you realize it's not the best destination for you after all?

Don't let your pre-planning impinge on the journey or constrict your story. Stay open to the route that's unfolding before you as you write.

74. "WHAT IF I DECIDE I NEED A DIFFERENT CLIMAX FROM THE ONE IN MY OUTLINE? HOW RIGIDLY DO I NEED TO CLING TO IT?"

Don't cling to it at all. Don't let your assumptions undermine what you've learned about the story while you've been writing it.

You may find it freeing to torch your outline (figuratively or literally) and let the story lead you to where it wants to go based on the characters' desires, even if that's to places you were never prepared to travel.

75. "WHAT IF I WRITE MYSELF INTO A CORNER?"

Hopefully, you will.

That's often where the best ideas lie waiting for you.

There will always be some degree to which you're writing toward something (as you anticipate where the story might go) as well as writing from something (as you consider where it's been), but when you find yourself in a corner, it's often best to take a step back from your intentions and take a deeper journey into the story itself.

Stop analyzing the story and start entering the scenes. Step into them and look around. Imposing preconceptions upon the story is a common problem. This happens when we bend the narrative toward where we want it to go rather than probing into it to find out where it would most naturally go if we weren't holding the reins.

Here's a question to ask yourself: "Am I letting the story grow from what's happening, or am I bending it toward where I want it to go?"

Fear will drive you back to an outline. It will lure you away from the story and into a formula. Don't let that happen.

Would you outline a symphony? Do you try to figure out its structure and start there—or do you end there? You start with a note or a tune, a musical progression that won't let you go.

Focus on causality and believability rather than structure. So, instead of asking yourself what should happen to move the story forward, ask yourself what would naturally happen based on what already has. Then, add some surprises to pivot into unexpected realms.

Take a deeper dive into the characters' desires and allow them to act in ways that are completely believable and that reveal more about who they are, their pursuit, and how deeply it matters to them.

If you listen, the characters will tell you what should happen next.

76. "WITHOUT AN OUTLINE, HOW CAN I KNOW WHAT TO WRITE NEXT?"

Ask yourself what the character would naturally do in that situation, then have him do it, or, if he must do something else, show readers that there's a better reason for that unexpected course of action.

For example, let's say your karate expert protagonist is walking down a dark alley and is suddenly attacked by four thugs. Readers will think he's going to fight back skillfully. So, you have two options—let him fight and move on, or avoid the fight and then justify that course of action to your readers.

Let's say he fights. What then? Does he win? Does he lose?

He wins? Okay, what would he do next? Call the cops? Go home and forget about it? Take the injured guys to the hospital? Whatever you choose has to be natural and believable for that character.

Now, as you move believably forward, tighten the tension. Look for ways to make things worse. How will that fight scene escalate the central struggles of the story—does he get into trouble with the law? With his sensei? Is he blackmailed? Injured? Does it bring to mind bad memories from his childhood? Does the city's entire criminal underground come after him?

Whatever the consequences, they'll affect his life or pursuit in tangible and surprising ways.

As those become clearer to you, you may need to rewrite some of the previous scenes to make them honest and integral to the actual progression of the story. As you do, stay flexible, nimble, and hold the story loosely in your hand. Nothing is in stone until the book is published, so enjoy the process as you watch the story unfold.

77. "THERE ARE LOTS OF PLOT TEMPLATES OUT THERE. WOULD IT BE HELPFUL TO USE ONE?"

It's probably best for you to hold back from the temptation to funnel your ideas into a plot template or formula, better to avoid cramming the story into a predetermined framework and number of acts.

Simply put, if you want to write formulaic stories, then follow a formula. If that's not what you want, then don't. Following a formula is a great way to pump out cookie-cutter novels.

Do you want to write ground-breaking stories or formulaic ones? What do you want to be known for?

(It's certainly true that some authors make a lot of money writing formulaic stories, so, in the end, you'll need to decide how you measure success and how that will affect your engagement with the creative process.)

Think about this: Why do so many movies seem the same?

Well, because so many of the screenwriters are working from the same playbook and forcing their ideas into the same three-act structure.

Even though it might be helpful for an amateur artist to start by using a paint-by-numbers approach, there comes a time when he's had enough of using that crutch and is ready to start working from an empty canvas. Evaluate where you are in the process and let your personal journey and goals inform your approach.

78. "THEN WHY DO SO MANY PEOPLE TEACH THAT I SHOULD USE THOSE TEMPLATES?"

It's easier to offer writers a formula than teach the principles that will allow them to master the art form for themselves. It's much less work to hand someone a recipe than it is to teach him to cook.

79. "MY CHARACTERS SEEM TO HAVE A MIND OF THEIR OWN AND ARE DICTATING WHERE THE STORY IS GOING. IS THAT NORMAL, OR IS THERE SOMETHING WRONG WITH ME?"

For many authors, this is the norm. It results from an intuitive approach, one that really attends to the story and allows the characters to run free.

This issue is more common for organic writers, but it happens with outliners as well—however, organic writers are more apt to listen to the voice that tells them to take the story in another direction, while outliners will often default back to the outline they've constructed.

80. "BUT HOW CAN YOU START A STORY BEFORE YOU KNOW HOW IT WILL END?"

Although you might have an idea of the pathway to the conclusion before you write the story, the path will often look different when you've finished writing than you thought it would look when you began your book.

As long as you understand how a character pursues his objective through the story, the ending will become clear to you as you write. You might even find that what you thought would be the beginning isn't the story's *true* origin, and you might need to change the opening as you work on the ending.

Responsiveness to the story as you nurture it on its way to being born is a vital aspect of the creative process.

81. "MY STORY DOESN'T REALLY GO ANYWHERE. THINGS ARE BELIEVABLE, BUT THEY DON'T ESCALATE. HOW CAN I SOLVE THAT?"

This is the result of asking one category of questions about story development but neglecting another. It's likely you've been asking questions that organic writers instinctively ask:

- "What would this character naturally do?"
- "How would she most likely respond?"
- "What would be believable?"
- "What effect does this choice have on the story's

progression?"

All of these questions revolve around *believability* and *causality*—two vital aspects of storytelling. Characters will act in congruence with who they are (believability), and scenes and action will progress in a logical way based on what has just happened (causality).

That's category one.

A second category of questions revolves around *escalation*. When looking for ways to escalate tension, you'll ask:

- "What could go wrong?"
- "How will this turn out badly?"
- "How can I make things worse?"
- "What would deepen this character's struggle?"
- "Can I raise the stakes?"
- "How can I tug this character in two directions at once?"

Regarding that last question, the tug might come from a physical obligation (being in two places at once), a moral obligation (having to choose between two things he despises), or a relational obligation (requiring him to serve someone he doesn't want to serve).

These questions will help move the story toward a stirring and fitting climax rather than allowing it to wander into an unsatisfying ending.

As your story unfolds, ask questions from both categories to tap into all three of these vital narrative forces: believability, causality, *and* escalation.

82. "CAN YOU ELABORATE ON THIS IDEA OF CAUSALITY?"

Stories are not lists of things happening; they are accounts of things being caused.

Examine the order of events and their movement from cause to effect. For example, consider the two examples below:

1. "He went immediately to the fridge for something to drink; he was parched after spending all day working in the blazing sun."

2. "After spending all day working in the blazing sun, he was parched and went immediately to the fridge for something to drink."

In the first example, the action occurs, and then there's an explanation for why it happened. In the second, we see desire (thirst) that leads to action. No explanation is needed. That's what you want.

Also, in the first example, there's a fraction of a second when readers will ask, "Why?" as they wonder, *Why is he going directly to the fridge?—Oh. I see. He's not hungry; he's thirsty.*

In the second example, the action moves the story logically forward, and readers are continually present in the story. No confusion results.

Ask if your scene moves from event to explanation. If so, you can often improve it by reversing the order of events to move from cause to effect rather than effect to cause.

83. "HOW DOES CAUSALITY AFFECT THE FLOW OF MY SCENES?"

Causality affects the movement of every scene as well as the outcome of the story as a whole by grounding everything in the contingent nature of fiction.

Contingency simply means that the events are caused by the ones preceding them rather than just randomly occurring. In fiction, things happen for a reason (rather than randomly), and then those things, in turn, cause what follows next.

Avoid describing a character taking an action and then telling readers why he did it. Instead, establish the reason first, and then let him act.

You might write, "Allison cut her finger while slicing the tomatoes and hustled to the bathroom to find a bandage." In this case, you have an event (cutting her finger) causing another event (her search for a bandage).

But you wouldn't write, "Allison hustled to the bathroom to find a bandage. She'd cut her finger while slicing the tomatoes." This example moves from an event (her search for a bandage) not to another event but to an explanation. So, instead of driving the story forward, you're stuck having to go back to explain to readers what's going on.

In essence, you're telling the story backward.

84. "CAUSALITY IS NEW TO ME. ARE YOU SAYING IT'S ALL ABOUT AVOIDING TELLING THINGS IN THE WRONG ORDER?"

That's part of it. More to the point, it's about keeping readers oriented and immersed in the story through the logical flow of events.

Remember, you don't want to keep explaining why something just happened; you want it to be clear to readers based on the context.

Move the narrative from event to event to event to event, rather than from event to explanation to event to explanation. This maintains seamless believability and natural dramatic escalation.

Do you find yourself explaining or rendering? Does each stimulus have a natural response? If an explanation is necessary, you might have things in the wrong order. In most cases, when you find a sentence that serves to explain why something just happened, you can improve the writing by switching the order.

So, instead of, "We hopped into my cruiser and took off for Sebastian Lincoln's house. The DNA had led us back to him," you'd write, "The DNA led us back to Sebastian Lincoln. We hopped into my cruiser and took off for his house."

Rather than reaction and then clarification, show the stimulus and then the response. One thing causes the next, which causes the next, which causes the next.

Whatever fictional world you've created or the context of your story, the events that occur will be logically and contingently related to the ones that precede them.

85. "WHAT ARE SOME OTHER WAYS TO FIX CAUSALITY ISSUES?"

First, introduce desire before action. Write: "I'd been up for nearly thirty hours. All I wanted to do was get some sleep. I collected my suitcases at baggage claim and headed to the hotel." Rather than: "I collected my suitcases at baggage claim and headed to the hotel. All I wanted to do was get some sleep. I'd been up for nearly thirty hours."

In the second example, the *context* (being up for nearly thirty hours) and *desire* (I wanted to get some sleep) follow the *action* (collecting the suitcases and heading to the hotel). This is backward.

Secondly, show what leads to a revelation or discovery rather than noting it afterward. Write: "When she read the letter to me, I immediately understood: Al was Meredith's secret admirer." Rather than: "I immediately understood that Al was Meredith's secret admirer when she read the letter to me."

In the second example, the realization precedes the event that causes it. Backward once again.

Finally, move the story forward by letting things play out in logical order. Write: "He punched me hard in the gut, sending me reeling backward. Gasping for breath, I tried to shove him out of the way, but he flicked out a knife and said, 'It's time we end this. My way.'" Rather than: "He told me it was time to end this his way. He had flicked out a knife and punched me in the gut. I was trying to shove him out of the way after reeling backward and gasping for breath."

See what a mess you end up with when you neglect logic and causality?

If readers complain that your story is too confusing or that it's not going anywhere, it might be because you're not managing causality well.

86. "WHAT ROLE SHOULD CHANCE PLAY IN MY STORY?"

As little of a role as possible.

If events occur with no grounding in what has come before them, readers will be turned off and complain that the story "doesn't make sense."

Why?

In fiction, we want to find the meaning and coherence that's so often lacking in "real life." That coherence comes from the causal relationships that exist in the fictional realm.

Don't let chance come to the rescue: the cops show up at the scene precisely when they're needed, the magic elixir suddenly appears, the character's friend or mentor arrives just in the nick of time to save the day, etc.

If your character suddenly finds what he needs right at the moment that he needs it, the story will reek of coincidence, undermine believability, and leave readers thinking, *Oh, that was convenient!*

87. "WHAT ELSE DO I NEED TO KNOW ABOUT CHANCE AND COINCIDENCE?"

The only uncaused event in your story will be the first one. Or, another way to look at it: the only coincidence will be the opening scene in the book.

At least, *ideally*, that'll be the only coincidence.

Since every story begins with coincidence, that's the scene you'll need to justify the least. The scene in which you'll want to include the least amount of coincidence is the climax—so, since foreshadowing is how we remove coincidence, the climax will be the scene that has the most foreshadowing.

So, the scene with the *most* coincidence is the opening scene; the scene with the *least* amount will be (or should be) the climax.

However, many authors get things backward.

Instead of allowing coincidence to start the story and a choice to end it, they spend all sorts of time dumping in backstory in chapter two to (unnecessarily) justify the story's opening and then, when the choice matters most at the climax, they use coincidence to solve the problem by having someone else show up to rescue the hero.

Exactly the opposite of what you want.

Though your story will begin with a coincidence (as all do), it should not end with one (as all too many do).

(Incidentally, whenever you introduce a new character, at least for a moment, coincidence is on your side. So, if you need to lean into having things happen in a slightly-too-convenient way, let that happen at the initiation of a new storyline.)

88. "HOW DO COINCIDENCES SNEAK INTO STORIES?"

Coincidences often crop up when you've decided on a plot point, and you're trying to get the story to lean in that direction, or you've written yourself into a corner and you don't want to go back and rewrite sections of the book to make the next event inevitable. If something becomes available right when it's needed, or someone appears right when they're needed, you have a coincidence.

That being said, if your story is about how God or destiny directs us, readers will give you more leeway when it comes to including coincidences. But apart from those instances, you'll want to avoid coincidences—especially at the climax.

89. "HOW CAN I REMOVE COINCIDENCES FROM MY STORY?"

Try one of these steps:

1. Identify the significant moments in your story—particularly where a character uses a special skill, tool, or resource to solve a pivotal problem. Then, foreshadow the skill or object earlier in the story so that when it's necessary, it doesn't appear "out of nowhere." Let a character use it in a contextually appropriate way in a previous scene so readers are aware of it but not focused on it.

2. If fate plays a role in your story, set the promise at the beginning that this story occurs in a world in which it's present or where the apparent coincidences always carry a deeper meaning. Perhaps angels are real and intervene in human affairs. Make that clear early on.

3. If it's important to the story for another character to be present at the climax, show that help is on the way before it arrives. You don't want someone to drop in all of a sudden and rescue your hero. It'll seem too convenient and won't satisfy readers.

4. Point out the coincidence. Have one character say to another, "Doesn't this seem a little too convenient to you?" Readers will agree and be curious what the bigger plan is that's at play.

5. Cut down on the number of scenes you interrupt with all-too-conveniently timed phone calls, text messages, ringing doorbells, alarms, etc. (You'll be the most tempted to do this during intimate encounters between love interests, especially in scenes that are subtext dependent. Perhaps once in a book is okay, but don't get into the habit of ending scenes by interrupting them.)

6. Avoid coincidences by writing, "A few minutes later," or "After I'd started looking through the files," or something along those lines to show the passage of time and make it clear that the event or revelation doesn't happen right when the character needs it to.

90. "MY STORY IS BORING, BUT I DON'T KNOW HOW TO WEAVE IN MORE ACTION WITHOUT RESTRUCTURING THE WHOLE THING. ANY THOUGHTS?"

Weave in tension rather than action.

Look for ways to promise that things are going to get worse, that there's danger just around the bend, or that the impending peril is getting closer.

Also, keep your promises early on to gain your readers' trust. Readers will be turned off if things are boring, but they'll be drawn in if they trust that everything ties together and if they believe that the climax will be unforgettable.

91. "SHOULD MY STORY HAVE RISING ACTION?"

Since storytellers save the best for last, the final sequence will have the most tension, the highest stakes, and the most morally complex or meaningful decision.

If the high point of the book comes in the middle, readers will feel let down when they get to the less-than-climactic ending.

However, simply adding more action by itself will do little to keep readers interested and, at a certain point, will start to bore them. Few things are as boring as relentless action, and few are as engaging as relentless escalation. The tension will rise; the action might not.

92. "IF I DON'T HAVE RISING ACTION, HOW WILL I BUILD THE TENSION AS THINGS MOVE TOWARD THE CLIMAX?"

Let's say that in your thriller, there's a final confrontation between the hero and the would-be suicide bomber. It might not include much action at all, but can it be tense?

Absolutely.

Well-meaning writing instructors often tell aspiring authors that they need to "make something happen" in their stories, in order to "keep things moving." Most of the time, however, that's not the case.

Stories aren't about happenings and activity but pursuit and progression. Instead of trying to "make something happen," start letting the characters be themselves in the pursuit of their goal. Don't just make more things happen, make more things matter. Also, rather than trying to "keep things moving," keep them escalating.

Focus on increasing impending peril, and then be sure to pay off the promises you've made. This is more effective than simply making more and more events occur—even if they include lots of action.

Are you contorting the story in the direction you want it to go, or are you letting it inform you as it unfolds? Rather than trying to put a bit and bridle on your story, cut the reins and see where the context takes you. It'll often be more interesting than what you first had in mind.

93. "HOW DO I WALK THE FINE LINE BETWEEN TELLING READERS SO MUCH THAT IT MAKES THE ENDING PREDICTABLE AND HIDING THE CLUES TO IT SO DEEPLY THAT IT BECOMES UNBELIEVABLE?"

It's vital to step into your readers' shoes. Look at every scene through the lens of what the readers know, are anticipating, and are hoping for.

Shade each scene toward the solution, using foreshadowing to remove the coincidences at the end of the story but balancing that out with not giving too much away too early.

There's no formula for this.

There's no way to say, "On page 50, give the first hint," or something like that. (Although there are plenty of people selling plot and story templates who will be more than happy to give you this type of advice—for a price.)

Every story is different, every climax unique, and every pathway leading to it is fraught with its own pitfalls and laced with its own disadvantages—and also its own unique opportunities for tension.

You may wish to foreshadow danger:

1. Through warnings: ("Watch out for...")
   "Be careful with that firecracker."
   "Always keep your arms straight during your dive."
   "Don't forget to block your tires when you change a tire so the car doesn't roll off the jack."

2. Through predictions: ("If... then...")
   "If the sleet gets any worse, the roads are going to be impassable."
   "If no one shows up soon, we're going to be trapped on this mountain overnight."
   "If my dad finds you here, he's gonna ground me for life."

3. Through observations: ("This has happened in the past and might happen again.")
   "The last time I went that far back in the hills, I had zero cell reception."
   "I once rolled my car when a deer jumped out in front of me on that very stretch of road."
   "And they say that since that night, Clarence the Killer Clown still walks these woods and searches for little campers who don't stay in their cabins at night. And if he finds them, they are never...seen...again...Okay, kids, time for bed. I'm gonna hit the hay! Goodnight!"

Study the context, trust the process of reading from a reader's perspective, and hone your instincts to tell you the timing of the clues and revelations to include.

94. "WHAT'S ONE SECRET TO ESCALATING MY STORY TOWARD AN ENDING THAT ISN'T TOO PREDICTABLE?"

Be on the lookout for unintended consequences. They can be great ways of escalating the plot in directions that the readers and the characters will believe but not foresee.

95. "I WISH THERE WAS AN EASY WAY TO REMEMBER THE PROGRESSION OF A STORY. IS THERE ANYTHING SHORT AND SIMPLE BEYOND THAT IT SHOULD HAVE A BEGINNING, A MIDDLE, AND AN END?"

Your story will move through four primary realms: orientation, disruption, escalation, and transformation.

First, *orientation* as you introduce readers to your character, setting, and the narrative promises regarding the genre, voice, mood, and direction of the story. It will answer the readers' questions, "Who should I care about? Why should I care about them? When are we? Where are we?"

Then, a *disruption* will either turn the protagonist's world upside down (a crisis) or invite her out of her ordinary life into an extraordinary adventure (a calling).

At that point, setbacks will arise. They'll heighten the tension and make the story's goal more and more difficult to obtain. This *escalation* will eventually lead to a moment of hopelessness when it appears to readers (and often to the character as well) as if all seems lost. This moment often comes after a moment when all seems solved, but the situation isn't actually resolved at all.

Stories are not necessarily about the ascent of action to the climax as more and more things happen but are often about the descent of hope as more things that matter go wrong.

While rising to the occasion, the character will make an unexpected decision or meaningful sacrifice that brings resolution. Typically, this means that there will be some sort of *transformation* of the situation, the character's primary relationship, or of the character herself.

Within the story, let your characters loose; don't constrain them. Trust that, when you're progressing through these four story stages, the characters will know better than you do about the direction the story should go. Ask yourself:

- What is normal life like for this character?

- What is the crisis that disrupts that world? Or, what is the calling that initiates the story's journey or pursuit?

- How do things get worse? What is the moment at which all seems lost?

- What does the character discover about his world or himself?

- How does this affect him or his relationships?

- How does he end differently (or in a different place or state of mind) than he began?

SECTION IV

DIMENSIONALITY AND TENSION

96. "HOW CAN I CONCEPTUALIZE A THREE-DIMENSIONAL CHARACTER?"

Often, writing instructors refer to stories as being "plot-driven" or "character-driven." While helpful in some instances, this isn't a robust-enough paradigm for understanding how characters relate to events in most stories.

Characterization is developed by how a character makes decisions, expresses desires, and faces obstacles. So, in the graphic below, those three aspects border the character himself.

Regarding *decisions*, ask, "What does he do?" Regarding *desire*, ask, "What does he want?" And regarding *obstacles*, ask, "What does he face?"

At the point where his desire meets up with an obstacle, *tension* is born. When his desire meets up with a decision, readers receive a *revelation* of what he's truly like. And finally, when his decision meets up with an obstacle, the story progresses through *escalation* of the struggles at the heart of the story.

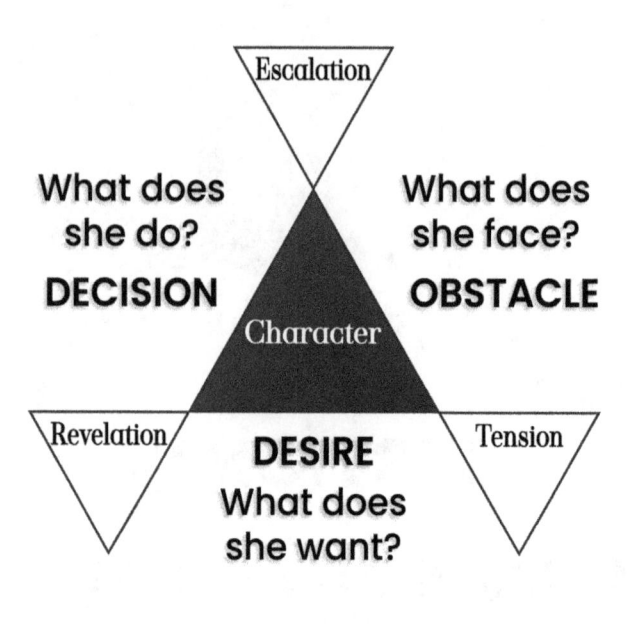

```
            Escalation
               /\
              /  \
What does   /    \   What does
she do?    /      \  she face?
DECISION  / Character\ OBSTACLE
         /_____\
  Revelation           Tension
         DESIRE
       What does
       she want?
```

97. "HOW CAN I CRAFT CHARACTERS WHO INSTANTLY COME ALIVE TO READERS?"

Remember, stories are not simply about what characters do; they're about what characters want and how they pursue those unmet desires.

Early in your story (preferably as soon as we meet the character), make it clear to readers what she desires or what she's seeking or avoiding. To quickly make her interesting: (1) Stick her in the middle of a struggle, (2) Give her an attitude, a quirk, or a unique voice (3) Let her show resolve, courage, or self-sacrifice (4) Put another character in peril and have your protagonist use her special skill or ability to help her, (5) Make her the underdog in a significant confrontation.

Also, delve into what really makes that character tick. Ask yourself:

- What holds her back from complete honesty—fear?

Expediency? Complicity? It can tell you a lot about the character.

- What does she cling to that she doesn't need anymore?

- What does she let go of that she should hang onto?

- What does she deny or ignore that she should confront? What causes her to do so? What relationships will be affected by that? What will that result in?

- Is she drifting from (or even running from) the direction she needs to go?

- What delusions is she under? What lie does she believe? Where will clarity come from?

98. "HOW CAN I MAKE MY CHARACTERS MORE UNIQUE?"

Think in terms of the idiosyncrasies, goals, catchphrases, hobbies, habits, special skills, and traits of each character.

1. The math professor only shaves on days that are prime numbers.

2. The runway model carries floss around with her everywhere because she gets stuff stuck in the gap between those two teeth that were never fixed because her family couldn't afford braces.

Think about food choices (vegan, anti-vegan, fruitarian), eating habits (always on the couch? Only with a spork?), or pet peeves (Velcro shoes, camouflage flashlights, people naming their cars after ex-girlfriends, etc.).

Often, a memorable protagonist will be finely drawn, with one-of-a-kind quirks, deep convictions, and a moral center that will direct his decisions and attract readers.

Sometimes you can look for contradictions between what readers would expect and what the character does in his free time: The accountant builds small imitations of famous buildings out of toothpicks, so whenever he goes to a restaurant, he brings some of the toothpicks back home.

Consider:

- When she's nervous, she...
- When he has a day off, he...
- Her favorite family recipe is...
- He relies on science, except for the home remedy for...

Is she a snob when it comes to coffee? Craft beer? Wine? Cheese? Jazz music? What else are people snobs about? Think of habits that annoy you. Start with people you've lived with. Tap into their habits. Let the character become someone interesting, one-of-a-kind, and memorable.

99. "ARE THERE OTHER WAYS I CAN ESTABLISH THE INDIVIDUALITY OF MY CHARACTERS?"

Each character in your story will have a unique package of quirks, inconsistencies, and beliefs.

The more central a character is to your story, the more important it'll be that readers see how he or she is a unique and irresistible individual.

Consider how your protagonist's backstory might affect her. Is she still living under the thumb of the past? For instance, she might still be trying to please her father, who has been dead for five years. Or is she obsessed with the future and worried about where things are going in her life rather than enjoying life as it unfurls before her?

To discover individuality, ask, "How would he respond to this challenge in a way the other characters would not?" That's where the uniqueness lies. Is there a defining attitude that he has toward the other characters in the scene or toward this type of situation?

(Incidentally, if your character has bad habits—and he very well might—they should be ones that your readers will forgive or overlook, given the context of the story.)

100. "DOES MY CHARACTER NEED A SPECIAL ABILITY?"

Not necessarily, but often, he will have a unique skill or trait that will come into play at the climax.

For a pivot, you can have the bad guy remove the protagonist's assets or special skill and leave him having to fend for himself at the climax without them.

Just don't build up a special ability throughout the story and then fail to pay off that promise. For example, if the archer happens to forget that he can shoot his bow at the rope to cut it and save the hanging man, readers will think he's an idiot and won't be on his side anymore.

101. "IS IT TRUE THAT CHARACTERS SHOULD HAVE INCONGRUITIES?"

Characters who portray the same attitude all the time are boring.

If your character is always loving and kind, she'll annoy your readers. If he's always impatient with everyone, he'll grate on readers. The secret is finding the moments when she *isn't* loving, or he actually *is* patient toward someone.

Apparent inconsistencies will draw readers in and, make them curious and keep you from portraying cardboard, one-dimensional characters.

Look for the exception to the rule. When isn't the generally happy person happy? When she's alone with her husband? If so, what does that tell you about her struggle and her story?

Contradictions invite reader interest and speculation. When readers begin to wonder, *Why is she like that? What's the story here? What's the reason for that incongruity?* it gives you a natural and unobtrusive bridge to backstory.

If you choose to include a flashback in your book, you might render the scene that shows the reason for the incongruity since readers are often intrigued by the origin stories of characters they enjoy.

Consistency is different from incongruities.

Readers want characters to act *authentically* in each situation they encounter. That is, the characters will consistently portray their incongruities. As soon as a character stops acting in concert with who she is or shows inconsistency regarding her core attitudes and goals, the story loses believability.

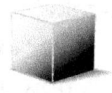

102. "HOW CAN I MAKE MY CHARACTERS MORE WELL-ROUNDED?"

You won't want to.

Most people are not well-rounded. Well-rounded people aren't very interesting. It's people who are neurotic, off-balance, who pendulum-swing from one interest or emotion to another who are the most interesting to readers. Rocky Road instead of vanilla. A roller coaster ride rather than a drive through the suburbs. That's what you're shooting for. That's where you want to take things.

When working on your characters, remember that:

1. Contradictions deepen characterization.

2. Quirks create empathy.

3. Believability engenders connection.

4. Shame arises from beliefs.

5. Secrets reveal fears.

103. "HOW CAN I SUBTLY INCREASE THE TENSION IN MY CHARACTER'S JOURNEY THROUGH THE STORY?"

Look beyond what the character wants and consider what that desire implies. In other words, what do his desires or his choices reveal about him or his priorities? Is he aware of that? Will that revelation be significant to the story? Or is his lack of self-understanding the core issue at stake? What's holding him back from becoming all that he could potentially be?

• What attitude or perception is keeping your character from getting what he wants?

• What external forces are stopping him? What societal or cultural pressures?

• What setting-specific liabilities are hindering him? What other characters or personal beliefs are intruding on his intentions?

Also, think of natural disabilities or hindrances. For instance, mental or physical impairments, familial pressure, emotional hardships (he's depressed, grieving, distracted, on the rebound), fear (of discovery, of consequences, of rejection), or self-perception (low self-esteem, self-loathing, lack of confidence). Secrets can also be effective. What is the secret? Why is it important to keep a lid on it? What will happen if it's exposed?

Secrets aren't essential, but the goal of keeping a secret can be a powerful way of driving a story forward. To show *how* she's hiding, put her in a scene with someone who's trying to get to know her secrets. To show *why* or *what* she's hiding, you may wish to include a flashback to delve into backstory and the painful moment or memory that's rooted there.

104. "DOES MY STORY'S CENTRAL DILEMMA NEED TO BE CLARIFIED?"

Clear to readers, yes.

Specifically stated, no.

Sometimes, there's a question that runs throughout the entire story or the moral dilemma that the story hinges upon. It might not be specifically stated, but will undergird every scene.

When you have a team of main characters, the protagonist doesn't need to be the one to ask the story's central question; one of his teammates can do so instead. This is common in series stories in which the same cast of characters appears.

Accentuate that the character doesn't simply face a difficult decision, but a moral dilemma. It will cost him dearly either way, whatever he chooses. Dilemmas add tension, so include deadlines and time constraints, countdowns, moral quandaries, distractions, dual obligations, and conflicting desires.

For example, the protagonist might have two goals, even in scenes in which the stakes aren't sky high: He might want to impress the girl but also not hurt her feelings. So, he tries to decide whether or not to let her win at the game of chess. (Regardless of his decision, it'll likely backfire to add tension to the story.)

One thing to remember: Moral complexity (involving a dilemma that matters) is not the same thing as moral ambiguity, in which no distinction is made between virtues and vices.

105. "HOW IMPORTANT IS DESIRE TO THE CHARACTER'S PURSUIT?"

As we explored earlier, without unmet desire, nothing within the world of the story will go anywhere. No matter how many conflicts or complications arise, as long as the character doesn't desire change or isn't willing to act in pursuit of that, the story won't get out of the starting blocks.

Story is more than conflict; it is pursuit in a specific direction. Fuse action with intention in every scene. Tension is born when conflict meets desire. It is the lifeblood of every story. Let it course through every scene.

Understanding what your characters want is essential. When you begin rewriting your novel, you might not know how far they're willing to go to get what they desire most—that uncertainty is normal and natural. However, as you work through your story, it'll become more and more clear to you. Don't hold back. Let your characters go all the way to the brink in pursuit of their desires.

106. "DOES EVERY CHARACTER NEED AN OVERRIDING DESIRE?"

Every point of view character will have a pursuit that'll eventually become clear to readers. Secondary characters will also have desires, but readers won't necessarily find out what they are, and those desires won't necessarily alter the story's trajectory.

107. "CAN MY CHARACTER DESIRE MORE

THAN ONE THING? CAN IT CHANGE AS THE STORY PROGRESSES?"

Yes, she can have multiple desires—in fact, if you can identify two primary desires, it'll provide an opportunity for you to weave moral dilemmas into your story.

For instance, if she wants both to protect the innocent (compassion) and to tell the truth (honesty) and she ends up in a situation in which she must choose between the two, you've ratcheted up the tension. Look for specific opportunities to allow dual desires to become dueling desires.

As tension deepens and the story develops, the primary desire might change, but as long as it does so logically, readers will accept that.

For example, the billionaire seeks more and more money until his wife is abducted, and he receives a ransom note. Now, his desire shifts to finding a way to secure her safe return. Complications in the story might alter his primary desire again as the story develops—perhaps to take revenge on those who abducted her.

That being said, remember that it's vital for readers to understand or easily discern the desires (intentions) present in each scene.

Also, a character's choices will always have an effect on her.

Additionally, as she seeks to fulfill her desire or accomplish her quest, she might learn that what she thought she wanted out of the situation is not, on a deeper level, what she really wants after all. The revelation would then result in choices of its own.

108. "I DON'T KNOW WHAT MY PROTAGONIST SHOULD DO IN THIS SCENE. HOW CAN I FIGURE THAT OUT?"

Ask what he would pursue rather than what he should do.

Remember, he'll take concrete, believable steps to pursue his desire. If you don't know what that is, odds are your readers won't either, and until they figure it out, they'll be lost.

Sure, they might be *curious* about what's going on, but they won't be emotionally enthralled in the story because they'll naturally be trying to figure out what the characters' actions imply. If that's the case, readers won't be worried about where things are going—because they don't yet know what the desire (or goal) is or why they should care about it at all. They will eventually become more confused than concerned about what's happening in the character's life and put the book down.

109. "CAN TWO CHARACTERS HAVE THE SAME GOAL IN A SCENE?"

Sure. Two detectives visit a crime scene and work together to find the killer. Or two would-be lovers flirt, looking for a way to deepen their relationship.

Often, when two characters are both seeking the same goal in a scene, they either go about it in a different way or show how they're unique in the steps that they take as the scene unfolds. Sometimes, only one of them will achieve the stated objective, resulting in tension between the characters.

110. "I CAN SEE HOW DESIRE IS THE ENGINE FOR STORIES, BUT I'M WONDERING—WHAT IF THE CHARACTER ISN'T AWARE OF WHAT HE WANTS? WHAT DRIVES THE STORY FORWARD THEN?"

Three types of desire exist in stories: actual, perceived, and expressed.

Let's say your protagonist shows up at a bar and the bartender says, "What can I get you?" The man replies, "Bourbon. Dirty. I'm here for one reason tonight: to forget that woman who just walked out on me."

He's expressed a desire, but let's say he actually showed up because he heard that the detective he's been hoping to interview for the true crime book he's writing comes here on Thursday nights. He wants to meet him but decides he needs to conceal that fact from the bartender for the time being. In that case, the protagonist's expressed desire and perceived desire would be different.

But what about his actual desire?

Well, it might be to interview that detective and finish the book, or it might be something else: maybe he's working so hard on this book because his marriage is in shambles and he doesn't want to face that fact. So his actual goal is to escape his problems, even if he's not aware of that.

Here are the questions you'll ask yourself related to the desires of your characters:

EXPRESSED DESIRE	1) What does he *say* he wants? 2) How will this affect the progression of this scene?
PERCEIVED DESIRE	1) What does he *believe* he wants? 2) How will this perception affect his choices?
ACTUAL DESIRE	1) What does he *actually* want (even if he's not aware of it)? 2) How can I make this clearer to readers?

As you write, explore the ways the character is in the dark about what he wants and, if his perceived desire and actual desire aren't the same, what scene or event could cause him to realize that and change.

111. "YOU'RE SAYING MY CHARACTER CAN DESIRE SOMETHING AND NOT BE AWARE OF IT?"

Just as in real life, characters in stories won't always know what they want or might be wrong about what they think they desire.

When it comes to desire, even if the character isn't clear on what he wants (or is confused about what he wants), readers will be lost if they don't understand what he's pursuing. They might actually cheer for his ultimate success, which means his momentary failure.

112. "CAN YOU GIVE ME AN EXAMPLE OF WHEN READERS WILL CHEER FOR THE PROTAGONIST'S MOMENTARY FAILURE?"

If he's pursuing a goal they know is counterintuitive to what he actually needs.

For instance, a character thinks that fortune and glory will bring him happiness, but as he achieves it, he begins to lose his family due to his greed. Readers can see that every step he takes toward what he perceives to be the pathway to happiness is actually a step in the wrong direction and is undermining what's truly important in life.

In that case, since readers care about the character, they'll be cheering for him to fail to get what he wants (more fame and fortune) so he can discover what he truly needs (better priorities and closer relationships).

113. "CAN READERS BE AWARE OF THE SUBCONSCIOUS DESIRES OF THE CHARACTERS?"

A character's subconscious (or actual) desire is often more evident or visible to readers than it is to her. Sometimes, it's possible (and valuable) to let readers in on what the character actually wants, even if that character isn't aware of those desires.

This can be done through showing the destructive nature of their current priorities, by letting others show by example what he needs, or by appealing to readers' natural sense of right and wrong or of virtue and vice.

For instance, readers realize the character really desires forgiveness even though he believes that he needs to enact revenge on those who have harmed him.

Also, readers might be able to infer from the actions of the character that she probably doesn't desire what she thinks she desires or won't be happy if she achieves what she's currently pursuing.

As you explore the yearnings and desires of your characters, take things deeper by allowing your protagonist to answer the following questions (perhaps have him write you a letter answering them as you brainstorm your story):

1. What dreams am I pursuing? What dreams have I postponed?

2. Where does my passion lie? What brings me the most joy and satisfaction?

3. What am I yearning for most? What steps am I taking to obtain it?

4. What desires or convictions clash inside of me? Which

ones am I feeding by my choices?

5. What moral inconsistencies exist in my life (that is, incongruity between what I confess/claim and how I live)?

6. What fears are holding me back from pursuing the things that I believe are important? Why do I have them, and what will I do about them?

114. "SHOULD I LET READERS IN ON WHAT CHARACTERS KNOW?"

In a mystery, don't let readers notice more clues than the detective, or they'll think he's not very bright. However, you can make readers *think* they've solved the case before he has, but then, after the twist or the big reveal, realize that they were wrong.

Often, you can draw readers into a story by allowing them to discover something significant about the character before that character is aware of it. This might be an understanding of the character's true nature, a revelation of her deepest desires, or an awareness of impending danger she's about to face.

Play with this dynamic and allow readers to see more meaning in the character's life or choices than the character is aware of, as long as your protagonist doesn't come across as stupid or clueless.

115. "IS IT POSSIBLE FOR MY CHARACTER TO HAVE MULTIPLE, CONTRADICTORY TRAITS OR DESIRES AT THE SAME TIME?"

Yes. A character might be both strong and vulnerable at the same time, in need of both mercy and justice, both selfless and selfish, both stubborn and yet easily manipulated, both protective of others and also self-possessed. He might be courageous yet timid, confident yet insecure, idealistic and also pessimistic, jaded as well as sensitive—and he might be all of them at once, just as people in real life are.

Often, a character will have more than one emotional response to a scene. By delving into this internal tug of war, we can engage reader empathy, create more nuanced characters, and better reflect reality.

Paradox is always interesting, as long as it's honest.

You will be told to show and not tell, but in this case, it's okay to tell readers that the character feels conflicted as you clarify her paradoxical desires. For instance, she might think…

> *I'm looking forward to…but also apprehensive about…*
> *I'm relieved that…but also worried that…*
> *I love to…but also hate…*
> *I desire…but also fear…*
> *I regret…but I learned to…*
> *I am hoping for…but also doubt that…*
> *I am afraid of/anxious about…but I'm also…*
> *I feel excited to…but also…*
> *I'm nervous about…but also…*
> *I'm thankful for…but also…*
> *I admire…but also…*
> *I'm saddened…but also…*
> *I have noticed that I am often…but also…*

116. "I'M NOT SURE WHAT MY CHARACTER WANTS MOST. HOW DO I FIGURE THAT OUT?"

Often, the character's desire will become clearer to you as the story progresses and you get to know him more intimately, both from spending time with him and by delving into his actions and responses to what's occurring in the story. Step out of the way. Stay open to the movement of the story. If you listen to the character and watch what he does, you'll begin to discern more about his desires.

Don't worry if the desire isn't crystal clear to you from the start. If you pay attention, it'll become more evident. Just acknowledge that as it does, you may need to go back through your manuscript and alter the things he said, thought, or did in order to direct them more inexorably toward the primary driving desire/s you've uncovered.

117. "CAN KNOWING WHAT MY CHARACTER FEARS HELP ME DISCOVER WHAT HE WANTS?"

Fear and desire are cousins. Identifying one will help reveal the other.

So, if you know what your character fears, you'll know what he desires. For example, if he fears loneliness, then he desires intimacy; if he fears a stifling work environment, he desires the freedom to explore his creative nature.

The fear of being consumed by the personality of another would reveal the desire for individual expression. Some people are afraid of losing themselves, others of finding themselves. Some people fear risk, others failure, still others security or success.

It works the other way as well—if you know what your character desires, you'll also know what he fears:

FEAR	DESIRE
Boredom	Adventure
Depression	Joy
Rejection	Acceptance
Disrespect	Value

Exclusion	Belonging
Hypocrisy	Authenticity
Irrelevance	Significance
Meaninglessness	Meaning
Deception	Truth
Emptiness	Fulfillment
Death	Survival
Injustice	Justice
Danger	Security
Failure	Success

118. "MY PROTAGONIST DOESN'T HAVE A 'FATAL FLAW.' DOES SHE NEED ONE?"

Characters need unmet desire, the ability to make meaningful choices, and a uniqueness that sets them apart from other characters, but they do not need one overriding "fatal" flaw.

They might be vulnerable in certain areas, but if you create a character who has that one glaring, obvious weakness, you've also made your story more predictable because the character will likely have to address that flaw, usually at the climax. You've let readers see your hand.

Evaluate if your character will have an Achilles' heel or not. If so, identify where she's the most vulnerable, then press the forces of antagonism against that vulnerability. However, don't feel obligated to include a "fatal" flaw. Only include one if it's vital to the story and authentic to that character's life.

119. "WHAT TYPES OF VULNERABILITIES CAN CHARACTERS HAVE?"

The sky is the limit. Here are three areas where we often find vulnerabilities:

1. *Physical impairments*: He can't walk, or has only one arm, or is slowly losing his mind. He might be battling depression or substance abuse. He might be suicidal. Think of anything believable that would be a disadvantage to your character in his pursuit or in his clash against the story's forces of antagonism, and it can become a vulnerability.

2. *Reliance on others*: In coming-of-age stories, the protagonist will often have to come to terms at the climax with the idea that she must be self-reliant, that her choices matter, and that no one is going to bail her out or swoop in to save her.

3. *Personal temptations*: Tempt your character to give up on his convictions. He'll be most vulnerable when he's alone, hungry, in a distant land, frustrated, or tired. Take him to the brink so that he (and your readers) can see what he's made of.

120. "HOW CAN I MAKE MY PROTAGONIST MORE VULNERABLE WITHOUT MAKING HIM WEAK?"

Consider what strength of his can be twisted around to become a vulnerability by the villain. For instance, compassion is a vulnerability. It's not a weakness to love others, but it does make you more vulnerable. It requires you to act for the good of others, while the villain might only act for the good of himself.

When the villain harms or threatens the hero's beloved, he's attacking the hero where he is most vulnerable. While villains might act in cold-hearted ways, your hero will be inhibited by his concern, empathy, and love for other characters.

What is the character's attribute that readers will most admire? What makes him vulnerable in ways that they can understand and empathize with—in ways that don't make him weak? That's what you're looking for.

Also, ask, "Where does he allow himself little indulgences?" Those are areas where he could be blackmailed or ransomed.

In fiction, to make a character do what he doesn't want to do, have another character either bribe him (offer him what he desires) or extort him (threaten to take away what he values). Nearly all inter-character manipulation in novels occurs either because of promises (bribery) or threats (extortion).

121. "HOW IMPORTANT ARE CHOICES IN REVEALING MY CHARACTER'S DEVELOPMENT?"

A protagonist might not always change, but he will always *choose*. And his choices might lead him to learn, grow, adapt, or perhaps—in some cases—succumb.

Our choices don't define us, but they do impact us. Every mistake leaves its mark. Every second chance is there to give us hope to try again.

It's the same for story characters. Choices reveal us even as they shape our lives.

By the way, focusing on one moment in the character's backstory and making that the impetus or determinant moment in her life isn't necessarily a good idea. Readers know that our identities aren't shaped by one incident or decision. We're affected by those things, but our personalities and identities aren't ultimately determined by them.

You'll often see this when an author introduces an intrusive flashback just to include the reason for the character's motivation. These usually aren't necessary.

Instead, focus on the story that's being told now and on the choices that are currently being made rather than on a scene that happened beforehand, in the character's past.

122. "REGARDING THAT, HOW MUCH OF MY CHARACTER'S BACKSTORY OR HISTORY SHOULD I INCLUDE?"

Backstory isn't the same as the character's history. Identifying applicable backstory requires putting her history through a sieve and sifting out only what is vital, relevant, and necessary for this story.

Figuring out backstory isn't so much about inclusion but about purposeful exclusion.

You might not know the character's backstory until you realize what's significant to this story—which might not happen until you're done writing your first draft. Only then will you know what aspects of this character's history have impacted this current story.

Not all stories need to include backstory. The "past coming back to haunt you" or "dealing with demons from the past" motifs appear in some stories, but not all.

Backstory is a promise of significance, so don't give detailed backstory to characters who are insignificant or who simply get killed off at the end of the scene they appear in.

Backstory is closely tied to interrelationships. It'll often affect the current state of the relationship with other characters as well as the relationship's trajectory.

123. "HOW CAN I SUBTLY BRIDGE TO THE BACKSTORY?"

Often, bridges to the backstory are clunky and awkward: For some reason, on this day, the character decides to suddenly—at this all-too-convenient moment—reminisce about her past. Usually, there isn't a valid impetus; it's just the gimmick the author is using to get the backstory in: studying the picture on the wall, feeling nostalgic while going through memorabilia, etc. Readers basically know they can skip the next section.

Motivate the rumination. Don't just let someone reminisce for no reason. What causes her to do so on this day, at this time?

So, either (1) give her a contextually compelling reason for the bridge, (2) let the pursuit become the bridge, or (3) use dialogue as the bridge.

Hinting at the backstory can be effective. Note the difference in each couplet of sentences below. The first introduces a struggle. The second also introduces backstory and the effect it's having on the present:

1. I couldn't stand the thought of saying goodbye.

2. I couldn't stand the thought of saying goodbye again.

Now, readers know that this character has had to say goodbye before. What happened? What's that all about? It's a story that readers will look forward to being let in on.

Or, take this example:

1. There was no reason to think there would be a cobra in our bed.

2. There was no reason to think there would be a second

cobra in our bed. Before that night, it'd always just been one.

Perhaps give your characters a scar or a tattoo. Both allow for an origin story: Something caused the scar; something influenced him to get that tattoo. What lesson did he take away from the situation?

Or, let him have a phobia. Often, a phobia is a type of scar. It can result from a traumatic past experience. (Unless it's of clowns, which are just plain universally creepy.) So, phobias can be clues or bridges to a character's backstory.

For some reason, hair brushing is a common (and clunky) bridge to backstory: "She brushed her lush, shoulder-length, brandy-colored hair and stared in the mirror, admiring the milky soft features on her face and the high cheekbones she'd inherited from her maternal grandmother, Ethel, who was widowed when she was nineteen when her husband, Ricky, was shipped off to war…" Or, "He brushed aside a strand of his auburn hair, and it reminded him of the time his mother used to ruffle his curly locks when he was a young lad in Scotland…"

Yeah. You get it.

Don't do that.

124. "HOW DOES THE LENGTH OF A STORY AFFECT THE AMOUNT OF BACKSTORY?"

The more compact your story is in terms of the time expanse it covers, the more backstory you may need to include. So, a story taking place over a weekend might need a flashback.

On the other hand, the broader the scope of your story in regard to the time it takes for it to happen, the more you can have events happen "onstage" rather than preceding the novel's initiation. A story spanning decades could include the potential flashback material organically within the narrative.

Serving up the backstory all at once may make readers want to walk away from the table. Instead, sprinkle it in little by little as you move the story forward. Do so by (1) overlaying promises, (2) introducing multiple storylines, (3) verifying that the story remains believable, and (4) turning the story in an unforeseen direction rather than making readers relive what they already know.

125. "HOW DOES BACKSTORY RELATE TO FLASHBACKS?"

Some writers include flashbacks to fill in the backstory of the characters, but often this isn't necessary or advisable.

We're all impacted by our past. It's impossible to separate ourselves completely from the choices we've made, the emotions we've felt, and the traumas and triumphs we've experienced. It's the same for your characters—their past impacts their present condition—however, that doesn't mean that you need to rehash it in this current story.

The iceberg of your character's past will always be larger than what you can contain on the pages of your book. Ask yourself: "What part is sticking out of the water? What part do readers really need to see?" A flashback might be used to render a pivotal scene, but only if readers long for that scene to appear on the page.

126. "HOW MANY FLASHBACKS SHOULD I INCLUDE?"

As few as possible.

Some stories, especially those that alternate between present and past storylines, might have a flashback every alternating chapter. If you choose this technique, be aware that some readers will simply skip or skim the flashback sections.

Why?

While there might be some mystery as to why things are the

way they are in the present storyline, there'll often be little suspense in the flashback since readers know the characters survived and made it to the present.

Flashbacks stop the forward momentum of the story, can easily become a distraction, and are often used simply to fill the reader in on backstory or context that the author wrote up in the outlining stage and doesn't want to "waste."

If the flashback is there just for mood or backstory, or to show why a character is a certain way, it can probably be dropped.

127. "DO I NEED TO KNOW MY CHARACTER'S MOTIVATION?"

Not necessarily. And neither does your character. And neither do your readers.

Intention (the goal), rather than motivation (the reason for it), drives every story.

To understand motivation, ask, "Why does this character view the world as he does, notice the things that he does, and do the things that he does?"

Motivation is often embedded in backstory. If your character is afraid of snakes, readers won't wonder why since fear of snakes is such a common thing. If he's afraid of marshmallows, however, they'll be more curious to know the backstory to understand the cause of that fear.

Usually, it's enough to say, "As far back as he could remember, he'd always been afraid of heights." You don't need to render a scene where he falls out of a tree house.

The point? Backstory and motivation are only essential when something unique or pivotal to the movement of the story is at stake. If there's no necessity or natural opportunity for a flashback for this character, don't bend over backward trying to include or clarify motivation.

Rather than thinking about what a character might be motivated to do in a scene, ask what that character's intentions are. What is he trying to achieve or withstand right now in the story? That's what matters more.

128. "YOU DIFFERENTIATE BETWEEN MOTIVATION AND INTENTION. THAT'S A LITTLE CONFUSING. CAN YOU CLARIFY THE DIFFERENCE?"

Regardless of what motivates an action (nature, nurture, environmental cues, and so on), what matters most in a scene is intention rather than the origin of that desire.

For instance, if an intruder is threatening your character with a knife, the aggressor's intention is to kill her, and her intention is to escape. Why is he motivated to kill her? Who knows? And does it matter?

No. Not in this scene.

What matters is his goal: If he gets what he wants, she doesn't get what she wants; if she gets what she wants, he doesn't get what he wants.

Their mutually exclusive goals create tension and life-and-death stakes.

Stop worrying so much about motivation and focus more on intention.

Many authors do precisely the opposite. They try to delve deeply into motive, attempting to pin all of the character's current situation on a single past (typically traumatic) event, but they don't take the time to clearly delineate what's at stake in the current scene.

As soon as you try to blame the serial killer's actions on his controlling mother or justify the terrorist's actions by having a family member get killed by a drone strike, you create a simplistic picture that won't satisfy your most astute readers.

As Sidney Lumet noted in *Making Movies*, "In the early days of television…we always reached a point where we 'explained' the character…'Someone once took his rubber ducky away from him, and that's why he's a deranged killer.' That was the fashion back then, and with many producers and studios, it still is. I always try to eliminate the rubber-ducky explanations. A character should be clear from his present actions…If the writer has to state the reasons, something's wrong in the way the character has been written."

Avoid rubber ducky moments in unnecessary flashbacks.

When developing your story, focus on the friction created when your character's desire meets up with the forces of antagonism. That's where the heart of the scene will be found.

129. "CAN FEAR BE A MOTIVATOR FOR MY CHARACTERS TO ACT IN A CERTAIN WAY?"

Fear is not a motivator; it's a response to threatening stimuli. We can manipulate people to do almost anything if the threat factor is high enough. In that regard, fear can be a mechanism of control, but it doesn't motivate us per se.

As you consider the impetus that'll get your character to act, think about the natural desires that we all have. Self-preservation is one of the most basic core instincts that humans have. It's also a goal that can be leveraged to your advantage—just alter the degree of, the nature of, or the proximity of the threat. Put a character in a perilous situation, and he'll seek relief or escape from it.

How will your character respond to the threat? What type of danger will he perceive himself to be in? What steps will he take to find safety? Saving himself first, or trying to save others?

Think of a belief or priority your character has that's greater than his desire for self-preservation. Is it his concern for or love for someone else? How does this deep belief or priority affect your story as it stands now? How will it affect the direction it's heading in? How can you force your character into a corner where there isn't any good way out?

Rather than focusing on fear, focus on the response to being afraid and what that response reveals about this character.

SECTION V

SCENES AND STRUGGLES

130. "WHAT EXACTLY IS A SCENE?"

Stop thinking of scenes as simply being about a progression of events. Just like stories, scenes are essentially about clashes of desire. Sometimes, desire can collide with doubts or limitations. Often, we are the biggest obstacle to our own success.

The manuscripts of aspiring writers often follow the pattern of chat/emote, chat/emote rather than desire/pursue, desire/pursue. A story is forward-facing and tension-driven. It's not just reminiscence.

Great scenes lean forward. The prose presses into the future, the possibilities both narrowing and expanding—narrowing because one choice is made, expanding because multiple choices are consequently possible. They are born of the forward propulsion of the story.

Ask yourself, "Is my scene currently concerned with thoughts or setbacks? With movement or with reminiscence? With what was in the past or what is happening now?" Once again, stories always lean forward, one sentence into the next, within the logic of what precedes them into the possibilities that lie before them.

As things move forward, scenes often progress along a pathway through intention to action to emotion to reflection.

Intention gives the character a pursuit, something to shoot for. This is his goal. *Action* reveals the steps that he takes toward what he desires. These are initiated by meaningful choices. *Emotion* results from the setbacks that he faces and his deepening relationships and interactions with other characters. His reaction to the setbacks he faces and the emotions they evoke will lead him to *reflection* that results in a decision that moves the story to the next scene.

131. "WHAT NEEDS TO HAPPEN IN A SCENE?"

In every scene, you'll want to accomplish four things:

1. Clarify the character's intention. This is vital because readers need to know what the scene is about, what the pursuit is, and what core desire the character is acting from.

2. Justify the choices he makes. Every choice will be naturally caused by what precedes it and will be logical in the character's mind (as he seeks his perceived goal) and in the readers' minds as well. If the choice doesn't make sense to the character, he won't make it. If it doesn't make sense to your readers, they won't buy it.

3. Reiterate or amplify the significance of the pursuit. Let readers see how important the choices made in this scene will be to the fate of the character they're cheering for.

4. Specify the stakes. Make it clear to readers what tragedy will ensue for the character (or those he cares about) if things don't go as planned in this scene. Desire is closely tied to stakes, and there's a natural progression of questions that can uncover them both. Ask, "What does the character want? How is he attempting to get it? Why isn't it working?

What negative consequences will result if he doesn't obtain it?"

To reiterate, if the desire isn't clear to your readers, they won't know what the scene is about or why the character is choosing to act as he does. If there's nothing getting in the way of him getting what he wants, there won't be any tension. If he acts in inexplicable ways, readers will be confused. If nothing is at stake, there's little reason for readers to care about the outcome of the scene.

The choices in the scene will all be suffused with desire, and the actions will be permeated with intention. If the action isn't intention-infused, the scene might be unnecessary, or even worse, a distraction from what matters most in the story.

132. "HOW CAN I TELL WHEN I SHOULD RENDER A SCENE AND WHEN TO SUMMARIZE ONE?"

A scene should be rendered whenever something vital to the story is altered, revealed, or transformed.

If the character's attitude and situation is the same at the end of the scene that you're drafting as it was at the beginning of that scene, you might not need to render that scene. Just summarize it instead.

For instance, if someone is trying to make a decision, briefly explain the consequences of each possibility and then write something like, "I debated what to do and finally decided that I would just stay home for the day." Don't create an entire scene out of a simple decision, especially one that only leads to an extension of the current condition.

Take a close look not just at what happens in the scene but at what is changed as a result of the inherent struggles contained within it.

If you have a scene in which nothing tangible or significant is altered, you may wish to deepen the subtext. Allow the tension to come through in the characters' relationship in ways that aren't specifically stated but are rather made clear by the context.

In regard to a scene's content, for the most part, you'll want to tell intention and show (that is, render) emotion. Show it physically by revealing its results in the physical world. Play it out. Don't just have characters emote or explain how they feel. Show the emotional impact of the scene while avoiding melodrama.

But when it comes to intention—let readers know what the characters want before the scene begins so they'll know what it's about as it plays out.

133. "HOW DO I TAP INTO MY SCENE'S EMOTION WITHOUT MELODRAMA OR MANIPULATION?"

Melodrama happens when you ask readers to feel more emotion than the scene would naturally elicit. (If you can insert, *"Dum, dum, dum, duuuum..."* it's melodrama.)

As Frederick Buechner once noted, "To sentimentalize something is to savor rather than to suffer the sadness of it, is to sigh over the prettiness of it rather than to tremble at the beauty of it."

Manipulation occurs when you ask readers to do what they're not ready to. Readers will only laugh (or cry) if the story rings true about life.

Don't ask, "What would be dramatic?" but rather, "What would be honest?" Readers will respond with a smile, a shiver, or a tear, not because of how impressively you've written, but because of how true the scene is about life or human nature.

Also, readers won't cry if they don't care. And they won't care if they don't want what's best for the character—so developing a character that readers will worry about and want to succeed is vital.

When it comes to eliciting emotion, don't simply inform readers. Move them. Rather than telling them something is sad, sadden them. Rather than telling them something is horrifying, horrify them. An authentic emotional response must be earned through genuine concern for the character's well-being.

134. "HOW CAN I MAKE MY SCENE MORE INTRIGUING?"

A scene isn't made more intriguing by sticking in something "interesting" or "exciting"; it's made more intriguing when you have a character who's striving for something meaningful that's out of reach—something that he cares about and that readers care about as well.

To add intrigue, look for what doesn't belong and let it blossom into something important. For example, you might have a character notice something in an environment or relationship that's a little out of place. The more you draw attention to this, the more readers will attribute significance to it. They'll assume it's relevant even if they can't determine yet why it's important.

Also, you may wish to allow characters to act in ways that appear, at first glance, to be incongruous with their circumstances. For instance, the master detective observes the sunlight coming through the window, dusts off the piano, studies the wine in his glass and announces, "I've solved the case." Readers will think, *What? How? I don't understand!* But they'll also want to find out from that detective what the significance of each of these clues was, and they'll read on to find out.

In that instance, you've added intrigue by letting the character act in a way that seems at first to be inexplicable.

When using this technique, remember that readers eventually need to know the reason behind the detective's seemingly incongruous actions and will lose patience if you don't allow them to see the meaning soon. Respect them. Don't drag things out too long in an attempt to "keep them in suspense." Let the "why?" become the impetus to an explanation, not to readers' frustration.

135. "YOU'VE HINTED AT USING SUBTEXT TO CREATE MORE TENSION. HOW DOES THAT WORK?"

Subtext is what's meant but isn't being said. It's most often present in romantic encounters.

For example, the guy is teaching the woman how to play the piano (external action), and he's pausing as he corrects her finger position, as he gently leans over her shoulder and murmurs in her ear. This is a scene that's not primarily about a piano lesson, but about deepening and accentuating the sexual or romantic tension.

If your scene seems flat, it might be because you're simply letting all of the meaning of the scene rest there on the surface. You might need to imbue the scene with meaning that lies beneath what's seen in order to bring more depth to the journey of the characters toward each other.

136. "I HAVE TOO MANY SCENES OF PEOPLE SITTING AROUND TALKING. IS ADDING MORE ACTION THE KEY TO SOLVING THAT?"

Unless it's driven forward by strong subtext, there's very little dramatic tension in a scene compromised mainly of people chatting. For the most part, you'll want to avoid that.

The solution doesn't involve adding more action; it lies in adding more tension.

Remember, tension is created by unmet desire. It's what lies at the heart of stories and keeps readers flipping pages. So, three things are key: making sure that (1) the character is pursuing a goal, (2) readers know what that goal is, and (3) something (an obstacle, setback, etc.) is getting in the way of the character's pursuit.

Consider the scene in question. Rather than asking what the characters could discuss, ask what each of them is trying to accomplish.

137. "HOW CAN I FIX THOSE TENSIONLESS SCENES?"

To inject more tension into scenes that consist mainly of discussions or dialogue, try any of the following five steps.

1. Introduce more subtext.

2. Clarify the perceived desire of the characters, then look for ways to let them clash with each other.

3. View dialogue as a place to let characters contend with each other, not so much as a means of information dissemination.

4. Give your characters an external goal to accomplish during the conversation. For example, one person is trying to cook while the other wants to talk. The confluence of conflicting goals creates tension and allows one character to externalize her emotion (through the way she interacts with the cooking utensils she's using—smashing the potatoes or perhaps gently massaging the dough), offering you more ways to move the story beyond just dialogue.

5. Increase suspense by layering in more promises of peril rather than simply adding more action. Many times, readers want to see that danger is right around the bend, and this apprehension keeps them more interested than if you were to keep throwing more and more events at them, as exciting as these activities might be.

138. "SO THERE SHOULD BE TENSION EVEN

IN CONVERSATIONS?"

For the most part, yes. Remember that when characters are in a conversation, they have a goal and that objective flavors all that they say in the scene. Don't let them simply talk to each other, let them spar with each other. Silence, interruptions, and diversions can speak louder than words that are shouted. Ask yourself:

- What does each character want out of this conversation? Why can't he get it? How will he try to get it anyway?
- How can I show this goal to readers through his word choice, body language, and actions? Can I create a dilemma rather than just a discussion?
- How can I add subtext to the scene so it isn't ultimately about the action "onstage" but about the state of a relationship or the inner desires of the characters?

To add tension, have characters hint rather than make requests (as Anne does in the example below) or avoid answering questions (as Bryan does).

Anne: "Don't you think it's hot in here?"
Bryan: "It's cooler than it is outside."
Anne: "I know, but aren't you hot?"
Bryan: "Are you trying to ask me to do something?"
Anne: "I'm just asking if you think it's hot."
Bryan: "Women always do this."
Anne: "Always do what?"
Bryan: "Hint at things rather than just saying what they mean! Why not just ask me to turn down the heat?"
Anne: "There's no need to get snippy! Why do you have to turn everything into an argument?"

Notice how the tension escalates as Bryan makes a judgy generalization about women, and Anne accuses him of *always* starting arguments. Tension saturates every line of that dialogue exchange.

139. "CAN I INCLUDE A SCENE JUST FOR CHARACTERIZATION?"

Avoid bland scenes in which nothing is sought or altered, but the actions are just there "to show characterization." The best way to show characterization is when a character is attempting to overcome something vital or has to rise to the occasion when something significant is at stake.

If a scene in your story exists just to show what a character is like, it's going to annoy readers because they might very well complain that "nothing is happening!"

Something is happening, of course—the character is ruminating as she jogs, or having a chat with her friend over coffee, or driving around thinking about what just happened in the previous scene. But—and here's the key—she's not trying to *overcome* anything. Without a setback or goal, you have no tension.

Every character enters every scene, hoping for something. If readers can't discern what it is, they won't know what the scene is ultimately about.

Think in terms of what the characters hope for, what they expect, what they face, and then how they respond.

Consider the scene in question and ask, "What could she be trying to accomplish? What could she be hoping for? Working toward? Attempting to acquire or avoid?" As the character faces the challenge before her, she'll have to respond when things don't go her way—or go her way so well that it becomes suspicious and ends up as a promise that things are about to get a whole lot worse.

Stick her in a situation in which she desires what she doesn't have, or position some roadblocks in the way and force her to deal with them.

Press your characters. What would it take for her to capitulate morally? To give up what she desires or deeply values? To abandon her pursuit? These are some of the best roadblocks you can use.

Make her face those choices head-on.

The best scenes for revealing what a character is truly like are those that show action with intention or choices in the face of meaningful challenges. Look for how your character would respond based on what she wants. If you have specific attributes you're hoping to portray, brainstorm setbacks that would allow her to respond in revelatory ways that bring out those attributes.

140. "CAN YOU EXPLAIN MORE IN-DEPTH HOW SCENES WORK?"

Simply put, a scene is the account of a character working toward an objective that he wishes to accomplish and trying to overcome the obstacles toward achieving it.

A scene begins either because of a decision of his own or an obligation thrust on him by another that places him in this specific situation where he must accomplish this certain task. The task might be almost anything: picking up a pizza, negotiating a good deal on a new car, seducing a co-worker, saving a child who fell into the lake, and so on. In a scene, there's always a *task* that's related to a *goal*.

Scenes are made stronger when they include tension, struggles, setbacks, and clearly specified unmet desire.

To have a scene without desire or pursuit or setbacks is to have a scene without tension, and that'll typically leave readers confused or bored. Most often, in a scene, the character will seek something, fail to get his ultimate goal, regroup by processing what just happened, and then make a decision that drives the story forward to the next scene.

In the scene, they seek and fail. During the interlude, they process and proceed. This is the path your character will take through the story: seek, fail, process, proceed.

141. "YOU MENTIONED INTERLUDES. IS THAT JUST WHAT HAPPENS BETWEEN SCENES?"

Scenes are strung together by those moments during which the character regroups and reassesses his pursuit. During these interludes, characters will think through what just happened in order to understand its importance (if there was an accomplishment), or process its implications (if it was a negative experience).

For instance, after escaping from the serial killer's lair, the victim might process the emotions of what just happened to her (reviewing them and finding relief from the fear she experienced) and then make a decision regarding what to do next.

Or, the team fails to win the big game, and now you're writing what happens in the locker room. What does the coach say? How does it help or hurt the cause? What's the next step now?

These interludes aren't just breathers or breaks in the action; they're essential moments for characters to process the conflict and setbacks in order to evaluate their feelings or adjust to the consequences of what has just occurred. Interludes allow the character to make an informed choice that moves the story logically and inevitability to the next scene.

Managing the length of the interludes and making sure they don't weigh the story down too much requires understanding the genre conventions and reader expectations regarding the ideal pace for this type of (or genre of) story.

142. "WHAT IF I FIND THAT THE INTERLUDES BETWEEN MY SCENES ARE DRAGGING DOWN THE PACE?"

Most scenes end in one of four ways: with a revelation, a decision, a promise, or a tragedy (that is, the characters don't get what they ultimately want).

So, the scene might end with new information (a clue) that

leads the characters in a new direction; it might end with a defining choice; it could include a narrative promise regarding the direction of the story, or it might end without the characters getting what they set out to get. Tragedy and failure require us to reorient ourselves. That's what your story characters will do during the interludes.

Most of the time, the interludes will be quite brief, but in coming-of-age stories and romances, they'll typically be longer since these two genres revolve around personal growth (acceptance, belonging, competence, and emotional development), or the initiation or restoration of an intimate relationship.

Whatever genre you're writing in, the processing can be internal, occurring solely in the thoughts of the character, or external, as two characters discuss what just happened and form a plan on how to deal with the setback and move forward.

To shrink the interludes and make sure they don't kill the pace of the story, zero in on the emotions, results, and consequences of the scene's ending. Then, immediately move on to the choice that leads to the next scene.

Rather than spending a lot of time reviewing the actions that just occurred, focus on the current state of affairs and the forward movement of the story. For instance:

- "Everybody take a breath. We need to figure out what to do next."

- "Can you believe he said that to me? How can I ever look him in the eyes again?"

- "Okay, things have definitely changed here. What are we supposed to do now?"

Allow the length of the interlude to (1) adequately deal with the pain of loss or the setback that has occurred in the scene, (2) give readers (and characters) a chance to sort out the consequences of what just happened, and (3) clearly drive the story in a new direction or make a decision that leads to the next scene.

The Four Questions That Will Solve Any Plot Problem You Ever Have

	Organic Writing	Outlining
Instinctive questions	1. What is happening? 2. What would naturally happen next?	1. What needs to happen? 2. How can I escalate to the climax I'm trying to build toward?
Strengths	1. Logical, contingent, believable. 2. Strong continuity.	1. Tension escalates exponentially. 2. Mind-blowing climaxes.
Weaknesses	1. Stories can wander and not escalate. 2. Stories can end abruptly. 3. Climaxes can be anticlimactic.	1. Scenes aren't always believable. 2. Transitions between scenes are weak. 3. Climaxes can seem contrived.
To solve the problems, ask:	1. How can I make things worse? 2. How can I make the end of the scene and the story as a whole surprising?	1. What would this character na do? 2. How can I make the ending related to what precedes it'

143. "BESIDES INTERLUDES THAT ARE TOO LONG, WHAT ELSE CAN STALL A STORY OUT?"

In many stories, characters spend too much time debating what to do before taking action. It's more important to let them act—get them *moving*—even as they process the implications of what has just happened or the setbacks they've encountered. Here are five more things that stall out stories:

1. Chase scenes that go on too long without meaningful escalation.

2. Detailed descriptions of settings that readers are already familiar with.

3. Rumination or internal reflection that readers couldn't care less about.

4. Unnecessary flashbacks.

5. People sitting around gabbing, caught up in conversations that are meant to convey information to readers rather than accentuate or sharpen the tension between the characters or redirect them toward their goals.

Make and keep promises when readers expect them, relentlessly escalate the tension of the story, raise the stakes, and balance the amount of exposition so it occurs after climactic scenes when readers want a break and need a chance to reorient themselves before the next scene.

Time is elastic in a novel, so to fix pacing issues, stretch out the time when you're in an intense scene and leap over time in transitions between locations. Readers don't need to see the character driving in her car, musing about what has just happened.

Don't let scenes—or interludes—go on too long. Kill them while they're still kicking.

144. "HOW SHOULD I START MY SCENES?"

You'll probably have a tendency to *arrive* your way into scenes and *interrupt* your way out of them—especially with a phone call or text or with a perfectly-timed (and very coincidental) arrival of someone.

Readers are wise to these gimmicks, and they'll become frustrated if you overuse them. For the most part, you'll want to avoid beginning scenes with an arrival (of a character, a car, a plane, a ship, a bus, a galactic star cruiser, etc.) and ending them with an interruption.

Instead, strive to begin scenes in the midst of movement, action, or tension and end them with a decision rather than a perfectly timed disturbance or disruption. Strive to arrive at the scene as late as possible and leave as early as you can.

145. "HOW DO I KNOW IF I SHOULD INCLUDE A CERTAIN SCENE OR DROP IT?"

Ask yourself if this scene is a means to an end or an end in itself. Look for ways to make every scene an end in itself. If the scene is just there to serve another scene, to set something up that you're going to pay off later, it often won't hold up its own weight in the story.

You may find that, in the early stages of writing your story, you leap from event to event as you excitedly pour out your ideas. Later, as you reread your work, you'll notice gaps and transitional jumps that need to be smoothed out so readers don't become disoriented. This is normal and natural.

Transitions between different settings of time and space can be tricky. Just remember that when you move your characters to new places, you'll need to provide a good reason for them to go there. Transitions of place need to be justified by the context and by the character's unmet desire.

Your story isn't here to serve you, it's here to serve your reader, so ask yourself, "Is this scene in the story because I want it in there or because readers will want it in there?"

146. "ARE THERE WAYS TO TRANSITION TO NEW SETTINGS OR SCENES WITHOUT BORING OR JARRING READERS?"

Yes. Here are four:

1. Try using chapter breaks. So, one chapter ends: "We jumped into the helicopter," and the next chapter begins: "We landed."

2. Have the character engage in a meaningful and contextually appropriate activity en route: "We talked about the Thanksgiving dinner all the way to the airport."

3. Have two activities going on at the same time: "As she maneuvered through traffic, I pulled up the precinct's website and logged into it. By the time we reached the police station, I'd familiarized myself with the case file."

4. Simply let the character sleep or reflect during the transition: "I was deep in thought all throughout the flight, and before I knew it, we were landing in L.A."

147. "HOW DO I REACH A GOOD BALANCE

REGARDING HOW MUCH ACTION OR REFLECTION TO INCLUDE IN EACH SCENE?"

Things that happen for no reason won't help your story; they'll distract and confuse your readers, no matter how "action-packed" the scene is.

Think through readers' expectations, the story's genre, and its inherent promises: What will readers expect in this genre? What will they be assuming or anticipating? What will they want to see? What will the action be promising as far as what's yet to come in the story?

Some stories have lots of things happening, but eventually, the action just becomes boring. Other stories have little happening, but they're infused with tension, and readers can hardly put them down.

Tension often lags during meal scenes, so drop them or increase the tension within them. Many times, you can improve your story by having it progress despite meals rather than during them.

For instance, suspense is built on promises of peril and can lead readers deeply into a story without much action occurring at all. Walking across the ice on a frozen lake and not being sure if it will crack can create plenty of suspense. There doesn't need to be a car chase across the ice.

Although the amount of action depends on the genre, it's often wise to include less action and more promises of peril. Action alone can lead to boredom. As they say in Hollywood, "People can fall asleep on the edge of their seats." So, stop thinking about making more things (or more *exciting* things) happen, and start focusing instead on making and keeping promises, especially early in your story.

The more personal the struggle and the more impending the danger, the more suspenseful the story. Look over your manuscript to see if you've clarified the central struggle of the story early enough. Beware of spending too much time setting the stage before you introduce the struggle or clarify the stakes.

148. "WHY DO SCENES TYPICALLY ONLY HAVE A COUPLE OF CHARACTERS IN THEM?"

Let's say you have two people in your scene—Abel and Krissy.

You would need to deal with and balance out Abel's attitude and goal toward Krissy, and Krissy's attitude and goal toward Abel. Perhaps Abel is in love with Krissy and wants to ask her out, but she's upset with him for talking about her behind her back and wants to avoid him.

Now, add one more person—Frank—and weave in his attitude and goals toward the other two. Suddenly, you're dealing with six interwoven attitudes and relationships instead of just two:

- Abel's attitude/goal toward Krissy
- Abel's attitude/goal toward Frank
- Krissy's attitude/goal toward Abel
- Krissy's attitude/goal toward Frank
- Frank's attitude/goal toward Abel
- Frank's attitude/goal toward Krissy

Now, add another two or three additional characters, and you can see how, with exponentially increasing relational dynamics, it would be extremely difficult to keep everything straight and write a strong, focused scene.

For the most part, you'll want to keep your scenes manageable by limiting how many characters you keep "onstage" at any given time. Two or three is usually plenty.

149. "WHERE DOES THE CHARACTER'S HISTORY WITH OTHER CHARACTERS COME INTO PLAY?"

Characters typically have a HAG (that is, a History, Attitude, and Goal) toward the other characters in a scene. (They might also have a HAG concerning the setting and any environmental obstacles or unusual objects that they might interact with during that scene.)

Depending on the story's context and flow, these HAGs might be simple: order a burger at the greasy spoon diner down the block, or much more complex: navigate past that alluring woman's defenses and woo her.

	OTHER CHARACTERS	THE SETTING	OBSTACLES
The protagonist's **history** with…	How does his past intersect with this other character's? How will that history affect this scene?	How will his past experiences with this setting affect his current reaction to it?	Does his past give him any insight on how to handle this current challenge?
The protagonist's **attitude** toward…	Is he afraid of her? Angry at her? Happy to see her? Sad? How will his attitude affect his actions?	How does he feel about being in this place at this time?	How will he emotionally handle a setback this severe at this point in the story?

The protagonist's **goal** toward...	What does he want from this person (or what does he want this person to do)?	What does he hope to get out of this setting?	What is he hoping to accomplish with regard to this obstacle?

Ask yourself, "What would this character be thinking at this time, in this scene, based on what he's just been through? What would he be processing, planning to do, or preparing for? How will his HAGs be affecting him and revealing what really matters to him?"

150. "WHAT ABOUT HER SELF-PERCEPTION? WILL THE WAY THE CHARACTER SEES HERSELF AFFECT THE WAY SHE SEES OTHERS?"

Yes. Every character will have a perception of herself, a perception of others, and a perception of how others view her.

Explore how she views herself, how she views others, and how she thinks they view her. If they were to describe her, what would she think they would say? For instance, "If Mom were to describe me, she'd say I was fatter than I needed to be." See how much this simple line tells you about the girl, her mother, and the state of their relationship?

Or, "He'd made it clear to me in the past that he thought I dressed like a slob. I call it 'beach wear,' thank you very much." Here, you also see a touch of attitude in the character's description of his preferred outfits.

151. "HOW CAN I BETTER UNDERSTAND MY CHARACTER?"

Delving into the depths of your character's life can help you figure out the most honest and authentic way for him to act in the story. It'll also inform the choices he's urging you to let him make.

How does he handle stress? Does he run from it? Deal with it head-on? Exercise? Take drugs? As he experiences more and more stress in your book, show how it affects his emotional stability and how he continues to try to cope with it. Let one of the things that he does surprise you.

Psychologists will sometimes say that no one can make you angry, that you choose to be angry, that it's all up to you. Is that true? If so, what are the implications for your character? If it's not true, how does that affect your character when he faces anger-producing situations?

Think about your character's present situation. Is he married? Divorced? In a committed relationship? Looking for one? Does he have children? In what ways does the person he loves the most know him the least? What would happen if all of his secrets were finally out in the open?

Asking any of these questions will deepen your understanding of the character.

152. "WHAT'S THE KEY TO FIGURING OUT MY CHARACTER'S CORE IDENTITY OR VALUES?"

Spend time with her. Ask her what matters to her, where she's hurting, what she's hiding, what she regrets, and what she's dreaming of becoming. Then, write up the responses in letters that she addresses to you.

Explore her backstory. Is she the sum of her choices and experiences? If so, how does that limit her? If not, where else does her identity come from? In other words, who is she despite (not because of) her choices and experiences?

Examine her aspirations. How do they affect her daily life? What beliefs does she hold most dear? What would it take for her to give those up?

Moral choices reveal the beliefs, priorities, and vulnerabilities of your protagonist. Struggles make those choices inevitable. So, use setbacks and obstacles to create the struggles that are necessary for your character's true self to emerge.

153. "BACK TO THE PROTAGONIST FOR A SECOND. WILL READERS ALWAYS KNOW WHO HE IS?"

They need to know who to worry about. If there are multiple main characters, you'll need to entice your readers to cheer for them all until the protagonist becomes more evident.

Sometimes, the story's true protagonist will only be revealed at the very end of the narrative—sometimes, at the same moment that the genre is revealed in a twist or shocking narrative pivot.

If readers don't know the genre or the length of the story, you might be able to use that to your advantage in creating a twist at the end that they won't soon forget.

For instance, readers might not be sure if the story is a thriller or a horror story, and only when one of the main characters is killed in the final scene and evil wins is the genre—and the pivot—revealed. So, in stories or short stories with a dramatic plunge at the end, the protagonist might not be divulged until the last scene, and only in retrospect does it make sense that this person was really the story's protagonist after all.

In a down-ending story like this, you might have a reverse resurrection—where the new life (or metaphorical resurrection) readers thought was going to occur is lost in one final, desperate, plummeting moment.

154. "DO MAIN CHARACTERS NEED TO BE UNIQUE?"

The more central a character is to your story, the more important it is for readers to see how he's an individual unlike anyone else they've ever met while also being someone they can intimately identify with.

In this way, the main character is both someone readers can relate to and also look up to, both true to life and bigger than life at the same time. In other words, there will be something extraordinary about her, yet also something honest and relatable.

The challenge is crafting characters who are irresistible, memorable, and inviting to be around.

155. "HOW OPEN SHOULD MY MAIN CHARACTER BE WITH THE OTHER CHARACTERS IN THE STORY?"

There's a difference between openness and honesty. Though we might strive to be honest in our dealings with others, that doesn't mean we're 100% open with everyone all the time.

People navigate relationships by understanding what to reveal and what to conceal about themselves to others at any given time. People who are "socially awkward" tend to misjudge things, revealing too much or not enough.

Evaluate how your character will respond to other characters based on his agenda, goals, social aptitude, and the context of the specific social encounter you're portraying.

Sometimes great dramatic moments (and comedic ones as well) can result from misunderstanding, from characters taking things the wrong way, saying too much (or too little), innuendo, and misjudging how much openness or honesty to express.

156. "THERE ARE TOO MANY CHARACTERS TO KEEP STRAIGHT IN MY STORY. HOW CAN I SHRINK THE NUMBER WITHOUT DISMANTLING THE PLOT?"

You can solve this by conflating several characters into one, eliminating unnecessary characters, or decreasing the importance of insignificant characters.

Conflation: If two or more characters play the same role, they can often be conflated into one character. If your story is about a teen girl who wants to exhibit more freedom in her life, and both of her parents are against it—why are they both in the story? Could you eliminate one of them? Or maybe add more tension by having one parent support the girl and one of them act as a roadblock?

Elimination: Some characters might be able to be eliminated if doing so doesn't alter the storyline of your book. Drop or recast the scenes in which nothing significant is altered—in other words, where a character makes a choice that doesn't end up affecting the direction of the story. Maybe you just included that scene because it was interesting to you, or you thought it was clever, even though it wasn't necessarily relevant. Consider removing it to make your story leaner.

Deflation: If you've created scenes during which you're introducing minor characters and making them significant or intriguing, you may wish to flatten out those characters a bit so readers aren't thinking that they have to keep all of those characters in mind as the story progresses. Make the less important characters more forgettable. Let the restaurant server or airline attendant or receptionist or nurse (or so on), play a smaller role. In a sense, let them become set pieces to the story.

157. "IS IT STANDARD TO TREAT MINOR OR SECONDARY CHARACTERS IN THAT WAY?"

The taxicab driver who only appears in one scene, the soccer mom who drives past your protagonist in her minivan, the person in the cubicle next to your main character's love interest—all of these might only be placeholders in your story. However, you don't need to make them completely generic. Perhaps mention a single trait in their description:

- She walked in a way that showed she knew what men liked.

- He cleared his throat at the start of every sentence.

- I'd never spoken to her when she wasn't chewing bubblegum.

Also, remember, a name is a promise. When you name characters, it's a clue to readers that this person has a significant role to play in the story.

Readers don't necessarily need to know what characters are thinking or doing all the time, but it's important for you, as the author, to remember that as soon as a character enters the story, he has become a cog in it—one that's both being affected by and affecting the direction of the scene. Their actions and choices inevitably alter the trajectory of the protagonist's pursuit.

158. "HOW DO MY READERS' BELIEFS ABOUT STORY AFFECT SCENE PROGRESSION?"

Since readers expect that things in stories are not always what they appear to be, the more you assure them that everything is okay, the less they'll believe you.

The more eloquent a character tries to sound, the more readers suspect he has something to hide, and the less authentic he becomes. Also, if a character is smiling all the time, readers will begin to suspect that he has an ulterior motive.

The more you tell readers that something is impossible, the less they'll believe you. The more guilty you make someone seem, the less readers will think he is.

Also, when a character makes a promise, it's often a clue to readers that something is going to go wrong—or at least that things are not going to turn out as planned.

1. "Everything will be okay this time, I assure you." Readers are thinking, *Oh yeah? I don't think so.*

2. "I'll see you at five. I'll be there. I promise." *Oh no, you won't. Something's going to come up to make you break that promise.*

3. "I will never leave you for anyone else. I vow to be there for you forever." *This is not going to turn out well. I just know it.*

4. "There's nothing to worry about." *Oh, yes, there is!*

5. "I've only had a couple of drinks." *She's sloshed.*

6. "I would never do anything to hurt you." *He already has—or is about to.*

7. "I won't share that with anyone." *He's on his way to say it to someone right now.*

8. "I'll get that proposal to you by Monday." *She's not gonna see that sucker for at least a week, so she better not hold her breath.*

9. "I retire in six months." *Fat chance.*

10. "I'm as healthy as a horse." *This guy is literally about to die.*

159. "WHAT'S THE KEY TO CREATING EMOTIONALLY CAPTIVATING CHARACTERS?"

In a story, readers journey with the protagonist through the struggles inherent at the heart of the narrative and find new insight into themselves through their identification with or concern for the protagonist. Emotion is elicited through *empathy* (feeling the emotions along with the character) and *sympathy* (feeling emotions for a character).

Either can be a powerful way to draw readers more deeply into your story.

Readers vicariously feel emotion when they identify with the deep questions characters are asking of themselves or their world, so strive to find a connection between the lives of your characters and the lives of your readers. To create empathy, give your character a question we all ask, an aspiration we all have (a universal human desire), or a specific struggle we can all identify with.

The more your readers identify with the internal struggles of your characters, the more empathy they'll experience. If they see the character is hurting but in a way they don't necessarily identify with, they'll be more apt to feel sympathy for that character instead of empathy.

To develop sympathy, strive to put your characters in situations that your readers will care about, even if they can't personally identify with them. You want your readers to care so much about your character that when they read about her struggle with depression and suicidal thoughts, they'll want to reach into the story and wrench the bottle of pills from her hand.

160. "HOW SPECIFIC SHOULD MY CHARACTER'S GOALS OR STRUGGLES BE TO CREATE EMPATHY?"

As specific as possible.

In one of the paradoxes of writing, the more specific you are in depicting the struggles of your protagonist, the more universal they'll become and the broader appeal they'll have.

Readers make the emotional jump from the specific to the universal more easily than from the universal to the specific. If your story touches on how to deal with shame, that's too broad. Let your character deal with the shame of insulting her best friend in a social media post. Then, readers will identify with it in a more personal and intimate manner.

Look for specific ways to hone in on your character's attitudes and internal struggles. Make them as clear and unambiguous as possible.

TOO BROAD	MORE SPECIFIC
"He's greedy."	His garage is full of things he never uses, and he keeps buying more stuff.
"She struggles with self-doubt."	She keeps putting off applying to grad school because she's afraid she won't be accepted.
"He deals with lust."	His addiction to online porn is driving a wedge between him and his wife.
"She judges others."	She refuses to go to the family reunion because of all the conservatives who'll be attending.

161. "HOW CAN I ENHANCE READER EMPATHY WITH MY PROTAGONIST?"

Readers will feel emotion as the natural result of identification with the characters' desires.

Shoot for ways to find commonality between your readers' lives and your characters' struggles. Shared goals create commonality; commonality leads to identification; identification engenders an emotional response on the part of readers.

For example, the character might experience the sting of losing out on a job to someone less qualified, getting chosen last at recess, or not finding anyone to sign her high school yearbook.

Or, he might feel the bittersweet mixture of joy and sorrow when he drops his daughter off for her first day of kindergarten, or relief when he welcomes the prodigal child back home again, or elation when he hears his girlfriend say "I love you" for the first time. He might learn to let go or, say goodbye to a loved one, or embrace a new dream or relationship.

None of these situations are manipulative because they naturally evoke certain emotions in readers. Strive for...

1. ...writing that elicits a mood that captures your readers' attention,

2. ...showing how a character struggles with issues your readers deal with or have dealt with in the past,

3. ...establishing that the amount of emotion the scene intends to evoke is justified (or even underplayed) in the writing,

4. ...maintaining tension by allowing the character to hold back the tears or emotion that readers are feeling.

162. "WHAT ARE SOME ADDITIONAL WAYS TO INVITE READERS TO IDENTIFY WITH THE CHARACTER'S STRUGGLES?"

Readers understand and will identify with loss. So, think of ways you could have your main character lose something that's important to him. What does he desire most? (Security, adventure, autonomy, love, etc.) What are the consequences of not getting it? (Depression, loneliness, despair, death, etc.)

Often, the loss of faith or family will matter more to readers than the loss of fortune or fame. Could you have your character lose a family member (either physically—through death, for instance—or relationally, through emotional resistance) or lose her moral grounding and the security of her belief system?

If you're having trouble identifying the broad struggle or a specific example of it, write a short scene that serves as the genesis for your character's struggle. Maybe you'll include it in your manuscript, maybe not, but use it to clarify in your own mind the specific nature of her unmet desire or pursuit.

163. "HOW IMPORTANT IS IT FOR THE PROTAGONIST TO MEET SETBACKS ON HIS WAY THROUGH THE STORY?"

It's vital. If he solves his problem on the first try, you don't really have a story, you just have an example of his proficiency or special abilities.

On the other hand, the antagonist might succeed all throughout the story and then, only at the climax, fail.

In a sense, the journeys of the protagonist and the antagonist mirror each other. So, if your story has a happy ending, it might look like this:

CHARACTER	JOURNEY
Protagonist	Fails on his way to eventual success.
Antagonist	Succeeds on his way to eventual failure.

If your story doesn't have a happy ending, the pattern might look like this:

CHARACTER	JOURNEY
Protagonist	Fails on his way to ultimate failure.
Antagonist	Succeeds on his way to ultimate success.

164. "WHAT DOES A CHARACTER'S FAILURE DO FOR THE STORY?"

It gives fuel to the story's flames.

It isn't just that your protagonist will face conflict, setbacks, and difficulties—she will also face failure. If your character doesn't fail on the way to success, the pathway there is too easy.

Think of what events created (or called forth) the courage, resolve, or sacrifice the character exhibits at the climax. The list will usually include setbacks that seemed to cause him to fall further behind in his quest, even as he took steps toward completing it.

Each setback will motivate or further equip him to tackle the biggest quest of all when all the cards seem to be stacked against him at the climax.

Think of a way to let him fail.

Then, think of a way to let him succeed by doing something readers don't expect but that makes perfect sense within the context of the story and resolves the story in a satisfactory way. Do that, and your ending will feel surprising, honest, and satisfying.

165. "BUT IS FAILURE REALLY ESSENTIAL?"

Failure of some type, yes.

Let's say your story begins with your main character landing a new job at a high-tech Internet company. Everything seems to be going her way.

Is this a setback?

No. But, since readers understand that stories are about things going wrong rather than simply chronicles of things going right, they'll intuitively know that the setbacks are about to come. If those difficulties don't come, you have no story. You only have an announcement of good news. A list of events with no setbacks isn't a story.

Think of how boring it would be if things continued to progressively get easier or better for the protagonist: He takes a small step, succeeds. Takes another. More good news. And so on: "He worked tirelessly to move up the ladder of success. Every year, things got easier and easier for him. He received regular promotions. Through it all, he invested wisely and met his financial goals. He cared for his family and retired a happy, satisfied, self-actualized man."

This might be the picture that some people have of success in the "real world," but it wouldn't make a very good fictional story. In fiction, true success has scars.

166. "EXPLAIN THAT—SUCCESS HAVING SCARS. WHAT EXACTLY DOES THAT MEAN?"

Success comes through trials, and it always comes at a cost. Though in real life, people might learn best by example, fictional characters don't learn the lessons that matter most the easy way. The more valuable the insight, the more costly it'll be and the more important it is that they learn it personally, through experience, not by being told the answer and successfully implementing the advice right away.

Instead of solving a problem in a story step by step, it's done setback by setback. A story includes an account of struggles being overcome rather than simply listing a series of good things happening.

Because of the nature of narrative escalation, a story's progression means coming up to "road closed" and "bridge out" signs and finding the route home getting harder and harder to navigate rather than easier and easier.

Insight is earned through suffering. Growth comes through pain. And scars are the result.

167. "SO, STRUGGLE IS THE INCUBATOR FOR GROWTH?"

In a sense, yes. Your protagonist's truest, deepest convictions will be learned in the fires of trials and temptations.

The bigger the revelation your characters have about themselves, the more difficult the circumstances in their lives are going to become prior to them learning it. The depth of the revelation will be determined by the enormity or severity of the struggle.

Epiphanies won't result from random, sudden flashes of insight.

In real life, "Eureka!" moments might seem to come out of nowhere, but in a fictional story, they're earned through suffering and caused logically by what precedes them.

Look for ways to drive the protagonist deeper and deeper into a seemingly impossible situation (emotionally, physically, or relationally) that you eventually resolve in a way that both surprises and pleases readers.

168. "CAN BALANCE OR EQUILIBRIUM IN THE PROTAGONIST'S LIFE BE A PROMISE?"

Readers will naturally anticipate that if everything is going right for the protagonist, something is about to go terribly wrong, and (since stories escalate in tension) if everything is already going wrong, things are about to get even more difficult before they get any easier.

Stories emerge from the ways that imbalance and disruption affect characters. If your protagonist is happy and emotionally stable at the beginning of the story, readers know something is about to happen that'll disrupt her normal life and throw her headfirst into the central struggle of the story.

If your character is wounded at the beginning, readers anticipate that there will be healing at the story's end—or some sort of "death." Something will be changed. If things come easily for your protagonist at first, you're making a promise that he's heading in the wrong direction or is on his way toward unintended tragedy.

These are implicit promises you make.

Escalation is one of the most powerful narrative forces. We build upon the tension, scene-by-scene until we reach the dark moment right before the climax—typically, a moment at which all seems lost—and then we let the protagonist make an unexpected yet logical choice that leads to (or through) the climax—the moment of highest tension or most significant sacrifice in the story.

169. "CAN RELATIONAL PROBLEMS BE THE DISRUPTION THAT INITIATES THE STORY?"

Certainly. Think in terms of the status quo, of what disrupts that, and how the character's pursuit affects the trajectory of her life or the transformation of her situation.

- Your character trusts the wrong person. What happens as a result?

- Your character fails to trust the right person. How does that cause more trouble?

- Your character decides never to trust anyone ever again. Where does that decision take her?

Stable and healthy relationships early on in the story can also become implied promises. When things go well, it's actually a promise to readers that they're not going to remain that way for long. Soon enough, the rug is going to be pulled out from beneath the scene, and the characters will need to adapt and try to deal with the consequences of the resulting disequilibrium.

170. "SO, DISRUPTION GETS A STORY MOVING AND ACTION KEEPS IT MOVING?"

Disruption often initiates pursuit. Unmet desires result and action comes from meaningful choices in the service of those desires. Action serves a purpose, but it's not the main source of the story's forward movement—tension is. Action often comes as the fulfillment of emotionally charged promises.

Rather than thinking in terms of action alone, think in terms of the natural choices necessary to drive the story forward and toward transformation.

The main character will spend the majority of the story striving to accomplish something elusive. And, since stories are built not just on events but on anticipation and the journey through escalating tension, promises of even greater setbacks coming down the pike will propel the story forward even more.

As you write, ask yourself how well you've used setbacks and promises to move the story forward.

171. "REGARDING ACTION AND SUSPENSE, HOW DO YOU CRAFT AN ACTION SEQUENCE THAT WILL ENGAGE READERS?"

Through (1) clarity about the protagonist's pursuit, (2) emotional resonance, and (3) relentless cycles of escalation.

At their core, action scenes are not about action but rather about solving problems. Once the struggle is resolved, the story is over. One exciting event happening after another doesn't make an intriguing action story. In fact, it'll eventually bore readers unless they can see what's at stake and can understand and identify with the unfulfilled desire of the main character.

Thrillers aren't as much about scary (or even thrilling) things happening as they are about impending peril and the promise of pain. The key isn't necessarily to include more action or violence, but to make more promises that things are going to get worse. Then, add more and more threatening situations that characters whom readers care about must face.

172. "HOW CAN I SCARE MY READERS?"

Think about a place where your character feels safe being alone—perhaps at home in bed, or working late at the office, or beachcombing by herself at dawn.

Then, consider how that illusion of safety can be shattered—someone enters her house while she's asleep and photographs her in bed, the killer is waiting for her in the backseat of her car, a stalker identifies her habit and follows her along the beach or watches her through binoculars.

Insert danger and uncertainty into the place where she feels the most invulnerable. Odds are, your readers will feel the same unease because they likely feel the same sense of safety in those locations or situations.

173. "AT ITS CORE, WHAT IS SUSPENSE?"

Suspense is apprehension born of concern.

Suspense contains the promise of impending peril. It's the space between expectation (or the promise) of something dreadful and the actual event itself. Your readers' worry and apprehension will keep them flipping pages. In a suspenseful story, it isn't the action per se but rather the stillness between the promise of peril and the payoff that draws readers in and leads them to keep reading.

When they care about a character and worry about the impending danger or peril to that character's well-being, they'll be in suspense. Simply put, if readers don't care, they won't worry. And if they don't worry, they won't be in suspense.

The peril doesn't need to be life-threatening. It might be that the character is in danger of losing the account to a competitor, or being embarrassed in front of her friends, or getting in trouble for something she didn't do, and so on.

Suspense isn't movement. It's not activity. It's the wire of apprehension that stretches between the promise of pain and the payoff—whether that painful event comes or is cleverly averted by the hero.

174. "HOW CAN I ADD MORE SUSPENSE TO MY STORY?"

Allow readers to be in on the secret. Show them the danger that's waiting just around the corner. If you can do this without allowing the story characters to become aware of the impending peril, it'll often be even more effective at building apprehension.

For instance, you let readers know that the killer is waiting behind the door, but you don't let the protagonist know about him. As she reaches for the doorknob on the other side of the door, readers will be thinking, *No! Don't open it! He's right on the other side!*

If you don't make it clear to readers what the threat is, you won't be keeping them in suspense; you'll actually be keeping them *from* suspense.

Suspense is created through revelations; mystery is sustained through concealment. In this way, suspense and mystery are opposites of each other.

Anxiety can grow from a feeling of foreboding, the sense that things are going to get worse, and there's really nothing you can do to stop the dominoes from falling. When your readers feel helplessness in the face of danger or the inevitability of disaster, they'll be in suspense.

175. "HOW MUCH VIOLENCE DO I NEED TO MAKE MY STORY SUSPENSEFUL?"

None. However, at least one character whom readers care about will be in peril.

Violence alone does little to create suspense. Often, it's more terrifying for readers to imagine violence than see it played out on the page.

So, you don't necessarily have to show every tendon ripping apart and the blood spurting out if someone is beheaded—unless you're trying to disturb readers and give them a visceral reaction. Instead, showing the lead-up to the crime and the aftermath might be more appropriate for your genre. When it comes to the violent act itself, it might be better in your story to tell (summarize) than to show (render).

Leverage fear of the unknown. In monster movies, audiences typically only get glimpses of the monster until the big reveal at the climax—and that monster better have been worth the wait. Often, the more screen time the monster has, the less frightening he becomes. This is also true for villains, killer sharks, alien invaders, and so on. Limit the page time of your villain and let mystery swirl around the amount of pain he's capable of causing.

As you determine ways to endanger characters, evaluate your story in terms of what readers would be thinking and experiencing in each scene. Many times, inserting more blood and gore will numb readers and undermine, rather than incubate, the suspense. Inserting more promises of impending danger is the key. To increase suspense, develop more apprehension about potential violence than inclusion of acts of violence. To increase disgust, include more graphic depictions of the violence occurring.

176. "WHAT'S THE SECRET TO DEVELOPING MORE SUSPENSE?"

To develop suspense, make the stakes of failure clear to readers. Also, give the protagonist a goal that readers can worry about him accomplishing.

Things cannot come easily for your protagonist. Or, if they do, readers need to see that he's actually heading in the wrong direction.

We sustain tension when we have different levels of promises relating to the protagonist's journey through the story. These promises revolve around the stakes (that is, the potential negative consequences failure would result in) that she might face as she deals with herself, with others, and with the world around her.

If readers can't see the scene, they won't care about what's happening in it. For suspense, they need to visualize the scene, care about the character, and be worried about what will happen next. Rather than plowing forward to incubate suspense, slow things down, and show readers the setting—the more atmospheric, the better.

Anything that the protagonist achieves without a setback (or without deepening subtext) will not serve the story's forward progression.

177. "CAN YOU ELABORATE ON THAT?"

Don't let your protagonist solve an important problem on the first try. If she does, it's an event, not a story. In other words, if plan A works out just fine, you have a plot flaw.

Evaluate each scene, asking yourself if it's completely clear what the character wants and what occurs to keep her from getting it.

As we covered earlier in the discussion of scenes and interludes, move your character from goal to obstacle to failure to a decision that drives the story forward once again. Typically, in every scene (except the final one), the protagonist will fail to reach his ultimate goal, even if it might appear to him that, at the time, he has solved it.

Action is the avenue for revelation; it is not the be-all and end-all of the story.

178. "WHAT WILL KEEP READERS MORE ENGAGED IN MY STORY?"

Readers will stick with a story as long as they're curious, concerned, intrigued, or entertained. (Sometimes, they'll also keep reading it if they feel obligated to, but that's never a response you're going to be shooting for!)

Readers will forgive all sorts of narrative stumbles as long as they're enjoying themselves.

WHAT KEEPS READERS FLIPPING PAGES				
Curiosity	Concern	Anticipation	Entertainment	Obligation
"I'm wondering where this is going."	"I'm worried about where this is going."	"I can't wait to see where this is going."	"I don't care where this is going. I just want to read it—it's that good!"	"I have to finish this because I started it/was told it was good/was assigned it."
intellectual engagement	emotional engagement	future enjoyment	current pleasure	limited investment
found often in mysteries	found often in suspense	found often in romance	found often in humorous stories	found often in classics / literary

good for creating intrigue	good for creating tension	requires a satisfying climax	necessary during flashbacks	never a good thing
Readers don't know what will happen.	Readers think they know what will happen.	Readers look forward to what will happen.	Readers care most about what's currently happening.	Readers desperately hope something interesting will happen.

179. "CAN HUMOR OR LIGHTHEARTED MOMENTS HELP MY STORY?"

Absolutely. If you can make readers laugh out loud (at the right times), you have a rare and enviable gift. Most stories, no matter what genre, can benefit from moments of humor. A few reminders:

1. If you have to explain why something is funny, it's not. Let the humor stand or fall on its own merits.

2. If you have your characters laugh about something that your readers don't think is funny, they'll lose faith in the believability of the story. So, don't make your characters laugh at a joke unless you're showing that they perhaps laugh *at the wrong things*. This can be used to build the tension or reveal traits of your characters.

3. Humor often comes from showing readers the ludicrous nature of a situation through understatement or exaggeration. With comedy, foreshadowing serves as a

setup for the punchline.

4. Humor is often truth that no one has noticed yet or observations that point out the incongruities of life. Shoot for that, rather than telling jokes.

5. If you do include jokes, you might show how someone was trying to be funny, but it was backfiring. That can lead to comedic misunderstanding.

180. "IF I MAKE READERS ASK WHY SOMETHING IS HAPPENING, WILL THEIR CURIOSITY KEEP THEM READING?"

In a mystery, the detective will often pursue lines of inquiry that only become obvious later in the story, but in other genres, forcing readers to ask "Why?" will usually confuse them—which is something you'll want to avoid, since, while readers are confused, they're not worried. It's pretty tough to be, at the same time, both confused about why things are happening and also worried because you're anticipating how they might turn out.

Mystery creates curiosity; suspense creates anxiety. Remember, mystery conceals; suspense reveals. Decide which you want readers to experience, then give it to them by how and when you provide details about the danger that the characters are in or the peril they are facing. (A dark mood or a foreboding scene can create anxiety even if there's uncertainty what to worry about—bringing both mystery and suspense to the scene.)

For the most part, readers won't worry until they know what's going on. To create concern, you'll want to provide enough information so they don't have to ask, "Why?". When developing suspense, lead them in with promises of peril, lure them forward by endangering empathetic characters, and provide a satisfying payoff at the end.

SECTION VI

SETTINGS, TRANSFORMATIONS, AND DILEMMAS

181. "WHAT KIND OF A SETTING SHOULD I INCLUDE IN MY STORY?"

One that's congruent with and integrally related to your character's pursuit.

And, since it can play a significant role in either hindering or helping the character in that pursuit, setting is more than simply the backdrop of the action. Because of this, it can play a role in revealing (or transforming) the protagonist.

Some stories only require a small, intimate world; others need to be told with a sweeping, expansive landscape. Whatever setting you choose, it will typically be indispensable to the story's progression and impossible to extricate from the character's pursuit.

Readers want it to be as central to the narrative as any of the characters are.

182. "WHICH DETAILS ABOUT THE SETTING SHOULD I INCLUDE IN MY STORY?"

Ones that evoke an appropriate mood and ones that invite readers to picture the scene and care about what they see. You'll also want to be aware of the narrative promise that the details are making and invite readers to catch a glimpse of the character's attitude toward the scene.

To draw readers into the scene, ask:

- What details will help them envision this without being drowned in minutia or descriptions that don't ultimately matter?

- How can I lead readers to grasp what the narrator's view of or attitude concerning the scene is?

- What promises are the details making about the importance of what's to come later in the story?

Avoid the urge to describe everything. Some writing instructors teach that details bring life to a story, and while that can be true when they're not used properly, details can also bring death to the tension.

Trust readers to fill in the gaps. Too much description insults readers and causes them to critically analyze every detail, trying to keep track of it and evaluate how important it might end up being. This can lead readers out of the emotional and immersive world of the story.

183. "CAN SETTING BE A PROMISE?"

Yes. The more you draw attention to a specific setting, the more significant readers will assume it's going to be to the story. You're creating an implied promise of importance.

Despite what some people might say, setting is not a character. Don't treat it as one. It has no pursuit, no desire, no struggle, nothing that really makes a character interesting. Reveal your character's attitude about the setting by allowing him to interact with it. Rather than a paragraph of description, let the description emerge naturally as your characters move through and physically encounter the setting.

By the way, since descriptions of locations take time to read and eat up page space, you'll typically introduce the setting for the climax before the final sprint to the finish at the story's closing since that's not where you want to undermine the pace by slowing down to describe the location.

184. "IT'S HARD TO SEE THE SETTING IN CERTAIN SCENES. WHAT ARE THE SECRETS TO FIXING THAT?"

Setting is a vital aspect of storytelling. It allows readers to picture the characters, and it allows the characters to naturally interact with their environment as they move the narrative forward. Ask yourself, "How does the setting make this character feel?" And then show what that feeling causes him to say, think, or do.

When establishing your setting, ask if readers will be able to picture this scene as you've described it. Consider the lighting, the time of day, the time of year, and how familiar readers will be with that setting. If it's a contemporary living room, it'll only require minimal description; if it's an 18th-century parlor or a 25th-century spaceship, it'll require more work.

Use details to evoke, not just to describe. You're trying to do more than guide readers to simply visualize a scene. You're also trying to help them feel something about that setting. *How* you describe a setting is just as important as *what* you describe. Always consider what mood you're trying to convey in this scene. For example, describing a forest as "draped in shadows" creates a whole different mood than saying it was "graced with shafts of sunlight."

Finally, evaluate if the characters have an attitude about this setting and explore how you can bring that out. Readers want the setting to affect the characters in ways that aren't just physical but also psychological. Let's say your character enters a packed subway. If she's used to the subway, it might not bother her. If she's new to the city, it might really unsettle her. Take all of that into consideration as you describe the setting and show how the characters feel about or react to it.

185. "MY SETTING SEEMS TOO GENERIC. WHAT STEPS CAN I TAKE TO MAKE IT MORE MEMORABLE OR RELEVANT?"

To fix this, allow the point-of-view character to describe it from her perspective. This will allow her attitude to shade the description and allow for characterization.

Also, you may wish to combine unlikely elements to create memorable locations: the fudge factory/rum bar, the indie bookstore/pizza joint, the aquarium/waffle restaurant, and so on.

Finally, root the story in an indispensable location—the only city in the country that could host this convention, the world's most expensive bed and breakfast, the last wildlife reserve on the planet that has white rhinos, etc.

186. "DOES A STORY'S PURSUIT ALWAYS INVOLVE THE SETTING?"

To some extent, yes. However, while settings affect pursuits, the characters' pursuits don't need to be physical ones. They might be on a metaphorical quest instead, though they'll always be pursuing something that matters to them in some specific location.

Stories are often about adventures (journeying out, often toward change) and homecomings (journeying home, often toward self). They can show the importance of exploring the world, and also of returning to our roots.

Adventures: The character moves from one place in life to another. Perhaps away from pain and toward healing, or away from a sensible yet constrained life and toward risk.

Homecomings: A character returns to his hometown for some reason and must reunite with estranged loved ones, reconnect with his roots, find hope and a fresh start, or learn a lesson about what it means to be human.

In both of these scenarios, setting is used to help facilitate (or perhaps to mitigate against) the character's pursuit.

187. "CAN YOU EXPAND ON THIS IDEA OF JOURNEYING OUT OR RETURNING HOME?"

As you uncover your story, consider how your character has wandered away from home (literally or figuratively) and how the journey through this story might lead him back. Or, identify how he's on a journey (emotional, psychological, physical) away from an old life and toward a new one. Explore if your character is returning home or venturing forth. (In some stories, to some degree, he might be doing both.) Does your story focus on him reconnecting to something lost or finally establishing something new?

If the character returns home, consider sharpening the images, tone, mood, or verbs in the story's beginning and at the end so they reflect a strong connection with each other. Whether venturing forth or returning home, your character will be seeking happiness or her definition of success. (Though that definition might very well change during the story.)

188. "WILL MY CHARACTER EVER PURSUE ANYTHING OTHER THAN HAPPINESS?"

The pursuit of happiness is a broad umbrella that includes many facets.

Just like real people, your character will make choices related to his pursuit of happiness. He wants to be happy and successful (however he might define that). The pathway he chooses toward happiness might include pursuing justice, love, vengeance, or enlightenment. It might be a quest to do something noble, establish a new relationship, conceal a crime, reveal a secret, or any number of things.

His pursuit will be influenced by his beliefs about happiness and the role he decides is the best way to obtain it. At the beginning of the story, he'll have a certain view of what success, or a happy, fulfilled life, looks like. Some stories will challenge him to change that *view*; others will challenge him to change *himself*.

Ask these questions to analyze your character's understanding of and pursuit of happiness:

- What does he think will bring him happiness? Is he right? If not, how will the story affect his perspective? (It'll change somehow, either to become more harmonious with true happiness or to twist his life farther away from it.)

- How has the pursuit affected how he views his situation or how he perceives himself?

- What challenges his perspective concerning happiness? What reinforces it? How will his views have changed by the end of the story?

- Does each step in the process of moving toward this new understanding make contextual sense (in regard to both causality and believability)?

- Does he struggle enough throughout the story to justify

the revelation that he comes to at the end? (If the lesson was learned too easily, readers won't be satisfied because the story won't ring true and will seem agenda-driven.)

189. "WHAT CAN CHOICES REVEAL ABOUT CHARACTERS?"

Choices reveal at least four things: beliefs, priorities, goals, and wounds.

When a character chooses one thing over another, he shows either what he believes, values, desires, or what type of pain he might be trying to avoid.

People make time for what's truly important to them. To find out what matters to a person, don't ask him. Instead, examine what he spends his time doing and what he puts off doing. (*Why* he puts something off is another matter; the fact that he does so tells you that something else matters more to him in that moment.)

Unlike choices, which reveal what's valued, an epiphany is not so much a moment of revelation *of* you as it is a sudden, unexpected, life-altering revelation *to* you about your place in the world.

And through it all, characters often resist the very thing they need in order to grow—change.

190. "ARE CHARACTERS ALWAYS RESISTANT TO CHANGE?"

Typically, a character will initially resist change, just as real people do. If she isn't resistant to change, she won't seem realistic or believable to readers. She'll be too mutable and too willing to mature. It'll also decrease the tension of the story and the need for the story to occur in the first place.

Life is change, yet most of us resist it. We all have a lot of emotion and psychological investment tied up in the status quo and in the belief systems that we currently have. People will put up with an incredible amount of mental suffering rather than risk change and what it might bring. So, regarding change within your character, ask:

- What's holding him back from change? Why is he resisting it so strongly?
- What (or who) is calling to him to set him free? What would this freedom look like?
- What obstacles does he need to personally overcome to reach his goals (or dreams) and become all that he was meant to be?

191. "HOW CAN I BETTER UNDERSTAND THIS RESISTANCE?"

Delve into the lies your character believes, especially those that readers realize are lies. For instance, "If I just make enough money, I'll be happy," or "If we have a kid, it'll fix our relationship problems," or "It's not really a big deal. It was just a one-night stand."

Explore his integrity: Who is your character in the dark when no one is watching? What does he get away with or (contrarily) hold himself back from doing? What does that tell you about him?

Examine his sense of right and wrong: Where's true north for your protagonist? What part of his moral compass is broken? Is he aware of that? What would it take for him to reorient himself in the right direction or to veer off course for good?

We rarely change our lives while we're comfortable. Discomfort, tragedy, crisis, suffering, loss—it's in those times that we find ourselves shaken into considering the stark realities of life and the questions of where hope and meaning lie. Let that truth about human nature inform your development of your character. Ask, "What will it take to impel this character to change? What would realistically cause him to finally embrace it?"

192. "HOW WILL READERS KNOW THAT MY CHARACTER HAS CHANGED?"

He will make a choice that evinces the change. However, after your character makes a major decision to improve his life, test his resolve. Typically, things won't go so well at first.

Why?

It would be too easy and predictable for the story to be framed in this way: *Struggle (Eek!). Decision (Bravo!). Victory (Yay!)!*

It's more likely that the character will meet up with defeat at first, or else the story will read like a morality lesson.

His initial failure might lead to a discovery, despair, or deeper resolve.

193. "CAN THE CHARACTER SIMPLY COME TO A NEW CONCLUSION, OR DOES THAT GROWTH NEED TO BE SHOWN SOMEHOW?"

Don't tell us she has changed. Show us.

If your story is about internal transformation, the only way to show if the character has truly learned the lesson or accepted the insight is for her to act on it, not reflect on it.

Show the revelation and the change through what she does, not simply in a speech that she gives or through dialogue or inner reflection.

This act doesn't signal that the character's problems have all gone away, but instead that she has taken a significant step toward solving them—or that she is becoming (or emerging as) the kind of person who can better understand and cope with them.

Look for ways to have her make a decision that puts this new attitude or insight into practice. You want readers to be thinking, *Ah, yes. She really is different. She never would've done that at the beginning of the story*, rather than, *What was the point of this story after all? Does she change her mind or not?*

194. "HOW CAN I TEST MY CHARACTER IN A WAY THAT SHOWS WHAT HE'S CAPABLE OF?"

Convictions or beliefs that remain untested contain the promise of change but not the change itself. Let's say your character is a sinner who becomes a saint during the story. Tempt him to return to his old ways. He'll fail and find new direction through his mistakes.

If you're writing a faith-based story or one that has a moral message that you're hoping readers will walk away with, make sure that you test your character's conviction, shatter it, and then, at the end, rebuild it in a way that readers won't anticipate, but that they'll agree with and appreciate.

In a sense, the character will go through an eight-stage progression. Let's say your story spans four acts: Act 1 - revelation of the insight and initial rejection, Act 2 - struggle and acceptance, Act 3 - test and initial failure, Act 4 - new understanding and new direction (evidenced through a revelatory decision).

By the way, if there's an "answer-giver" character, the true lesson won't typically be the one that she gives to the protagonist. When tested, that advice (usually a cliché like "Follow your heart!") will be found to be lacking or incomplete. There'll be a deeper truth that the protagonist will discover in the end—one that rings true to readers as well. Perhaps: "Your heart can't always be trusted. Follow something bigger than your heart."

In all truth, it's easy to write in an all-knowing advice giver or a benevolent problem solver, but that doesn't excuse doing so.

If you must have advice being offered, let it come from the oppressed or from someone with low situational status rather than the characters with high substantive status.

Sometimes, it's even interesting to let the advice come from the villain. It's fascinating to have a villain state what seems to readers to be a good moral argument or reason for his actions, only to have the hero conclude that it's not—and then show that to readers as well. Consequently, readers will realize that the villain's justification or reasoning was flawed or insufficient in the first place.

195. "REGARDING CHANGE AND ALTERED RELATIONSHIPS, HOW CAN I SHOW THAT TWO CHARACTERS TRULY LOVE EACH OTHER?"

To show love...

1. ...explore intimacy. Love results in courage (the willingness to sacrifice for the beloved) but also vulnerability. In a very real sense, intimacy is the privilege you give to someone to hurt you the most. How open and intimate are these two characters with each other? Is it possible to have intimacy without openness?

2. ...include destiny. Readers want to feel that this relationship is special, not just random and that it has a deeper purpose. So, if your story is a love story, it might include the convention that fate (or the universe or a divine power) has brought the two lovers together.

3. ...show faithfulness. When lovers face temptation, they choose to remain faithful to each other. Look for ways to press your lovers to abandon their relationship and show how they respond. If they fail, they will seek (and receive) forgiveness.

4. ...reveal devotion. In real life, it doesn't matter how much you say you love someone; when it comes right down to it if you're not devoted to the other person, you don't love her. It's the same way in fiction.

196. "HOW IMPORTANT IS THAT DEVOTION IN EXPRESSING LOVE?"

Love sacrifices for the beloved and asks for nothing in return. As soon as there are strings attached, or someone becomes simply a means to an end, you've stopped loving them and are only in love with what they can provide you instead. (That is, you are primarily in love with yourself.)

Also, if love costs you nothing, it might be attraction, but it's not yet love. Giving spare change to a homeless man might be a form of kindness, but it's likely not a sacrifice—it's just leftovers. Ask, "What is this character willing to give up in the name of love?" The more costly the sacrifice, the more revelatory it is.

Brainstorm assets or beliefs that are precious to your character: What can she sacrifice for others? A family heirloom? An object of great value? Could she make a physical sacrifice? Then, consider ways you could force her into a corner in which she must choose whether to make that sacrifice for the benefit of her beloved. How can this sacrifice seem to lead her further from her overriding story goal but actually bring her closer to it?

197. "WHAT ARE SOME KEYS TO WRITING A LOVE OR ROMANCE STORYLINE?"

Here are four thoughts to keep in mind:

1. Readers want the couple to get together.

2. Readers care whether the couple does so.

3. At some point, readers won't be able to see a realistic way for them to get together. (Typically, this moment will come right after it seems like the couple truly is destined to be together, but before the climax.)

4. The couple will connect at the end in a surprising way that pleases readers (or the couple will learn that they aren't right for each other in a way that does the same).

In love stories, the lovers will often exchange gifts or give each other symbols of their undying devotion or affection. These objects might subsequently show up several times in the story as evidence of the lovers' commitment to the relationship.

198. "SHOULD I LOOK FOR WAYS TO GET THE LOVERS TOGETHER?"

Not exactly.

In fact, you're going to do the opposite.

Writing romance isn't about finding ways to get couples together but about finding believable ways to keep them apart. That's how the romantic tension builds. After all, if the two characters love each other, why don't they just sleep together, get married, or run off together? What obstacles are preventing them from doing so? Clarifying those reasons—and keeping them believable—is one of the keys to developing romantic storylines. Those obstacles might include parental pressure, cultural or societal norms, physical distance, age differences, other love interests or obligations, and religious views about sex and marriage.

As you strive to show heightening romantic tension, remember that it needs to escalate, it needs to remain believable, and each event that develops or deepens the relationship needs to follow naturally from the one that precedes it.

Let the lovers chat each other up. Let them flirt with each other. Let them excite each other.

But keep them apart.

Why?

Because as soon as they kiss or sleep together or get married (depending on your genre and that specific story's conclusion), the tension you've been building up is lost. You've resolved that story thread.

Where will things go from there? Where will that moment of resolution leave the lovers? Since unfulfilled desire creates dramatic tension, hooking up (however you might define that) will need to either end their relationship or lead to more problems, more tension, or more difficulties than their relationship had beforehand, or else the story's tension will de-escalate.

199. "CAN LOVE STORIES BE AN AVENUE FOR EXPLORING MORAL DILEMMAS?"

Yes. In fact, they are one of the best places to do so.

Love storylines do not need to deal with romantic love; they might explore brotherly love, parental love, platonic love, etc. Evaluate your storylines to see if they allow for the authentic expressions of affection, devotion, and self-sacrifice, and then search for ways to insert moral dilemmas to challenge and test the love between the characters. For instance:

- What is love? If it's attraction, what happens when the attraction is gone? Is there truly love left, or only the remnants of it? If it's devotion or sacrifice but not attraction, what happens when attraction toward someone else occurs?

- What's more important: romance or commitment? If

you're married but fall in love with someone other than your spouse, do you leave the marriage to be with the one you love, or do you abandon the one you love to remain in your marriage? Why?

- In a struggling marriage, what are the reasons that the couple should divorce? What are the reasons they should stay together?

- What is the truest cost of love? Is it worth offering yourself when you know the person you're loving doesn't love you in return? Ultimately, what does love require of us?

- What's more important, love or freedom? What if you knew that being with the person you love would cause her to lose her freedom? How much of your lover's happiness would you be willing to sacrifice to be together?

- How can platonic love best be shown to others? What are the appropriate or inappropriate ways to express it? What warnings or insights does that give regarding those relationships?

200. "WHAT ABOUT OTHER TYPES OF MORAL DILEMMAS?"

Sometimes, we have desires that aren't healthy. (Or, they may be normal, healthy desires, but we pursue them in unhealthy ways.) Those desires can lead to all sorts of moral quandaries and dilemmas.

Also, sometimes, needs masquerade as desires. For instance, we might desire vengeance (but really need justice instead), respect (but need integrity), admiration (but need acceptance), or sex (but need love).

Ask yourself, "Would this quest make a good story?" If the character is simply pursuing a more comfortable life for himself or more self-love or more money, power, prestige, possessions, fame, or a good reputation, readers will anticipate that the quest will backfire on him. If your character is consumed with seeking these things, you'd be making an implicit promise to your readers that he won't get them but will learn to pursue instead the things that matter more.

Or, the story could serve as a cautionary tale in which the character gets what he selfishly desires, but readers discover the tragic results of that pursuit. Someone will see the light in the end—even if it's only the readers.

201. "I CAN'T SEEM TO FIGURE OUT WHAT MY THEME IS. HOW IMPORTANT IS THAT TO THE STORY?"

Being able to state your theme isn't nearly as important as being able to state your dilemma.

Stories aren't driven forward by themes; they're driven forward by tension. Avoid trying to tell a story about something abstract (love, forgiveness, hope, despair, etc.) and start looking for specific struggles that your main character can face that will reveal her priorities, transform her, or enlighten her.

Include moral quandaries. Maybe your character must choose between two undesirable outcomes, keep two mutually exclusive promises, give up what she loves the most, or face what she fears the most.

Allow readers to see the dilemma through the protagonist's eyes.

Rather than looking for a way to have your story teach something, focus on the excellence of the narrative and the depth of the dilemma. Readers will reach a conclusion about the theme based on the character's choices and the consequences that result.

202. "WHAT IF I WANT TO GET A MESSAGE ACROSS? HOW DO I DO THAT?"

If you can distill your story down to a theme statement, you probably don't need to write the novel. Just print out some bumper stickers, pass them out, and be done with it: *Pursue your dreams! Work as a team! Be true to yourself!*

Why spend a year or a decade of your life on something so cliché?

Art isn't measured by how clearly it conveys a message but by how compellingly it draws us toward the truth. Agenda-driven fiction often falls flat and turns off readers who aren't already committed to that point of view. A theme can be something you examine or explore, but it shouldn't necessarily be a message you're trying to proclaim or prove.

Art doesn't try to convince. It doesn't have to. Art is the point at which arguments become moot, and truth becomes clear.

When you build your story out from a theme statement, you're starting with a solution. However, tension comes from questions, not from answers, so if you start your story with an answer, you're undermining the very dramatic tension that your story relies on to be compelling.

203. "WHAT OTHER OPTIONS ARE THERE BESIDES USING A THEME?"

Don't start with an answer, but a question. Don't start with an agenda, but a dilemma.

Rather than asking, "What theme can I share?" ask, "What virtue can I explore?" As acting coach and improv instructor Keith Johnston has pointed out, "Moral messages are not as interesting as moral decisions."

Most readers don't care if there's an easily discernable theme, but they do care about credulity, verisimilitude, entertainment value, the logical progression of the story, tension, humor, etc. If the story doesn't make sense, ring true, or entertain them, well, they'll notice that right away.

Just as an author can intrude on a story, so can the tools of his trade—metaphor, symbolism, parallelism, imagery, and so on. If they're visible in anything more than in a momentary, fleeting way, or if they draw attention to themselves rather than to the story, then they've stopped serving it and have started impinging on the reader's experience instead.

Rather than trying to teach a lesson, spend more time and attention on your protagonist's pursuit in a morally complex tale and let any thematic elements grow naturally from the story's inherent struggles.

204. "WHAT IF READERS DON'T UNDERSTAND WHAT MY STORY IS TRYING TO SAY?"

Trust the story and trust your readers. They like to piece things together; they don't like being clobbered over the head. A story becomes propaganda when it becomes polemic, when it stops asking questions that challenge us and starts offering answers we see coming. Propaganda is all about trying to convince someone to think like you rather than dilemma-driven storytelling, which invites readers to think for themselves. Don't try to manipulate your readers, just try to embody the truth in a way that they cannot turn away from.

As long as you write your story with the goal of trying to persuade someone of something, you run the risk of driving readers away from the narrative rather than inviting them into it.

Shoot for clarity, honesty, emotion, and depth.

In a way, you cannot help but convey a message, but often, the harder you try to do so, the less effective it will be. As strange as it may sound, you're actually trying to make the meaning in your story both unstated and unforgettable at the same time.

205. "SHOULD MY CHARACTERS REPRESENT SOMETHING?"

Characters aren't in your story to personify anything, to represent Politics or Religion or Society, or things of that nature. They're in the narrative to act and be revealed.

Literary tools are there to help deepen the narrative, not replace the core story elements of characterization, tension, escalation, and revelation. Again, focus on unmet desire and pursuit rather than on getting some sort of message across.

If you have a message you're trying to teach, write nonfiction. That's what it's there for. If you have a question you want to explore, a dilemma you want to examine, or an aspect of the human condition that you want to expose, then write fiction.

206. "WHAT ABOUT SYMBOLISM?"

Some writing instructors encourage authors to use symbolism to reach the subconscious. But that brings up a whole slew of thorny questions:

1. How much symbolism do you need? How much is too much?

2. How do you hide the symbolism so it doesn't become visible and distracting?

3. How many times does that symbol need to appear so that no readers consciously notice it, but all of them are subconsciously affected by it?

4. If the symbols, to retain their power, must remain hidden,

then how do we know they work on the subconscious? There's no way to test that.

5. Will the symbolism affect different readers in different ways? If so, how can you ever anticipate how much to include?

6. How do you keep astute readers from noticing the symbolism? How do you find out if you've achieved the desired effect? What *is* the desired effect?

The more keen-eyed your readers are, the more they'll be able to ferret out your themes and, symbols and takeaways. And as they do, they'll be on the lookout for instances of them showing up rather than remaining immersed in the story itself—which is the opposite of what you want.

So what to do instead?

Build your story on dilemmas and desire, and stop trying so hard to be symbolic or reach the subconscious mind of your readers. Instead, reach the *conscious* mind with vibrant prose, intriguing characters, engrossing storytelling, and unforgettable climaxes.

207. "CAN I USE EVENTS FROM MY OWN LIFE TO INFORM THE DILEMMAS IN MY FICTION?"

Dilemmas that you have faced (or are facing) might inform your story but shouldn't overtake it. Fiction isn't autobiography, but you can dip into your memories to find emotionally resonant moments that can deepen your story.

If you do use events or moral dilemmas from your own life, make certain that they're believable in the story world and contextually relevant. You can't justify poor fiction by claiming, "But that really happened!"

In essence, fiction is all about engaging readers' emotions in struggles that don't exist and with characters they know aren't real.

Readers willingly care about them and abandon, for a brief time, developing actual relationships in lieu of immersing themselves in imaginary ones. They come to fiction to be moved by something they know isn't true toward something that they know *is*: insights about the human condition and the world in which we live.

208. "HOW CAN I INCLUDE MORE MORAL DILEMMAS?"

The deepest tension comes from being forced to choose between two passionately held but mutually exclusive convictions or beliefs. So, require your character to do two things at once—to the detriment of one of them: Save two people, uphold two ideals, or be in two places at the same time.

Look for contextually justified reasons to force a character to give up something he believes in or to betray someone he cares about. For instance...

"How can I...while also...?"	"How can I make it to my son's baseball game in time while also adhering to the speed limit?"
"Is it ethical to... when...?"	"Is it ethical to deceive others when it's for a good reason?"
"What if I must sacrifice...in order to save...?"	"What if I must sacrifice my highest ideal in order to save the one I love?"

"What would it take for me to...?"	"What would it take for me to cheat on my taxes? My Graduate Record Exam? My résumé? My spouse?"
"When is...justified?"	"When is vigilantism justified?"
"If...is wrong, then why isn't...?"	"If infanticide is wrong, then why isn't late-term abortion? After all, the baby is still alive, it just hasn't been born yet."
"What moral conviction would you give up in order to...?"	"Would I betray my true love to save my child? Would I kill a stranger to save a loved one?"
"At what point does... become...?"	"At what point does a 'preemptive strike' become a war crime?"

209. "THESE DILEMMAS ARE FASCINATING BUT KIND OF TOUGH TO COME UP WITH. CAN YOU GIVE ANY MORE EXAMPLES?"

Again, force your character to choose. Ask yourself, "What's more important...or ...?"

> 1. ...happiness or freedom? This is common in science fiction and dystopian stories in which societies give up freedom in order to have "peace." (But is the enforced lack of conflict really happiness, or another kind of prison?)

2. ...justice or truth? For instance, does the character lie on the stand in order to make sure the rapist is convicted, or stick to the truth even though it will result in an acquittal, putting more women at risk of being attacked?

3. ...truth or hope? An injured person is dying. Do you comfort him by telling him that he's going to be all right and give him hope, or do you bluntly tell him that he's going to die and snatch hope away, giving him the stark truth instead?

4. ...truth or happiness? Does the young man share the truth and tell his family about his brain tumor, or protect them by keeping the news to himself?

5. ...privacy or security? There's always a tradeoff between the right to privacy and the need for public safety. How much personal freedom should we give up in the quest for national security?

6. ...authenticity or morality? Does the married man have an affair because he's attracted to someone else (to pursue his dreams, to be authentic), or does he stay faithful to his wife even though he doesn't love her? Is love a justifiable reason for an affair? Do motives matter in this case?

Remember, with a moral dilemma, you're looking for what the character must give up, not what she might gain. Perhaps she might gain insight (about the world or about herself) through the sacrifice, but that's not the reason why she makes it. To find out what your character is really made of, threaten the beliefs she clings to most passionately, the person she loves most dearly, or the safe place (emotionally, psychologically, spiritually, or physically) she goes to when she feels most afraid.

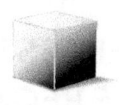

210. "IS THERE ALWAYS A DILEMMA IN FICTION?"

Not always, but there will always be a challenge presented and a choice required.

Every story has a moral fabric to it. It happens within a world in which some actions are justified and others are condemned. So, ask yourself what is celebrated in your story. What is reviled? Who does this story vilify? What behavior does it condone? What meaning does the ending convey in regard to moral issues?

Remember, the cost of the pursuit of any ideal will make a statement about its value. Ask yourself, "Is the statement this story is making about the world true? Is it a message that serves my readers? Is it offering them what they came to this story for?"

- Truth, valor, courage—these will be affirmed.

- Lies, betrayal, cowardice—these will be condemned.

For instance, readers want the villain to suffer for what he's done—and death might not be enough. They want justice, and sometimes that looks different than simply taking the villain's life: Readers want the villain to suffer pain commensurate with what he has caused. If they think the pain he caused outweighs the good accomplished by the hero, they'll leave the story believing that evil won out in the end.

For example, if your hero is slow to act and the villain wreaks havoc on the city, indiscriminately murdering dozens of people, the message readers will take away is "Justice cannot stop the pain caused by evil," rather than "Justice prevails, but there is a cost." In essence, evil wins.

211. "IF I INCLUDE REPRESENTATIONS OF EVIL, WILL IT DESENSITIZE PEOPLE TO VIOLENCE?"

It depends on how it's portrayed. If you glamorize evil, make it look stylish and cool and intriguing, then yes, you'll desensitize people to it, and your story might even be seen by some readers as an invitation to emulate it.

(Also, if you skip over evil and pretend that it doesn't really exist or that it's not such a big deal, your story will lack believability since readers already know that the real world isn't like that.)

Always be honest about the world.

Your content will depend on your genre and your target audience, but if you're striving to tell the truth about the world, about the human condition, you'll likely need to include some representation of the evil that's present on our planet—and in a very real way—threaded into every one of our hearts.

Truth sensitizes people to violence; lies desensitize them.

212. "HOW CAN I TELL IF I'M DESENSITIZING READERS OR NOT?"

The question is not so much if you *portray* evil, it's if you're *promoting* it. To be honest about life, you need to portray evil, but you need never celebrate it or make it look enticing or alluring. Evil is real, and if we don't name it and stand up against it, we are either living in denial, cowardice, or complicity.

Ask yourself:

- Who commits the crime? Is it an empathetic protagonist, or is it the antagonist? How am I meant to feel toward him?

- Is the crime justified in the eyes of the readers? Is there a point to this violence? Is the violence grounded in a moral universe?

- Are there consequences for the violent act? Does evil win in the end? Is that what readers have come to my story to see?

- Is the most interesting character the villain? What message does that convey?

- Is the violence glorified or made to look inviting?

- What is the context? What are the consequences? Does this violence serve this story?

- Is the story a dark comedy? Am I making light of violence? How will readers respond?

Stories can serve as siren calls luring readers closer to evil or as warning beacons floating in their consciences to keep them clear of the rocks. It often depends on how, not if, you portray virtues and vices.

213. "HOW SHOULD I DEAL WITH DEATH IN MY STORY?"

As honestly as possible.

The value of something in the narrative world is measured by the amount of pain it causes when it's lost. So, if you want life to appear trite, then deal with death in a trite way. If you want readers to sense that life is important, then let the loss of life in your story matter. Let people grieve. Show the shattered lives of the people the young man's suicide impacted. Show the mother mourn over her stillborn son.

A story about an action hero who indiscriminately kills people without any remorse or regret undermines the dignity and value of human life.

By the way, when you think of death in the narrative world, don't just think in terms of physical death. Other things might die—marriages, hope, careers, love, and so on. Really, anything that might matter to your readers can die in a story. But that's the key—letting it matter and making it count. Ask yourself, "What effect would this death have on my character? What does that tell me about him or about what matters to him? Will readers care? Will this draw them closer into the story or repel them from it?"

214. "WHAT IF MY STORY OFFENDS SOMEONE?"

There's a good chance it will.

Every story worth telling will offend someone. (However, don't let the quality of your storytelling be what offends people. Step out of the way so that the story's impact comes through naturally as a result of the characters' struggles and choices.)

Stories that matter often bring up difficult or thorny questions that some people just don't want to think about. Or, your story might contain material (sex, profanity, graphic violence, etc.) that will turn some readers off.

However, there's a difference between stepping on people's toes and purposely trying to stomp on their feet. Some authors seem to go out of their way to piss off, mock, or demean members of one political party, social class, religion, ethnicity, or demographic.

Avoid that.

Get your agenda out of the way and let the story do its work.

Go ahead. Write something worth being afraid of, worth banning.

Write something so good, so true, that it will unshackle people's chains. Write stories seared with so much truth that they become a threat.

Rage against mediocrity and moral diatribes. Embrace brilliance.

What is staying your hand? What is holding you back from excellence?

A single tear can change the world. Honest fiction can do the same.

Start a revolution with your words.

SECTION VII

STATUS, TENSION, AND BELIEVABILITY

215. "PEOPLE TELL ME MY PROTAGONIST IS ONE-DIMENSIONAL. WHAT SHOULD I DO?"

Deepen his desires and vary his status.

216. "WHAT DOES THAT MEAN?"

We've covered desires already. Regarding status, essentially, it's the degree of dominance or submission that a character has within a scene. While he might initially have low status in a certain situation or relationship, that can change. Substantive status is more determined by choice than by circumstances and is best shown through reaction rather than description.

Putting someone in a place where he has low *situational* status will often bring readers to his side. For instance, though your hero is abducted, chained to the wall, and about to be tortured (a predicament that puts him in a terrifically low-status situation), he keeps his cool and refuses to be intimidated (raising his substantive status above that of his captors, despite how much the odds are stacked against him).

If a character is outnumbered in a fight, readers will tend to be on his side—even if he isn't the hero. When considering status, ask:

- Who's calling the shots in this scene? (This person has higher status.)
- Who's *trying* to call the shots? (This would indicate lower status.)

The character who doesn't care who's in control shows that he isn't needy and so elevates his status; the character who's constantly striving to "one-up" others ends up undermining his status because of his lack of contentment and his self-focused attitude. Status isn't so much about demanding respect but earning it.

Giving your characters different degrees of situational and substantive status in their varying relationships, work environments, and interactions with each other will imbue them with dimensionality and will help humanize them.

When story characters have multiple levels of status with different characters (a spouse, a boss, family members, strangers, work associates, etc.), they'll seem more believable and more realistic.

217. "HOW DO I RAISE A CHARACTER'S STATUS?"

To raise substantive status, think in terms of stillness, self-restraint, and compassion.

Regarding *stillness*, look for places where the character can pause. Nothing speaks louder than silence. Slow her down; show her confidence and moral resolve. Courage in the face of danger and poise under pressure both raise status. Impatience and cowardice lower it. The person who's the most patient in a scene will claim the highest status.

With *self-restraint*, ask what she's refraining from doing that she could do. For example, holding back from returning an insult for an insult or refraining from striking out against her oppressor when she's taunted or attacked will raise status. The most powerful person can do the smallest gesture and create the most change. In a scene, power isn't shown through posturing, but through reservation. Often, he who says the least communicates the most. When you want to portray power, don't do so through having a character being overbearing, loud, boisterous, and so on. All of those lower status. Show self-restraint instead. Meekness is not weakness; it is power that's restrained. A weak person cannot be meek. A strong person can.

Concerning *compassion*, ask what she could sacrifice for another, either through the pain that she experiences on another's behalf or the pain that she relieves by giving up something that matters. When a character shows honor or respect, it raises her status; dissing, disregarding, or belittling others lowers it.

218. "THIS IS INTERESTING. WHAT ELSE AFFECTS STATUS?"

Composure raises status. A nervous, unsure, placating, or boastful character ends up lowering her status. Someone else might be in control of a situation, but the person with the highest status has control of himself.

The strongest man does not flex his muscles or posture or show off. The toughest kid has no need to prove himself.

Showing joy or other positive emotions doesn't decrease your status, but being smug does. Chortling at your own jokes lowers status; being able to laugh at yourself raises it.

Plucky is good. Smart is good. Quipping is good. Cutting sarcasm is not. Don't let your protagonist be whiny, smarmy, or judgmental, all of which undermine status.

Making a character proud, self-congratulatory, and needy will all lower his status. Insulting others lowers status, as does wringing your hands, whining, and being judgmental. To raise status, let your character be unconcerned with what others think of him rather than clamoring for their praise, attention, or applause. To listen attentively to others will raise your status. To be dismissive of them will lower it.

To lower situational status, put your character at a disadvantage, either in an unfamiliar environment or with a superior force of antagonism. Expose her vulnerabilities to someone who can take advantage of them. Add urgency. Then, allow her to choose and let that choice matter in determining substantive status.

219. "IS THERE AN EASY WAY TO REMEMBER ALL OF THIS STUFF ABOUT STATUS MANAGEMENT?"

Here are eight ways to raise status:

1. Sacrifice for the good of others.
2. Stand up for the oppressed.
3. Turn the other cheek.
4. Exhibit self-control.
5. Show compassion.
6. Be courageous.
7. Slow down.

8. Marvel.

Here are eight ways to lower status:

1. Whine.
2. Give in.
3. Be judgy.
4. Be a coward.
5. Lose control. Mock.
6. Rush frantically about.
7. Show how needy you are.
8. Be self-congratulatory. Sneer.

220. "CAN CHARACTERS HAVE EQUAL STATUS?"

Yes. To balance status, add banter. When friends or lovers jibe or rib each other, readers recognize that they're at ease having the same status.

Even though they might engage in friendly competition, buddies don't vie for dominance over each other. They're comfortable being equals.

Here are eight ways to equalize status:

1. Banter.
2. Show their wit.
3. Engage in friendly competition.

4. Allow them to come across as equals.
5. Let the characters complement each other.
6. Lighten the mood and bring a laugh.
7. Show equal cleverness or acumen.
8. Level the playing field.

221. "DOES WORD CHOICE IMPACT STATUS?"

Word choice can either elevate status or undermine it.

Demanding to have your way will lower status (because it shows your neediness), while *making a request* would raise your status (because it shows your poise and respect for others).

Verbs affect status. Notice how the status is raised in each of these verbs: *tell*, *inform*, and *rebuke*. For example, "He told me the answer," "He informed me I'd gotten a ticket," or "He rebuked me for what I'd said."

Verbs often express an attitude as well as a need—both of which affect status. For instance, to *sashay* shows an attitude but might also indicate a need for attention. Be aware of the subtle differences in your choice of verbs relating to how characters walk. Consider what attitude and need are expressed in the words *saunter*, *swagger*, and *traipse*. See how they each lower status? Now, note how, on the other hand, the verbs *stroll*, *amble*, and *glide* show a relaxed attitude and raise status.

If you have one character ask a question *urgently*, you raise his status; if you have him *plead* with someone, you show desperation and, therefore, lower his status. To act *hastily* (showing lack of self-control) lowers status, to act *quickly* (showing a prompt response) raises it.

Would you allow your protagonist to sneer at the villain? No. It would lower his substantive status too much. However, he might stare him down and refuse to look away, showing boldness and steely resolve, which would raise his status.

222. "WHAT ELSE DO I NEED TO KNOW ABOUT STATUS?"

Choices tilt or flip status, so how a character responds will affect his substantive status more than anything else about his predicament.

Your character might make courageous decisions when he's outnumbered or when he's oppressed by those with more power or authority. In this way, even though he's in a position of low situational status, he can turn the tables through his bravery or unflappable resolve.

This will often happen at the climax, the moment when the odds are stacked most highly against the protagonist (in other words, when he's in his lowest situational status predicament of the entire book).

A few things to remember about status:

1. You won't want your protagonist to make a decision that lowers his substantive status beneath that of the antagonist.

2. To lower status, let the character require an explanation from someone; to raise it, have him deduce the answer for himself.

3. Self-perception affects substantive status. Confidence raises it. Cowardice lowers it. Also, a character might perceive himself to have higher status than your readers or other characters recognize him to have. This self-delusion only serves to undermine his status even more.

223. "HOW DOES STATUS RELATE TO CONFLICT?"

Use difficult situations and setbacks to press your characters to choose, act, and respond. Those actions, while the stakes are high, will reveal her status.

224. "WHAT IS THE ROLE OF CONFLICT IN A STORY?"

Conflict by itself does little to drive a story forward. If your story is simply about a character who has bad things happen to him, the story will fall flat. His misfortunes need to be paired with his desire for things to be better and evidenced by the choices he makes because of that desire.

Having a succession of bad things happen to someone who's apathetic or complacent won't create a gripping story, no matter how bad those circumstances become. So, your character's attitude and self-perception affect your story's tension.

Tension is key, and it doesn't *necessarily* come from conflict; it results from unmet desire.

225. "WAIT—TENSION *DOESN'T* COME FROM CONFLICT? CAN YOU EXPLAIN THAT?"

To play a meaningful role in the story, conflict must be wedded to desire—that is, the intention-infused pursuit of something other than the current state of affairs. This unmet desire is what creates the tension that will hold up your story.

For example, tragedies can keep befalling your protagonist, but if he's resigned to his fate, those events won't produce tension, just reveal acquiescence or express complacency. In that case, there would be plenty of conflict but no story.

Conflict is not enough.

Desire (that drives the story), not simply conflict (from undesirable events), affects the trajectory of the protagonist's journey through the story.

$$\text{Conflict + Desire = Struggle}$$

Without conflict, you simply have a desire that is being fulfilled. Without desire, you simply have bad things happening to your character. Show the conflict, convey the desire (what does your character want and what's getting in the way?), and you will have identified the struggle in that scene.

Facing challenges changes us while also revealing who we are. When evaluating conflict, ask, "Does this conflict have any effect on my character? Does it show how witty or clever or determined or ingenious he is? Does it escalate the struggle?" If so, and if the conflict clashes with the character's desire, then it has risen to the level of struggle and will benefit the narrative progression of the story.

In a similar vein, when your character's choices in pursuit of a goal meet up with an obstacle that holds your characters back, tension results.

$$\text{Pursuit + Obstacle = Tension}$$

A pursuit alone, with no obstacles, will simply result in immediate success. An obstacle that's put in the way of your character without his pursuit meeting up with it will only result in immediate defeat. Both a pursuit and an obstacle are necessary to produce tension.

226. "WILL I ALWAYS SUSTAIN THE TENSION IN EVERY SCENE?"

Scenes tilt upon the expression and pursuit of unmet desire, so tension in stories is rarely static. Instead, it's dynamic. It stretches and shrinks within and between scenes.

Trying to "sustain the tension" will tend to be self-defeating since tension isn't something you *sustain*; it's something you tighten or release.

No matter how much is happening, if tension is simply being maintained, it'll soon be lost. When there's no escalation, there's no increase in the tension. Tension's ebb and flow between scenes (action) and interludes (reflection) leads readers inexorably forward through the story toward the unforgettable climax—the scene with the deepest tension and greatest payoff.

227. "HOW DOES TENSION RELATE TO THE STORY'S STAKES?"

The "stakes" refer to what would be lost or the suffering that would occur if the character failed to succeed in resolving her struggle. If there are no negative consequences (that is if nothing vital or meaningful is at stake), why should readers care about whether or not the main character actually gets what she wants during the story? With no stakes, there's no tension.

Evaluate whether the stakes are high enough in your story and if the consequences of failure are well enough defined. Consider this: If the stakes are too *low*, readers won't care. On the other hand, if they're too *high*, you'll strain credulity, and readers might not buy into the premise of the story.

Clarify to readers what will happen if the characters don't achieve what they've set out to accomplish or if they fail to complete their mission: emotional devastation, the loss of something valuable, the suffering of many people, death, etc.

Also, work to keep the stakes believable by buttressing the story with credible and causally related events that retain the veracity of what's occurring.

228. "PEOPLE TALK ABOUT A PLOT 'THICKENING.' WHAT DOES THAT MEAN?"

It means that the complications increase, the stakes escalate, the tension tightens, and the struggles deepen. Some plot thickeners for certain genres might include:

- Romance – someone else intrudes on or threatens the couple's relationship.

- Sci-fi – the AI computer becomes self-aware.

- Suspense – the kidnapper demands a life for a life.

- Fantasy – the prince is captured and taken to another realm.

Although it depends on the context, the genre, and the point in the story at which those moments occur, you can typically make the plot thicken by adding tension, red herrings, clues, suspects, and setbacks.

229. "WHAT OTHER STEPS I CAN TAKE TO THICKEN MY PLOT?"

Often, you can do it by adding a twist, creating dual moral or physical obligations (where he needs to be in two places at once) for your character, inserting a deadline or a countdown, making the stakes more intimate (personal) or sweeping (universal), isolating the protagonist, or removing his assets or support system.

To be left alone with evil and have to face it by yourself, or to be within sight of freedom and get captured, can be terrifying.

Here are five additional steps you can take to thicken the plot of your story:

1. Let a choice from the past impact the present: A minister who has turned his life around finds out that he has a nineteen-year-old son from a one-night stand he had back in college.

2. Introduce a new question that grows from a previous question or revelation: The search in the forest for the lost girl leads not just to the discovery of her shallow grave but the graves of three other girls.

3. Weave together two or more storylines: "You know that guy who spoke to you on the bus?" "The one who hit on me?" "Yeah. That was my husband."

4. Set a deadline that requires action or would result in devastating consequences: If they don't find the terrorist by midnight, the city will be destroyed.

5. Give readers (or the characters) an unexpected revelation: He has cancer, his identity was stolen, he's really an alien, or his whole life is a lie. (But probably not all of the above in the same story!)

230. "HOW DOES 'PLOT-THICKENING' OR ESCALATION RELATE TO CHASE SCENES OR ACTION SEQUENCES?"

Imagine you're writing an amazing chase scene. Your protagonist, a scrappy detective, is on a foot chase after a killer through the murky back alleys of the city.

You could write *I bolted down the street and saw the Midnight*

Strangler duck into an alley bordering the old warehouse. Cornering the building, I sprinted after him, running down the narrow alleyway.

You might write that, but you wouldn't want to. Why not? Because the verbs "bolted," "sprinted," and "ran" de-escalate in their urgency. In other words, each of them carries less urgency than the one that precedes it. Instead, you would reverse their order so the paragraph reads: *I ran down the street and saw the Midnight Strangler duck into an alley bordering the old warehouse. Cornering the building, I sprinted after him, bolting down the narrow alleyway.*

We want the tension and urgency to escalate, even in scenes where there's continuous action.

231. "ARE THERE WAYS I CAN USE A COUNTDOWN TO ADD TO MY STORY'S TENSION?"

When using a countdown, think about the difference between a timer and a metronome. The timer is ticking down to when the pizza will be done (a specific goal or event that you can look forward to); the metronome is clicking away rhythmically but with no end or resolution in sight.

Let your countdown be a timer, not a metronome. In other words, countdowns will have a purpose beyond simply tracking the passage of time.

1. Explore unique ways of using countdowns. Timers don't always need to be on a bomb. What other types of countdowns are there?

2. To increase tension and suspense, shorten the time available to solve the problem.

3. To make a countdown serve your story, clarify the stakes, and then raise them as the story progresses.

4. Be aware of the drawbacks of countdowns. Whenever

you insert a time marker, some readers are going to evaluate how much has happened since the last marker and if they think the timing strains believability, they won't buy into the story.

5. Let there be a final reckoning at the end of the countdown. Once you've reached the deadline or the end of the time limit, pay off the promises you've made regarding the stakes or consequences.

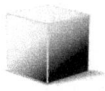

232. "I'M LOOKING FOR MORE STRUGGLES TO INCLUDE. ANY SUGGESTIONS?"

First, remember that struggles occur in three realms—within, around, and between.

Struggles *within* the character are internal; struggles *around* characters are external; struggles *between* characters are interpersonal.

Internal struggles might include the character's desire to overcome her past, learn to trust again or gain confidence in herself. They might be spiritual, emotional, philosophical, or existential and can deal with questions regarding identity, the meaning of life, or the search for significance.

External struggles often involve difficult or dangerous tasks, the removal of danger, or the quest for justice.

Interpersonal struggles deal with establishing or restoring relationships, often touching on issues of trust, friendship, commitment, love, sacrifice, and betrayal.

INTERNAL STRUGGLES	EXTERNAL STRUGGLES	INTER-PERSONAL STRUGGLES

To discover self/meaning	To embark on an adventure	To love and be loved
To find faith	To catch the villain	To reignite a friendship
To overcome shame/guilt	To complete a quest/journey	To start anew with someone else
To embrace a dream	To see justice meted out	To be understood
To accept help	To stop a threat	To belong
To be set free from self-limiting beliefs	To protect the innocent or rescue a victim	To relate to a difficult person
To find joy/hope/happiness	To obtain the object of desire	To initiate a relationship
To discover truth	To conquer a foe	To restore a relationship
To experience adventure/independence	To overcome adversity	To find acceptance in a group

Many stories deal with reinvention or redemption, or the discovery of self or the quest for love. What is it for your character? What is she searching for? A new start? New hope? Love? Identity? Examine her desire and let it inform her pursuit.

233. "HOW CAN I DEVELOP MORE TENSION IN EACH OF THE THREE REALMS?"

Search for ways to give the character two equally strong desires.

For an *internal* struggle, rather than just having a question that he's trying to answer, look for the tension involved in having two inner desires—to cling to an old way of thinking, a safe way, and also to pursue the truth regardless of where it takes him. The struggle is between the security of naivety and the "dangers" of knowing the truth.

For an *external* struggle, rather than just trying to solve one problem, he must choose between solving two equally important problems—save his daughter or his wife. One must die. Which one? How does he choose? How can you, as a writer, justify the choice while also ending the scene in a way that satisfies readers?

For an *interpersonal* struggle, explore not just how he can win the woman's heart but how he can both please his family, who doesn't approve of his beloved, *and also* win her heart. The tension: loyalty to family and the desire to be free of them (and also of stepping out into the world while still respecting your roots).

Rather than simply looking for what struggles your character has to overcome, think in terms of what your character will struggle with—given his multiplicity of beliefs, strongly-held convictions, and current situation in life.

234. "HOW DO STRUGGLES IN THOSE REALMS AFFECT THE CHARACTER'S JOURNEY THROUGH THE STORY?"

The three realms of struggles often merge and culminate in a moment of realization when a specific choice from the outer story world (the external struggle) helps the main character overcome her internal or interpersonal struggle.

Accentuate these moments of decision and illumination in your story. They provide some of the most satisfying moments for readers.

Incidentally, we sometimes desire seemingly contradictory things at the same time, and holding onto them both is essential for mental health and intimate relationships. For instance, we desire freedom (independence) as well as intimacy (dependence). If we only have one or the other, we're in trouble. If we only have the first, we become callous; if only the second, we become clingy. The only way to be mentally healthy is to dwell in the paradox of our own opposing desires.

235. "HOW IMPORTANT IS IT TO KNOW WHAT THE MIDDLE OF MY STORY IS ABOUT?"

If you don't know what the middle of your story is about, you don't know what your story is about. The middle is the beating heart of your tale. It isn't there to just take up space or act as a bridge between the beginning and the end. It's not just there to get you from A to B. It's the entire alphabet between A and Z.

236. "MY STORY SAGS IN THE MIDDLE. WHAT ARE SOME WAYS TO KEEP IT INTERESTING AND MOVING FORWARD?"

Layer in more storylines. Introduce one that readers will want to follow to the end, no matter how long the middle is. Every storyline will have its own trajectory, its own moments of suspense and revelation. As these moments happen at different times, readers will be drawn forward through the story.

This idea of stories having three acts leaves us with a problem: what to do with the long middle act. The "sagging middle." Don't let your story suffer because of blind adherence to a formula. Step back from, not further into, templates when you seem to have lost your way, and ask the characters what they are desiring, pursuing, fearing, or dreaming.

If your story is boring in the middle, it might be because it's too repetitive, too cyclical, or there isn't enough tension. Be sure that the stakes continue to rise in the middle of the book and that the tension continues to tighten. If your story has three acts with a long, sagging middle, recast the narrative to include four or five acts instead. Don't let adherence to a plot template negatively impact your story.

237. "HOW MANY SCENES SHOULD EACH ACT OF MY STORY INCLUDE?"

There is no *should*. The length of an act, just like the final story itself, is determined more by unmet desire, escalation, decisions, and pivots than it is by predetermined length considerations.

That being said, if you're writing for a prepackaged art form (for instance, a 50,000-word formulaic romance novel that's due every three months), you'll find that, while there is some flexibility, to complete your story in that timeframe, certain aspects of the narrative will naturally begin to emerge at certain places within the manuscript. Still, let the story rather than the structure have the final say.

Rather than trying to determine the number of beats, scenes, or acts before writing your story, let the story inform you, and be open to the direction that this specific story is taking you.

238. "IS THERE EVER A TIME WHEN I SHOULD USE TWO ACTS OR FOUR ACTS INSTEAD OF THREE?"

Some stories only require one act. Others naturally fall into two acts, three, four, five, or more.

When working on your story, don't chain it down by assuming that it must have only three (or four, or whatever number) acts. Be flexible, and remember that the story isn't set in stone yet. It's a work in progress. Don't tie yourself too rigidly to any plot paradigm.

Let the number of acts emerge as you write. How many you end up with is much less important than the story's believable and contingent progression. Don't let the straitjacket of preconceptions impinge on your story.

239. "HOW WILL I KNOW HOW MANY ACTS TO INCLUDE?"

Again, the number of acts is determined first and foremost by the story. Depending on the lens you use to view your story, it might move through...

- One act: Transformation

- Two acts: Disruption —> Resolution

- Three acts: Orientation —> Complication —> Resolution

- Four acts: Orientation —> Disruption —> Escalation—> Transformation

- Five acts: Orientation —> Disruption —> Escalation—> Transformation —> Resolution

Truthfully, readers don't care how many acts a story has; they care whether or not it's believable, makes sense, is entertaining, has some twists and surprises along the way, and has a great climax and meaningful payoff at the end.

240. "ARE YOU SAYING I SHOULD DISCARD THE IDEA OF ACTS ALTOGETHER?"

Rather than trying to unnecessarily conform your story to a certain number of acts, focus your efforts instead on your character's pursuit and journey of desire.

Stories naturally move through a stage of orientation, to a crisis or calling (developing or accentuating unmet desire), to an escalation of tension (which can, in itself, include numerous acts), and finally to a climactic encounter and resolution (or transformation).

Introduce readers to a character they care about and want to cheer for (or worry about), give her an obstacle to overcome or a goal to pursue, send a series of relentlessly escalating setbacks her way that lead her to a point of hopelessness. Then, allow her a chance to choose her fate and have her end the story in a different place (physically, spiritually, emotionally, or relationally) than she was at the beginning of the book. This might all happen in one act. It might happen in a dozen. The form of story is not the same as a formula for a story.

Astute readers can often tell when a story was written to conform to a certain template or pre-ordained plan. Strive to do better than that, to move past baby steps and tell fresh, original stories that chart new narrative paths instead of continually retreading the old familiar ones.

241. "SO THEN, REGARDLESS OF THE NUMBER

OF ACTS, DOES THE MAIN CHARACTER NEED TO ACHIEVE SOMETHING BY THE END OF THE STORY?"

He needs to take active steps to pursue something that he's convinced will bring him happiness or relief. A story can end either with the character getting what he wants or not getting it, depending on the genre. Generally speaking:

- Romance – She gets what she wants and (often) *even more than she dreamed!*

- Cozy mysteries – She gets what she wants (justice and a chance to cuddle with the cat).

- Thriller/literary – She gets what she wants but loses something precious in the process.

- Horror – She doesn't get what she wants and ends up *even worse off than she could have ever imagined!*

- Coming-of-age – She doesn't get what she wants, but rather what she needs—and learns something that makes the quest and sacrifice, in retrospect, all worthwhile.

242. "WHAT SHOULD THE CHOICES OF THE CHARACTERS INCORPORATE?"

Their choices will be intentional, logical, believable, and revelatory.

They'll be *intentional* in the sense that they aren't random but are centered around that character's desire-infused pursuit. Within the context, they're *logical* to readers and to the character. They make sense to the character and readers, making them *believable*. And finally, they're meaningful and *reveal* the priorities, attributes, and dimensionality of the character.

As you explore his choices, change the core questions you're asking regarding characterization so they lead you deeper into the true intentions of your character:

RATHER THAN ASKING...	ASK...
"What should this character do?"	"What does this character want?"
"How should this character act?"	"How would this character respond?"
"What is this story about?"	"What is this character pursuing?

243. "HOW IMPORTANT IS BELIEVABILITY THROUGH ALL OF THIS?"

When things aren't believable, events occur, but readers have no idea why. Characters make seemingly incongruous decisions. They pass through the story on their way to We Know Not What, constantly doing What Doesn't Make Sense.

Avoid that route at all costs.

In fiction, plausibility doesn't cut it. Probability doesn't either. It doesn't even matter if something is impossible or not. Your story events and the choices your characters make need to be believable to readers and logical to the characters.

Stories begin when characters act in a believable manner, given their personality, pursuit, and the situation they find themselves in. Then, that believability is sustained through logical, intention-directed choices as the story progresses.

244. "EVEN THOUGH THIS IS FICTION, YOU'RE SAYING THAT IT NEEDS TO REMAIN BELIEVABLE?"

Yes. If the characters are transformed internally, it should be in a believable way based on believable choices and natural consequences. If a character makes seemingly inexplicable choices, they must make eventual sense when taken into the broader context of the promise-woven fabric of your story.

Examine every page of your manuscript and ask, "Will my reader nod, or will he shake his head?" Your goal: Never make him shake his head as he discounts what you've written as unbelievable.

Believability is one of the most vital narrative forces.

245. "YOU'VE MENTIONED 'NARRATIVE FORCES' BEFORE. CAN YOU EXPLAIN WHAT YOU MEAN?"

Telling a great story requires keeping in mind five central factors: the *contingent* movement of the story from the origination to the resolution (that is, every event is caused by the one that precedes it), *believability*, *escalation*, *intention*, and *surprise*.

Let's explore them one at a time.

   1. *Contingency* – Are there gaps in narrative logic? Do things happen for no reason other than that you think they need to happen in order to make your outline work? If so, root them in cause and effect. Instead, stories are not just accounts of things happening, they are purpose-

driven, logically directed journeys of desire that unveil transformations.

2. *Believability* – Is everything that happens believable, even if it's impossible? Does the character act in a way that's in concert with his or her core attitudes, desires, inner turmoil, and external circumstances? Make sure every choice is believable given this specific character in this specific context.

3. *Escalation* – Are the stakes being raised? Is the danger becoming more imminent or more unstoppable? Is the tension building? Stories build in tension, or they fizzle out.

4. *Intention* – What drives this character to act? In other words, what does he want (or think he wants) more than anything else? How far is he willing to go to get it? Is every action that he takes sufficiently actuated by the context? Choices based on intention should infuse all of the action in the story.

5. *Surprise* – Do the scenes, the acts, and the story as a whole, end in a way that readers won't be able to predict? If not, what changes do you need to make to twist things in a new direction? Stories pivot in unexpected directions, or they become too predictable.

If a story lacks any of these five, it will suffer. If there is no causal relationship between events (that is, that things are not caused by what precedes them), the story will lack logical progression and seem outlandish. If there's no believability, readers won't buy it. If there's no escalation, it'll soon become boring. If there's no intention, the characters won't be dimensional. If there are no surprises, the story will be too predictable. Whatever else your story has or doesn't have, these five factors should be present in and affect the momentum of every scene.

246. "LET'S SAY THAT IN ORDER TO MOVE THE PLOT FORWARD, I NEED TO HAVE A CHARACTER DO SOMETHING THAT MIGHT SEEM UNBELIEVABLE. IS THIS OKAY?"

Not if it seems to the reader to be unbelievable within the story world. To address this unbelievability, you might have another character point out that the action is surprising. For instance, "I could hardly believe Lucy would say something like that! It really didn't sound like her at all. Something is off here." Readers will like that: *Aha! I thought that was strange, too. Let's see where this goes.*

Then, readers will trust you that there's a deeper plan at work rather than lose trust in you because you're asking them to accept something unbelievable.

247. "HOW WILL READERS REACT IF THEY DON'T UNDERSTAND WHY EVENTS ARE OCCURRING?"

As soon as something inexplicable happens, readers might either question your competence as a writer ("Things keep happening out of nowhere!") or lose faith in the acumen of the protagonist ("This guy's an idiot! Can't he see that there's something weird going on!?").

They might also complain that nothing is happening in the story, that it's too confusing, that it's not going anywhere, or that they simply "don't get it."

You're not placing your readers first if they're left thinking, *What was that supposed to mean?* or *How come he told us...and now we're supposed to believe that...?*

Consider whether you really want readers to ask "Why?" at this moment in the story. If you decide that you *do*, then keep the character's intention in that scene hidden from your readers. Otherwise, clarify the desire before the scene to bring clarity to readers concerning what the scene is about.

248. "HOW CAN I MAKE STORY EVENTS MORE BELIEVABLE?"

When something occurs that should elicit a response from your character, let her react immediately and appropriately to what happened.

As you evaluate the flow of your story, identify sequences in which characters don't make believable choices (that is, you've forced them to act in a way that doesn't allow them to remain true to who they are). Fix those instances by making the responses more believable, so you don't push readers out of the story.

Every action that your character takes should be genuine for her and not just a means for you to move the story in a new direction or to get to your next "plot point" or "signpost." Let her always respond authentically to stimuli in the story.

By the way, the more impossible you make something appear to story characters, the more believable it'll become to readers. For example, you're emphasizing how impossible it would be for someone to break into a certain high-tech government facility, and one character says, "There's no way anyone could get past their five levels of security. It's just not possible. That place is a veritable fortress. It's completely impenetrable." Readers are thinking, *Oh, no, it's not!* Those sentences become an implied promise that someone *will* break into that facility in a believable way that readers wouldn't have guessed.

While readers are making their way through your story, even if they're not aware of it, they're subconsciously asking if things make sense. If the events remain believable, readers will continue to "buy it." As they do this, they're constantly anticipating, predicting, and then recalibrating. When something isn't believable (or a solution suddenly comes out of nowhere), they'll naturally become either confused or frustrated—and neither of these are reactions you want them to have.

249. "HOW CAN I TELL WHAT MY CHARACTER TRULY BELIEVES?"

By how he acts, not by what he says.

In fiction, you can tell if a character believes something by the degree to which it affects him. If he claims to believe in the power of prayer yet never prays, readers will doubt the truth of his claim. If he claims to love someone but betrays her, he undermines readers' belief in his claims regarding his feelings toward her and his devotion to her.

You can't reveal beliefs apart from choices, and you won't be able to include meaningful choices without revealing a character's priorities or beliefs. A belief that's untested is simply wishful thinking. One that's confirmed by action is authentic.

Because of this, in a story, although a character might claim to believe certain things, readers won't be convinced of his beliefs until they're evidenced by his choices—the more difficult the choice he makes, the more revelatory it is regarding his beliefs.

250. "HOW IMPORTANT IS IT TO SHOW THE CONSEQUENCES OF MY CHARACTERS' MORAL CHOICES?"

It's vital. Every fictional story happens within a moral framework and assumes some understanding of human nature. If your story mocks virtue, celebrates vice, or equates them with each other, it won't ring true to readers.

Also, without consequences, you won't retain believability. You would be giving the impression that our choices don't make any difference in life, especially in matters of morality.

For example, if a character sacrifices his life for the protagonist and it makes no essential difference to the story or to the development (or revelation) of the main character, that would undermine the idea that selfless sacrifice is meaningful and something to be emulated.

251. "HOW FAR SHOULD I GO IN DEVELOPING (OR UNDERSTANDING) MY CHARACTERS' BELIEF SYSTEMS?"

Beliefs matter. They affect how we shape our lives, whether or not we have hope or find meaning, and where we ground our morality. Story can be a vehicle for more deeply and intimately exploring the beliefs of our characters.

1. *Hope* – Does he have hope for the future? If so, why? If not, why not? In what areas does it seem to him that change/growth/peace is hopeless? What gives him hope—God? Human potential? If he has no hope, how does he find motivation to tackle life each day? How does his lack of hope (or the presence of it) affect the way he approaches life?

2. *Faith* – Does she believe in destiny? In God? Fate? Chance? Is she a materialist? How do her beliefs give her reassurance—or don't they? What do they cause her to question? Does she pray? Why or why not? Does she believe that her prayers matter? Who (or what) does she pray to? What does she pray for? If she could have anything from God, what would it be? What does she pray for but is unwilling to be part of the answer to?

3. *Meaning* – Where does his sense of significance come

from? Does he believe that life has meaning? If so, what is it? If not, how does he live with that sense of meaninglessness? Is he searching for meaning? If so, how? If not, why not—has he found it, doesn't care, or just doesn't see the point?

Your character's beliefs will inevitably affect her pursuit and journey through the story. That doesn't mean, however, that you're trying to get readers to believe the same things as she does. If that ends up being the case, the story might easily come across as didactic or preachy.

252. "SHOULD I MAKE MY CHARACTERS RELIGIOUS?"

Whether they're religious in the traditional sense of the word or not, their beliefs will affect their choices—just as it is with real people in real life.

Consider how your characters' views and beliefs impact the way they relate to each other and influence the decisions they make as they pursue their unmet desires during the story.

QUESTION	CONCLUSIONS
What is the origin of life?	Creation? Evolution? Alien DNA? Chance? Divine design?
What gives us hope?	Effort? Natural Selection? God?

What is the problem with humanity?	Lack of enlightenment? Lack of education? Sin? There is no problem?
What is the meaning of life?	Every moment has meaning? There is no meaning? You make up meaning on your own?
Is there life after death?	Yes? No? What makes you say so?
Is there a God?	Yes? No? I don't know? It doesn't matter one way or the other?
Where do our views of morality come from?	Divine revelation? Society/Culture? The biological imperatives of survival and reproduction?

Even though they won't all likely make it into your story, plumbing the depths of your characters' beliefs about spirituality or religion can inform you about what matters most to them and how they would most naturally respond to different stimuli in the story.

253. "DOES MY STORY NEED TO ASK DEEP QUESTIONS?"

Fiction of lasting value asks questions that matter.

Only those writers willing to explore the oblique and often paradoxical aspects of human nature will end up writing the stories we remember for a lifetime. The stories that affect us the most, shape us, or change our views, are the ones that help us to examine who we are and how we might become who we long to be.

Fiction allows us to peer into the darkness and see it for what it truly is—to see ourselves for who we truly are. And then to catch a glimpse of the light.

Through fiction, readers enter into the experience of living vicariously and can learn to become better, more inspired, more integrated selves.

254. "I'M TRYING TO BE OPTIMISTIC IN MY STORY BUT ALSO HONEST ABOUT LIFE. ANY SUGGESTIONS?"

Often, writers fall into either the trap of naive optimism or that of fatalistic pessimism.

Some stories give us the message that if we just follow our hearts, pursue our dreams, and act in a way that's true to ourselves, then we'll be happy, self-actualized, and self-fulfilled human beings. But this simply isn't true. We all know people who've followed their dreams only to find them splintered apart at their feet. A story that ignores the shrieks and wounds of life on this broken planet isn't being honest.

On the other end of the spectrum, some storytellers focus only on the negative—life is pain and misery that you must simply endure until you die and exist no more. There's no ultimate meaning, no hope, no justice, no chance of redemption.

But this isn't honest about the world either. Because joy and beauty and hope *are* real. Love does bring meaning, the natural world does offer perspective and peace, laughter really does heal both bodies and souls—because this world is just as beautiful as it is horrifying, and stories that ring true will recognize, acknowledge, and honor that.

255. "HOW DO HONEST STORIES HANDLE

THAT PARADOX THEN?"

They both acknowledge the painful realities of life and also celebrate the hope that's available to us all. Ask yourself:

- Have I written from a moral worldview?
- Have I upheld the dignity, value, and honor of human life?
- Have I presented evil as disturbing rather than alluring?
- Am I glamorizing violence or sensitizing people to it?
- Does the story celebrate beauty, love, and imagination?
- Am I adding to the darkness, or am I showing people a glimpse of the light?

Think of it this way: Nobody goes up to a journalist who's doing a story on a murderer and says, "How can you report on that?" The reporter's goal is simply to tell the truth about what happened in that instance. Our goal as novelists is to tell the truth about what happens in our world. A journalist examines the crime, a novelist examines the human condition—not just an event, but the state of humanity. Journalists examine the results of human nature exposed; we explore the bounds of the human condition.

Stories that matter help us to open our eyes, avoiding both naivety and nihilism. Ours is a robust and tragic and terrible and glorious world, and well-crafted novels help us to rip off our blinders and see that.

It takes courage to tell stories like that. Be bold enough to tell the truth. Pull back the curtain and let readers glimpse the world as it truly is while also giving them a map to what it could one day become.

256. "HOW MUCH SHOULD MY FICTIONAL STORY BE TRUE?"

In your fictional world, you'll be attempting to capture truths about life in the real world. You're shooting to create stories that aren't necessarily true *to* life but true *of* life.

Remember, fiction differs from nonfiction: Fiction is a lie that must be believable; nonfiction is truth that doesn't need to be. In essence, through fiction, writers create a clearer view of reality by telling lies about it.

Truth in fiction simply means a reflection of life as it really is. Stories that only lament the pain of living in a hurting and hurtful world without also celebrating the wonder, magnificence, and love that's present, will soon become wearying to readers.

Incidentally, writing fiction will likely be taxing on your soul because you'll be wrestling with the stuff of truth every day. A writer can't help but stare slack-jawed at the world, both amazed at its glory and also shocked by its brutality—either of which might very well bring you to tears.

For most people, the majority of their lives are spent not in seeing the world as it truly is but as they wish it was. It's easy to close one eye to the suffering and live in self-imposed denial or to keep one eye closed to the glory and justify your despair.

If you never feel awe or despair, you're looking at life with one eye closed to the way the world really is. As the Japanese film director Akira Kurosawa said, "To be an artist means never to avert your eyes."

Writers learn to look at life with both eyes open. Because of that, you're going to identify with other people's suffering. You won't be able to ignore the homeless or the outcast. You won't be able to turn your back on those who are oppressed, those living in slums or garbage dumps or refugee camps. Yes, you'll feel their pain. Yes, you will, or else you won't be able to write honest stories about the world we share with them.

But even as you see how heartless the world can be, you'll also marvel and be astonished at the transcendence and wonder of all around you. You'll be in awe at a child's trust and a mother's love. So, you'll see all of life as a miracle and every sunset as glorious, even as you identify with the pain and heartache of those who are inexplicably suffering. And that's the most honest and also difficult place to be—to see the terrors around us while also refusing to give up the hope within us.

Do that, and your stories will ring as true, even though they are fiction.

SECTION VIII

DIALOGUE AND DESCRIPTION

257. "WHAT ARE THE NARRATIVE TOOLS I CAN USE TO TELL MY STORY?"

Here are four: (1) description, (2) dialogue (either external or in the mind of the character, sometimes called "internal monologue"), (3) narration (sometimes called "exposition"), and (4) formatting (how the text reads, spacing, and so on—think of how poets use this technique for effect).

Formatting isn't always thought of as a storytelling tool, but reading isn't just a cognitive experience; it's a visual one as well. People have certain feelings when they see a page with lots of white space or view pages without any. "It's a quick read" is usually a compliment. "It's a slow read" is usually a warning. (This obviously isn't true when listening to audiobooks, but the narrator is influenced by formatting and her inflection, timing, and emphasis on different aspects of the story still shine through.)

Most scenes will involve the inclusion of each of the four tools to some extent. However, it is possible to have a scene that's mostly dialogue (as long as readers can picture it and the context makes the setting clear) or mostly narration (as long as the characters' desires are evident to readers).

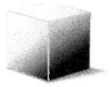

258. "HOW CAN I WRITE BETTER DESCRIPTIONS?"

Great descriptions do more than help readers see something, they invite readers to emotionally engage with the scene.

Try it right now.

Write a paragraph that describes the room you're currently in from the perspective of your hero. Then, do it from the perspective of the villain. How is it different? What are the connotations for readers in each case (positive or negative)?

Be wary, though. Don't get carried away with descriptions.

Unless the point of view, mood, and voice dictate otherwise, keep your descriptions short, pithy, and evocative.

259. "HOW CAN I MAKE MY DESCRIPTIONS BRIEFER AND MORE EVOCATIVE?"

1. Consider the verbs you use when describing actions that the character takes. Does she "put" her lipstick on or "smear" it on? When he shakes someone's hand, does he "pinch it lightly" or "crush it in his grip"? Did the sunlight "seep" into the room? Did it "bleed through the window," or did it "grace the bed"? Verbs are powerful conveyors of characteristics without requiring much additional description or explanation.

2. Subtly appeal to the senses. For instance, rather than telling readers what something smells like, simply mention what's present: "An open bag of cheddar-flavored potato

chips waited beside the couch" or "A sliced onion sat on the counter."

3. Stop thinking of details as ways to describe things and treat them as ways to evoke a response and establish mood. For example, you could certainly describe a coffee shop in great detail but fail to capture the essence of your character's attitude toward or interaction with that setting. It's not enough to just get readers to imagine something. Instead, strive to get them to *feel* something toward it as well.

4. Take into account that, paradoxically, the more you describe something, the more difficult it'll be for readers to picture it. For instance, the more you describe the micro-details of a character's face, the more you'll lose readers. A page describing someone's sweater isn't as effective as an evocative line, such as "She looked like she was wearing a dead llama."

5. Remember that all descriptions need to dovetail with the voice and viewpoint you're writing from. How would your narrator describe a hospital hallway? Would there be "a bright lemony scent" about it, or would it "reek with antiseptic"? A character's attitude and perspective will inevitably influence your word choice while you're writing from her point of view.

260. "CAN DETAILS BE PROMISES AS WELL?"

That's precisely what they are.

Keep in mind how significant this object, item, or location is and how much attention you wish to draw to it. Don't cause readers to needlessly dwell on minutia that doesn't end up having anything substantial to contribute to the story.

Descriptions of characters can also include promises. For instance, there's a big difference between saying, "I noticed that her left arm hadn't developed properly," and "I noticed that her left arm had been amputated." The first observation concerns something true of the character's past; the second delves into the character's backstory. The first example is an explanation; the second is a promise—readers will want to know why the arm was amputated—and they won't be pleased if you decide not to tell them.

261. "WHAT DOES IT MEAN TO WRITE 'ON THE NOSE'?"

That phrase refers to focusing on the minutia of what's being described rather than on its significance.

For example, when describing body language or facial expressions, elaborating on eyebrows wiggling and waggling and creasing and crossing and shooting up and narrowing, and so on, or describing every possible movement a character might take, leaning back in his chair, scrunching up his nose, folding his arms, etc.

For the most part, you'll limit this. Often, the more your characters emote, the less readers feel. So, avoid too much emoting with eyes snapping open or people screaming and crying and chortling all the time. When characters hold back on their emotions rather than releasing them, readers will engage on a deeper emotional level.

Think of *details* as those significant touches to show readers what they wouldn't typically notice and *minutia* as the insignificant traits that everyone would notice. Avoid minutia. Opt for evocative details instead.

262. "HOW DO I BALANCE OUT HOW MUCH INFORMATION TO GIVE READERS?"

As you write, you'll be both creating questions in readers' minds and offering them answers.

If readers are confused, you might be giving too many questions and not enough answers. If they're bored, you might be offering too many answers and not enough questions.

As you work your way through the story, keep asking what your readers are wondering about, what answers they're waiting for, and what resolution would ultimately satisfy them.

Remember that during every scene, your readers are both processing what has happened and predicting what will happen next. The pace and movement of the story will affect how much processing and how much predicting they're doing at any given moment.

During action sequences, readers will mainly be processing the events, taking everything in. During slower or more reflective scenes and interludes, they'll wonder where everything is heading and start predicting what's coming down the pike.

Use this understanding to your advantage when you're revising your work to help you climb into the minds of your readers and more aptly pace your story.

263. "REGARDING DESCRIPTIONS, I'M LOOKING FOR A BETTER WAY TO SHOW INSTEAD OF TELL. ANY SUGGESTIONS?"

If you have a character scream, "I hate you!" and then stomp off and slam the door, you don't need to tell readers, "She was angry." That's already clear from what has just happened, and it's insulting to readers to tell them what they've already discerned from the context. This is the difference between *showing* and *telling*.

When it comes to the character's intention or goal, however, it's often best to just go ahead and tell readers what the character wants (or at least, what she thinks she wants and is subsequently pursuing).

As we discussed earlier, show emotion; tell intention.

It's essential that your character's desire remains clear to readers. Some authors spend too much time trying to *show* what this desire is. Often, it's simpler and more effective to just *tell* readers outright what the character wants by allowing him to state it, think it, or express it to another character.

So, clarify your character's desire either (1) through his thoughts or choices, (2) by having him state his intentions, or (3) by simply telling readers outright what he wants during sections of exposition.

Stated to readers	I was going to find my daughter, and nothing was going to stop me.
Thought (internal monologue)	*You need to find your daughter, and you need to do it now.*
Stated to another character	"I'm here to find my daughter, and I'm not leaving until you tell me where she is."

264. "IS IT POSSIBLE, THOUGH, TO *SHOW* READERS THE GOAL RATHER THAN *TELL* IT TO THEM?

Sure. When you're looking for clearer ways to show intention, think in terms of setting up the situation through the context so that it's crystal clear to readers what the character's goal in the scene is: If a character is told by someone that he should buy flowers for his wife and then he goes online to look up flower stores nearby, you don't need to tell readers why he's doing that.

Don't tell readers what they can easily infer or deduce.

Vengeance and the pursuit of justice are two areas where context often makes it clear what a character wants, making it unnecessary to explicitly state it. For instance, if a man sees his wife get murdered and then goes off to buy a gun and begins to search for the killers, readers rightly assume he's seeking revenge. If a detective is assigned to a case, it's not necessary for you to state that she's trying to bring the culprit to justice. That's obvious.

265. "WHAT DO I NEED TO AVOID IN REGARD TO THE DESCRIPTIONS I INCLUDE?"

Self-assured writing is one of the most significant aspects of voice. Confidence is shown through trusting both the writing and the readers. Overwriting in terms of descriptions will turn readers off. Additionally, avoid...

1. ...explaining what can be assumed,
2. ...needlessly repeating an idea or situation,
3. ...letting symbolism or imagery impinge on the story,
4. ...dumbing down the story for any reason,
5. ...beating readers over the head with a theme or message you're trying to get across.

Instead, allow readers to draw inferences, identify interrelationships, and arrive at conclusions themselves.

266. "YOU MENTIONED VOICE. WHAT IS THAT, EXACTLY?"

Voice is the distinctive flavor of your storytelling. It's how you and you alone can tell this story. It's your signature style, and just like your actual signature, it's unique and personal.

Strive to say something that has never been said and to do so in a way that no one else can.

If you tell your story in a flat and generic way, that's what'll come across to readers. Instead, you'll want to walk the balancing beam of uniqueness while not drawing attention to the fact that you're doing so—because your story needs to be distinctive and original. At the same time, it should not be self-aggrandizing or draw attention to you as the author.

Think of it this way—if you died, is there anyone else who could finish your story with the same rhythm, grace, pace, and voice as you? If so, you might have some work yet to do in unearthing your voice.

267. "HOW DO I DO THAT? HOW DO I FIND MY VOICE?"

Write without pretense. Let your style come through in an honest and genuine way. Eloquence isn't about using big words or showing off your extensive vocabulary—and it shouldn't be your goal. Authenticity is.

Don't try to be literary or like any other writer. Listen to the story and then write what you hear. Be authentic, receptive, and perceptive, and you'll find yourself writing with a distinctive, individual style.

Also, let the journey into your story be a journey deeper into yourself. Let it be a path of self-discovery. The more you find yourself, the more your voice will begin to reveal itself to you and emerge in your writing.

268. "DOES THE POINT OF VIEW AFFECT THE

VOICE?"

Yes. For instance, you probably wouldn't write, "I meandered across the field and then sighed languidly as I studied the dreary clouds overhead."

People just don't talk like that. It sounds pretentious and inauthentic to write in first person in that way.

However, if you rendered that line in third person, it might work fine: "She meandered across the field and then sighed languidly as she studied the dreary clouds overhead."

269. "HOW DOES WORD CHOICE RELATE TO VOICE?"

Voice is established through and influenced by the words you choose.

Some politicians are fond of speaking in terms of "raising government revenue" instead of saying that they want to "raise taxes." The word "revenue" just sounds so much better. Who wouldn't want more revenue, after all? Does the character refer to the proposed policy as a "tax scheme" or a "tax plan"? Is it "crony Capitalism" or "free-market Capitalism"?

Or, think about this phrase, "Something wicked this way comes." You could write, "Something wicked is coming," or "A wicked thing is approaching us," or "Coming this way is something wicked," but none of those carry the same impact, the same feeling, as the original.

Does the smile "disappear" from his face, or "leak" from it, or "slide off it," or "drain from it," or simply "fade away"? Is the wall "cream-colored" or "bone-white"? Would the narrator describe someone as "clever" or "adroit"? Would he call the woman "petite" or "slight"? Or, perhaps, would she be "slender" or "spindly" or "willow" or "lissome" or "lithe" or "svelte"? All of that matters. Every word makes a difference and carries a different connotation.

Your character is a prostitute. Does she refer to the men she sleeps with as "Johns" or as her "clientele"? Does she think of herself as an "escort," a "courtesan," or a "whore"? What does that tell you about how she sees herself?

Let the impression come through in the words she chooses to use.

270. "HOW DO I MERGE THE NARRATOR'S POINT OF VIEW WITH HIS VOICE?"

Imagine you're writing a nighttime scene on a transatlantic flight. Your character is walking down the aisle of the plane, returning to his seat after using the washroom.

What's going through his mind? How he'll get through customs with those drugs in his suitcase? What his family is thinking of him for leaving them in Syria? How much he's looking forward to being home again in Chicago for the holidays? How badly he wants to leave his past mistakes in Cairo behind?

Taking the character into consideration, what does he notice, and how does that affect what he thinks, feels, or does? It'll be quite different if he's a flight attendant at the end of a sixteen-hour shift, a terrorist getting ready to storm the cockpit, or a twelve-year-old boy traveling to visit his father for the first time since the divorce.

Each of your characters will see the world through different-colored glasses, formed by their upbringing, mood, background, past wounds, pain, goals, and so on.

The primary question isn't what *you* would notice but what that *character* would notice in that specific situation. That's what you'll bring up. Then, when you're writing from his viewpoint, his voice will affect all that's narrated in the scene, including its vocabulary, tone, and perspective.

271. "HOW DO DESCRIPTION AND VIEWPOINT RELATE TO THE DETAILS I INCLUDE IN THE SCENE?"

Think of that flight from the last question. Here's the key: You're not going to try to describe all of what's on that plane. Instead, you're going to eliminate what you don't need to describe as you consider the point of view character's perspective.

An air marshal might be on the lookout for anyone with a computer logged on to the on-air entertainment system and who might be trying to hack into the flight computers. A woman who wants to be a mother might notice how many children's cartoons are being watched. When evaluating which details to mention, ask yourself what this character would notice, given what she wants.

If the character notices something, readers will assume there's a reason that it's brought up. Leave details out if they're not significant to the story or essential to the scene. Delete or rewrite whatever could become a distraction or might introduce narrative promises in the wrong direction.

272. "WHEN I'M IN ONE CHARACTER'S POINT OF VIEW, CAN I RELATE WHAT OTHER CHARACTERS ARE THINKING?"

Whoever describes the story's action is the narrator. If the narrator is one of the characters within the story, then she's only privy to what she can observe. So, clearly, she won't know what other characters are thinking unless they tell her.

For example, since the main character in a first-person point-of-view story doesn't know what other characters are thinking or feeling, when writing in her viewpoint, you couldn't write, "I watched her put the dishes away. She was disappointed and really wished I would've remembered our anniversary," because you don't know she's disappointed or what she wishes. You only *assume* you do.

However, you might write, "I watched her put the dishes away. The look on her face told me she was disappointed..." Or, "It seemed like she was disappointed..." Or "Considering the way she clattered the dishes, I figured that she was upset..."

The best that the protagonist can hope for is using his discernment to form an educated guess based on the context. For instance, he might say,

- "Janice appeared deeply troubled."
- "She looked annoyed."
- "I sensed that I'd hit a nerve in what I'd said."

In each of these examples, the narrator doesn't know for sure what Janice is thinking, but he expresses his own beliefs and impressions of the situation based on what he observes.

This is all he can do. As soon as the narrator, from his limited viewpoint, states something like, "Janice was troubled and annoyed. I'd hit a nerve," readers will be thinking, *How does he know that? He's not Janice!*

273. "THEN, SHOULD I SWITCH POINTS OF VIEW TO SHOW WHAT OTHER CHARACTERS ARE THINKING?"

When editors talk about "head hopping," they mean that the story is leaping from one point of view to another without a clear indication of whose viewpoint the readers are supposed to be present in.

So, you wouldn't write, "Jason watched curiously as Renita considered what she would do with Greg, who was thinking about asking her out." See how the introspection jumps from one internal world to another, to another?

Unless you're rendering a cutaway sequence in which readers get to see two different viewpoints alternating within a scene, you'll typically shift from one point of view to another only when there's a clear transition of time or place.

If you do choose to use multiple viewpoints, make it clear by chapter or section breaks that you're switching to another point-of-view character.

274. "HOW WILL I KNOW WHOSE POINT OF VIEW I SHOULD RENDER THE SCENE FROM?"

Choose the viewpoint that best serves your readers and your story, be consistent, and let the voice reflect what sounds authentic and most natural from that point of view. Typically, you'll stick with the story's central narrator unless there's an important reason to switch. Consider:

1. Struggle – Whose struggle is at the core of this scene?

2. Choices – Whose decisions or discoveries matter most?

3. Perspective – Whose point of view offers the most meaningful perspective on this scene?

4. Suspense – Is there a promise of peril that can be concealed from a character and yet revealed to readers?

275. "HOW MANY POINTS OF VIEW SHOULD I USE?"

As few as possible. Each of them will have their own pursuit, desires, struggles, and discoveries.

276. "WHAT ELSE DO I NEED TO KNOW ABOUT USING MULTIPLE VIEWPOINTS?"

Unless your novel is some sort of time-warping science fiction story, time will pass for all of the characters in your story at the same rate. So, when ten seconds pass for one character, ten seconds will have passed for every other story character as well. Keep this in mind, especially if you flip between multiple points of view, and make sure that you're not jumping forward or backward in time when you move to the new viewpoint.

This is such a common mistake that it bears repeating: time passes for all characters at the same rate. For example, during a fight scene, you might write, "He drew his fist back to punch me." And then you have a chapter break (presumably as a cliffhanger). Then, you shift to another point of view, where a woman is walking idly through a field. "Meredith wandered through the field of butterflies. She lilted among them for the rest of the afternoon until dusk gently settled over the meadow." Then you end her point of view section and get back to the fight scene: "His fist connected with my jaw."

See how the fight scene and Meredith's afternoon in the field of butterflies take a different amount of time? For the man in the fight, less than a second passes, but for her, a whole afternoon has drifted by. Don't do that. All too often, discerning readers will put your book down and not pick it up again.

277. "WHAT'S THE DIFFERENCE BETWEEN FIRST PERSON AND THIRD PERSON?"

When you write in third person, you might write, "He opened the door;" when you write in first person, it would change to, "I opened the door."

When writing in first person, you're really inviting the reader to intimately identify with the character in order to, in a sense, see things through that character's eyes.

Contrarily, when you're writing from the third-person point of view, you're allowing readers to watch what happens *to* the character rather than *through* the character.

The verb tense and the narrator's point of view work together to create an immediacy of effect. For instance, read the following two options for an opening line for a book:

1. When they write about what I did, they will call me a monster.

2. When they wrote about what he did, they would call him a monster.

See how the first example creates a more intimate connection with the story? Keep that in mind as you choose your verb tense and the narrator's point of view.

Think of a movie.

You might see a person running through the woods (third person) being chased by a vampire. That's one way to shoot the scene.

Another way would be to mount a camera on the potential victim's (or possibly the vampire's) head as she runs through the woods, so it seems like the viewer is running through the woods herself. That's the first-person perspective.

278. "WHAT ARE THE PROS AND CONS OF WRITING IN FIRST PERSON OR THIRD PERSON?"

First-person point of view really draws readers in and often helps to make them more empathetic to the character's plight or problem. For this reason, first person is often used in coming-of-age stories.

However, when writing in this way, you, as a writer, are limited because you can only reveal what that character would know at that time. If you stay in this point of view for the entire book, that character will need to be present in every scene that you render throughout the whole novel. This presents a problem for highly complex stories with multiple storylines, especially novels that have scenes occurring in different places around the globe (such as in an international thriller).

Since third-person writing creates just a little more distance between the reader and the story itself, the most obvious drawback to writing in third person is giving up some of the intimacy of the reader's engagement with the story that the first-person viewpoint provides.

The advantages of using multiple points of view include (1) being able to explore the feelings and thoughts of more than one character, (2) threading in multiple storylines throughout the novel that all come together at the end, (3) including scenes in which the protagonist doesn't appear, (4) creating suspense and dramatic irony by showing danger to the reader that the characters in a particular viewpoint are unaware of, and (5) adding variety to your word choice and writing style, since each point of view character will have their own distinctive voice.

279. "WHAT VERB TENSES SHOULD I USE?"

Although most stories are rendered in the past tense, whenever you slip into summoning up what has happened previously (a verb tense referred to as the "pluperfect" or "past perfect"), you slow down the forward momentum of the story. A story is mainly about what's presently occurring—the progression of events—not what happened at an earlier date. Imagine the story's narrator is recounting the scene to you:

Present tense	I approach the castle ruins. Ravens cry in the distance. Mists swirl around me.
Past tense	I approached the castle ruins. Ravens cried in the distance. Mists swirled around me.
Past perfect tense	I had approached the castle ruins. Ravens had cried in the distance. Mists had swirled around me.

Some stories make sense to render in present tense as it brings a certain immediacy to the scenes. Often, Young Adult novels and those told in first person utilize this technique. Let the verb tense grow from the story and what organically fits best within it. Choose one and stick with it to avoid needlessly (or inadvertently) switching back and forth.

280. "WHAT DO I NEED TO KNOW ABOUT ADJECTIVES AND ADVERBS?"

Some writing instructors are quick to disparage the use of adjectives and adverbs. However, it's not "wrong" to use them. Just be aware that the more adverbs and adjectives you use in a paragraph, the less impact each of them will have.

Adverbs often serve to restate what the reader already knows or can discern from the context, which is why you won't always need them. For example, the adverbs aren't needed in the sentences, "He shouted loudly" or "She whined annoyingly," since the verbs already tell readers all they need to know—a person cannot help but shout loudly, and there's no other way for someone to whine than annoyingly. Cut adverbs when they're redundant or aren't necessary.

Regarding adjectives, as we explored earlier, choose evocative ones, not just descriptive ones. For instance, rather than a "white" candle, how about a "vanilla-scented" one, or instead of "brownish" hair, maybe choose "earthworm-colored?" It certainly brings a different image and impression to mind.

281. "MY DIALOGUE IS OFF. WHAT ARE SOME SECRETS TO IMPROVING IT?"

Here are seven steps to developing stronger dialogue:

1. Read it aloud. See if it sounds natural. You may have too few contractions, sentences that are too long or too complex, or not enough interruptions.

2. Let the dialogue be a venue for characters to express attitude, desire, or frustration; not just relate information. Let them vent.

3. Add more subtext by allowing the main thrust of the conversation to be something that's implied to readers but not stated by the characters.

4. Give the characters an obstacle to overcome rather than simply a topic to discuss. Perhaps it's too noisy in the room, they're jogging and out of breath, or they're struggling to get their viewpoint across to a recalcitrant coworker. Think in terms of what to accomplish rather than what to convey.

5. Reduce the number of characters in your scene. Come up with a good reason for extra characters to leave so you have only two or three people in the scene. It'll be much easier to manage your dialogue if you limit the number of people in the discussion.

6. Search the scene for moments when a character might naturally state a goal or ask another character about her

goal. For instance, "I'm here to talk with you about my son and what you said to him the other day." Or "What are you even doing here anyway? Why did you drive all the way across town during rush hour when you could have just called?" The more that readers understand what the characters want, the more present they'll be in the scene and the more they can worry about whether or not the characters they care about will get what they're pursuing.

7. Let someone be misunderstood or get distracted. It's a simple and effective way to add more tension to a scene.

282. "WHAT ARE SOME ADDITIONAL WAYS TO ADD TENSION TO SECTIONS OF DIALOGUE?"

In all too many fictionalized conversations, the characters don't have any particular goal in mind, but the author does: to communicate information to the reader. Info dumps can stall out a story, kill the pace, and turn off readers.

Readers want the characters in a scene to desire something rather than simply discuss things. Tension naturally emerges in a scene when characters have a goal in mind, and setbacks occur, keeping them from accomplishing it. For instance, she's trying to discuss the marriage conference that she wants her husband to attend with her, but he's trying to tie his fly fishing lures and doesn't want to be disturbed. Their mutually exclusive goals create tension.

Make sure your characters have an obstacle in each conversation: Maybe she's in a hurry and can't talk now but is being forced to, or he's trying to impress his boss, but she's angry at him.

Notice that in all of those examples, there's a "but." That "but" creates tension. To add even more tension, show the character trying to...

1. ...avoid having his secret (or her true intentions)

revealed,

2. ...overcome the skepticism of others,

3. ...stay away from conflict, even though it's inevitable,

4. ...convince others of something they need to do,

5. ...sort out the truth for herself.

Perhaps you realize that you need to fill readers in about a historical event but also don't want to insult those who know about it already. You can have one character think he's familiar with the event while another character tries to inform him about the whitewashing or historical inaccuracies he has bought into. By doing that, rather than just having the character *explain*, you show her trying to *achieve* something meaningful within the context of the story—convincing the other character that he's been misinformed while he's resisting what she has to say.

283. "WHEN DEALING WITH DIALOGUE, HOW CAN I MAKE THE SCENE MORE INTERESTING?"

While taking the context into consideration, ask, "What would these characters *really* say? Why aren't they saying it?" Let them say it. Readers want honest reactions, friction, sparks, and visible results. Don't hold back.

Can you stack this scene with action, subtext, or multiple storylines? Can you infuse the scene with more tension by giving characters a meaningful *goal to pursue*, not just an *action to take*?

Look for ways to have the characters move through space while progressing through their conversation. They might be exiting a building—show them leaving the elevator, passing down the hallway, pressing open the door, entering the parking garage, etc.

Often, writers will have a character lean forward or back, cross or uncross her arms, raise their eyebrows, clench their jaws, angle their eyes, and so on during conversations. This meaningless activity does little to drive the story forward. If you do include posture and gestures, infuse the movement with meaning so that it adds to the tension and doesn't distract from the scene's progression.

284. "HOW CAN I GET IMPORTANT INFORMATION TO READERS WITHOUT HAVING A CHARACTER EXPLAIN IT TO THEM DURING DIALOGUE?"

Dialogue needs to serve a bigger purpose than just supplying data to readers. Let it build tension as well. For instance, two investigators arrive at a crime scene:

> They both stared at the body.
> "Looks like a Glock 22 was used over here."
> "Yeah, the shell casings come from a 9mm."
> "Exactly. As you can see, the entry wounds here speak to the caliber used."
> "And that tells us that the shooter was standing over there, near the wall."

Clearly, the author is using this exchange to pass along investigative clues to readers, rather than render tension, goals, or characterization. It comes across as flat, authorial, and insulting to readers.

If you find that you need to convey information through dialogue rather than through exposition, give the characters in the scene conflicting goals:

> They both stared at the body.
> "Looks like a Glock 22 was used over here."
> "You can't tell that by those shell casings."

"No, look at the exit wounds."

"That's not enough."

"But the diameter—I'm thinking a 9mm. And the shooter was standing over there, near the wall—"

"You're assuming too much. I've talked to you about this before."

In this second example, the information is still conveyed to readers, but there's also tension, characterization, a hint of backstory, and a status imbalance as the second speaker rebukes the first one.

285. "WHAT ARE SOME SUBTLETIES TO WRITING DIALOGUE THAT CAN MAKE IT MORE REALISTIC?"

To improve your dialogue, avoid having one character ask a question and another answer it, line after line, give and take, ping-pong, back and forth. Many authors fall into this trap. Avoid it by adding variety.

Can your characters get distracted? Refer back to what was said earlier? Imply? Infer? Communicate two things at once? Misjudge? Use sarcasm that carries a grain of truth with it?

Try one of these twelve techniques to make your dialogue more poignant and resonant. Rather than directly answering the question that's posed, try having the character:

1. *Pivot* – Change the subject. This often reveals a reticence to answer the question: "Huh. Say, what about those Cubs?"

2. *Evade* – Avoid directly answering the question: "I won't even dignify that with an answer."

3. *Refocus* – Restate the reason for the conversation in the first place or what the character is hoping to accomplish in this exchange: "That's all good and fine, but what I really want to talk about with you is…"

4. *Conclude* – Assume something that wasn't stated: "So, you think I look fat in this dress? Is that it?"

5. *Confront* – Make it personal. Turn the tables: "Are you calling me a liar?"

6. *Misunderstand* – Fail to grasp what's being discussed: "If I'm hearing you right, you're accusing me of…"

7. *Postpone* – Put off a reply until another time: "I'm not ready to answer that right now."

8. *Restate* – Use active listening to clarify: "So, what you're really saying is…"

9. *Conceal* – This can be done through silence or a spoken response: "I can't get into my reasons for saying those things. Not yet."

10. *Revisit* – Circle back to something that was said previously: "Hang on—what were you saying earlier about…?"

11. *Question* – Reply to the question with another question instead of an answer: "How could you even ask me a question like that?"

12. *Insult* – Take it personally and respond as if attacked: "All this coming from someone with your fashion sense?"

286. "ANY ADVICE ON SPEAKER TAGS—WHICH ONES TO USE AND WHICH ONES TO AVOID?"

This will, of course, depend on your voice and the genre you're writing in, but for the most part, you'll want to stick to the most common speaker attributions: said, told, asked, or replied.

A character might also occasionally explain, question, answer, exclaim, scream, holler, yell, shout, call, mumble, mutter, whisper, or gasp.

However, avoid having him croak, bark, yelp, roar, hiss, growl, and cackle. Using those verbs would diminish his status and also make him sound more like an animal than a human being. (Sneering, snorting, mocking, scoffing, jeering, and bellyaching will also undermine a character's status.)

287. "HOW DOES SUBTEXT RELATE TO DIALOGUE?"

As we covered earlier, subtext is what's meant but not said. It's what's going on in the scene that readers will discern as the actual intent of the characters rather than what appears there on the surface. It might even be contrary to what the characters state as their goal for the scene.

For instance, Tucker is in love with Andrea and she doesn't know it. He shows up at the high-end department store where she's working at the perfume counter.

"Tucker? What are you doing here?"

"I was just passing through on my way to check out the… running shoes." *(A lie. He's really there to see her, but he's not ready to tell her that yet.)*

"I didn't know you ran."

"I decided to step out on a limb. Dive into something I've never been very good at before." *(The truth—but not about running. He's never been good at talking to women, yet here he is.)*

"Nothing ventured, nothing gained."

"That's right."

"Would you like to try some cologne?"

"Um…Sure." *(A lie. He's not interested at all in cologne. He's interested in her and in prolonging the conversation.)*

She picked up a bottle. "Here. Give me your hand."

After a short hesitation, he held out his hand to her, and she took it in hers. *(Though he's ostensibly doing it so she can spritz cologne onto his wrist, his deeper goal is for her to hold his hand.)*

Readers understand that because of Tucker's goal of initiating a relationship with Andrea, there's a deeper meaning to everything that happens in this scene.

Silences can bring subtext to the surface. Often, in a scene rich in subtext, what remains unsaid speaks the loudest.

288. "HOW DOES SUBTEXT RELATE TO THE SETBACKS THE CHARACTER FACES?"

Things will never go quite as planned. (If they do, you probably don't need to render that scene, but could summarize it instead.)

No, things won't go exactly as planned, but they *might* go more wonderfully than the character could ever have hoped.

At first.

But then, everything is going to rip apart at the seams.

Typically, during a scene, a character will face some sort of setback or challenge. If, however, that scene is built mainly on subtext, he might very well achieve his apparent (external) goal, but the tension of his ulterior or deeper, subtextual desires will be sharpened.

If everything goes right externally in the scene, you'll want the tension (often romantic in nature) to escalate internally through subtext.

So, if your character stops at a gas station to fill up his car—and does—and nothing else really happens there, you could probably just mention in passing that he swung by to get gas on his way home. However, the scene might be significant if the character's intent is to flirt with the cute gas station attendant. Then, the romantic subtext could justify the scene.

289. "HOW CAN I DO A BETTER JOB OF TAKING MY READERS' EXPECTATIONS INTO CONSIDERATION AS I'M WRITING?"

Ask yourself these questions regarding your readers' state of mind before they even open your book:

1. *Mindset* – What will readers be coming to this story for? A puzzle? An emotional thrill ride? To unwind, escape, cry, laugh, shudder, deduce, shiver? To forget? To be inspired?

2. *Expectations* – From the other books in this series, the back cover copy, the title, the author bio, or the packaging and publicity, what will readers expect in this story? Have I given it to them?

3. *Assumptions* – As readers engage with the book before they read it (by looking at reviews, etc.), what genre will they anticipate it is? Are there disadvantages to being grouped into that genre? Will readers think, *Oh, that's just a beach read*, or *That's not for me. I'm not really into women's fiction*? If so, brainstorm ways to overcome those negative preconceptions as you develop your marketing strategy.

Keeping all of this in mind, rather than trying to pigeonhole your writing into one category—romantic suspense, political thriller, literary fiction, or whatever—shoot for engaging and delighting readers even if your story ends up landing in a genre that doesn't exist yet or is tough to define.

290. "HOW IMPORTANT IS PACKAGING IN PROMISING THE TYPE OF STORY I'M TELLING?"

Readers don't typically come to your book as empty slates. They've seen the cover, maybe checked out some online reviews, looked at the book's description or back cover copy, and so on. They come to the book with expectations shaped by all of those factors.

Packaging, buzz, hype, blurbs, anticipation—all of this occurs outside of the actual story you're telling, but all of these factors dramatically affect readers' expectations regarding the story. Channeling expectations in the right direction is vital, so be clear about the promises that your marketing and packaging are making.

291. "PUT SUCCINCTLY, WHAT IS MY STORY TRYING TO ACCOMPLISH?"

You're trying to tell a story that people will want to read but not want to finish—because they don't want to lose out on the experience of reading it.

They'll look forward to the climax with a sense of bittersweet anticipation, since, on the one hand, they want to know how the story will end, but on the other hand, they aren't happy that it has to. Even as they realize that closure is necessary, they don't want the pleasurable experience to be over.

Get your readers to that point, and you've nailed it.

292. "BESIDES ENTERTAINING READERS, CAN I HAVE OTHER GOALS FOR MY STORY?"

Certainly, but remember that if you're not entertaining your readers, you'll likely fail in any secondary goals you might have—inspiring them, creating thought-provoking dilemmas, deepening their marvel at the world, exploring human nature, and so on.

Your primary goal remains entertaining readers by moving them—either to laughter or tears or into suspense or delight. It isn't to inform them, impress them, or convince them to agree with you about something you think is important (politics, religion, social reform, etc.).

Instead, as novelists, we seek to render the truth of the human condition through stories that ask big questions and reveal the world to readers in ways they don't expect—all while entertaining them.

If readers aren't entertained, they have little reason to keep reading.

You might have the most scintillating dialogue, the most incredible descriptions, and the most fascinating characters, but if all you do is write beautifully, readers might be impressed but will remain unmoved, and your story might very well fall flat.

While readers may get distracted by sections of languid dialogue, a slow pace, flat characterization, and things that momentarily confuse them, as long as they're enjoying the ride, they'll overlook a multitude of plot flaws.

Whatever else might annoy readers, they'll never complain about being too entertained.

293. "HOW CAN I AVOID AUTHOR INTRUSION WHEN I'M WRITING ABOUT WHAT I KNOW?"

If you write material *because* you're an expert in something, you run the risk of showing off your expertise. However, if you write *despite* being an expert on that topic, you're probably focusing on the story first, and that's what you'll want to strive for.

Too many novels include information dumps about peripheral subjects (the life cycle of conch shells, Medieval weaponry, the history of lipstick, etc.), but if those things don't add to the narrative progression of the story, they don't belong. Readers probably don't come to your story for a vocabulary lesson or to be impressed by how much you know about Civil War buttons. Don't show off. Every time you do, you shatter, if only for a moment, the illusion of the narrative world by inserting yourself into it.

Authors intrude on their story when they...

- ...try to be funny, clever, or literary,

- ...resort to cheap tricks and overused gimmicks,

- ...dump in information all at once rather than sprinkling it in throughout the story,

- ...show off how much they know about a topic,

- ...propagandize a particular cultural, religious, or political viewpoint.

Regarding this last point, novels are not thinly veiled sermons. Sermons explain; stories explore. Sermons proclaim; stories ponder. Sermons exhort; stories expose. There's certainly a place for sermons; it's just not at the climax of a novel.

294. "WHAT DO I NEED TO KNOW ABOUT CHAPTER BREAKS?"

At the end of a chapter, give readers a good reason to turn the page rather than close the book. This can come through by introducing one of the 3Ds: a Dilemma, a Discovery, or a Decision.

Sometimes, a secret becomes known, backstory is revealed, or a significant choice is made.

Include as few chapters as the story needs and let the story's flow dictate the placement of those breaks.

If you choose to include chapter titles, use them as promises, not as spoilers. Allow readers to wonder what the title has to do with the chapter's content when they begin reading it. That can add a small, satisfying surprise—an "Aha!" moment—that clarifies the choice of that title to your readers by its close.

295. "WHAT ARE PLOT FLAWS AND HOW CAN I AVOID THEM?"

Plot flaws emerge in gaps between what readers would naturally expect and what actually occurs in the story. For instance, the events might not follow logically, and readers may be left complaining that the story doesn't make sense.

This can happen when:

1. A character states a goal and then doesn't pursue it. He says, "I need to finish decoding this cipher before bedtime." But then, for some unknown reason, heads off to play video games with his son instead.

2. Something unbelievable happens, and no one in the story seems to notice. In that case, the story characters will seem to be clueless, or the story will appear "contrived."

3. The story becomes either too predictable or too inexplicable. If readers can accurately guess what will happen, or if random events start occurring, readers will be turned off from the story.

4. Everything goes as planned for the main characters. If there aren't any setbacks, you don't have a story; you just have a litany of successes.

As you look through your story, be aware of problems with believability ("That would never happen!"), glitches in causality ("That came out of nowhere!"), de-escalation ("Well, that's anticlimactic."), gaps of logic ("That doesn't even make sense!"), and broken narrative promises ("I don't get it. Whatever happened with that one character who was the sharpshooter?").

Plot flaws often come from a lack of clarity, lack of intent, lack of tension, or they depend on early promises for too long without any payoff. Also, if there are no surprises and if choices don't make a difference, you still have some work to do.

Address those issues, or readers will become distracted and distanced from the story. Make the necessary changes so your readers will only notice the story and be drawn intimately and inextricably into another world. Don't let carelessness break the spell.

SECTION IX

PIVOTS, CLOSURE, AND NARRATION

296. "WHAT IS A PIVOT?"

To understand pivots, it's essential to understand that fiction is contingent; that is, everything that happens is caused by the thing that precedes it. When there's a break in that contingency, readers will be quick to point out that the story "doesn't make sense."

However, if everything always happens as we'd expect, the story would remain logical but would also be terribly boring and predictable. Yet, on the other hand, if things start happening out of nowhere, the story will be illogical, unbelievable, and ludicrous.

So, is there another option between a predictable story and an outlandish one?

Yes.

In *Poetics*, Aristotle wrote, "Reversal of the Situation is a change by which the action veers round to its opposite, subject always to our rule of probability or necessity."

While we might not use the same language today, Aristotle is pointing out an aspect of narrative that great writers and storytellers have included in their stories for thousands of years: the pivot.

It's a moment when the action tilts in a direction readers don't expect, but that makes logical sense based on what occurred before it in the story.

In other words, the moment is unexpected and inevitable, both. Some people have called this "retrospective inevitability;" others have labeled the concept "postdictable."

In truth, there are really only four options for every scene. It will either be too predictable (lacking surprise), too outlandish (breaking contingency), or it will be both surprising *and* believable. This is The Fourth Way. This is the pivot.

NARRATIVE FORCES AT PLAY			WHICH MEANS…	RESULT
Neither inevitable	nor	Unexpected	Somehow, nothing logical and nothing surprising happens. The "story" is just a chaotic collection of unrelated events.	Too nonsensical
Inevitable	but not	Unexpected	Everything is logical, but there are no surprises.	Too predictable

| Unexpected | but not | Inevitable | The story is full of surprises but lacks believability. Things happen for no reason. | Too outlandish |
| Unexpected | and also | Inevitable | The story is surprising yet also believable and logical. | Pivot! |

It's relatively easy to write perfectly logical, boring stories or ludicrous, unbelievable ones.

It takes real work to find, include, and hone pivots. But it's what your readers want, and it's your job to give it to them. So, ask, "How will things make sense in a way readers will not expect?"

297. "HOW DO PIVOTS WORK IN STORY PROGRESSION?"

A pivot is a moment we don't expect but that the story cannot live without. We don't see it coming, but, in retrospect, we can't imagine it not occurring. Yes, the story makes sense before it, but it makes sense in a deeper way after it.

A pivot will cause readers to review the story in their minds and then replay it with the new information that the pivot has provided—and (hopefully!) find that the story is deeper than they'd anticipated or imagined.

In this way, as pivots drive the story forward, they also reveal the true meaning of what has already happened within it.

Connecting two stories or two storylines in an unexpected and yet logical way is a type of pivot. To accomplish this, plant moments in your story that could lead the story in multiple directions or be taken in different ways.

Think of the pivot as logical and yet also as containing branches of believability. So, one event might carry more than one meaning to readers upon reflection later in the story.

298. "IS BELIEVABILITY IMPORTANT FOR PIVOTS?"

Only a believable storyline allows you to add pivots. After all, if nothing really makes sense anyway, nothing will end up being surprising. So, keep things believable even as you begin playing with the story's (or the scene's) ultimate, unexpected direction.

Pivots depend on inevitability. To make them work, you'll need two storylines that both seem inevitable, but when the second one is revealed, readers will see that it was really where things were heading all along and was, in the end, the most believable of all the possible routes through the story.

Even the best pivot will not save a poorly told story.

A twist relies on not confusing readers. If they're confused before the twist, it won't have its intended impact.

Because of genre expectations and foreshadowing, readers aren't always wondering how a story will end, but they are always wondering how they will be surprised before it does. For instance, in a romance novel, readers expect that the two love-struck lovers will get together at the end of the story—but readers don't want it to be in a way that they anticipate. In fact, they'll be annoyed and dissatisfied if they can guess all the twists and turns of the story.

When readers open a book, they're subconsciously asking themselves, "How will I be surprised?" If all goes as planned, it's a plot flaw. If you don't have a pivot, you'll let your readers down. But also, if you have things happen that are too "out of nowhere," readers won't be satisfied either. That's why you're always looking for The Fourth Way of inevitability and surprise.

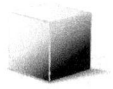

299. "HOW DO YOU EVEN COME UP WITH PIVOTS?"

Often, the moment of the pivot is an easy one to identify after the fact but a tricky one to come up with beforehand. Here are fifteen areas to tap into for a pivot for your scene or your novel:

1. *Appearances* – Who is not who they appear to be? What is not what it seems to be?

2. *Expectations* – What will readers expect in this genre of story—and how can I use those expectations to create a surprising payoff or chain of events?

3. *Surprise* – What surprises me about this situation or interaction (a character's response, their choice, or the unexpected result)?

4. *Duality* – What could mean two things at once, but in a way that readers won't realize at the time?

5. *Growth* – What unpredictable lesson did my character learn about himself, or how did he grow as a result of this?

6. *Despair* – What was the moment at which all seemed lost, and what logical event or choice (that readers won't anticipate) tilted things in a new direction?

7. *Plans* – What didn't go according to plan? How did that play out?

8. *Believability* – Is the end result inevitable yet also unexpected?

9. *Choices* – Can I pivot the story forward through unforeseen wit, grit, valor, or sacrifice?

10. *Depth* – Where in this story is there more than meets

the eye?

11. *Desire* – How can I give my readers what they didn't know they wanted?

12. *Revelations* – How did something external (an event) lead to an internal revelation (an epiphany)—and what unforeseen choice did that lead to?

13. *Logic* – How can I keep things logical and contingent, always moving forward from cause to effect?

14. *Twists* – How will things make sense in a way that readers don't expect and twist toward a believable ending that they won't see coming?

15. *Perspective* – How could I include a unique point of view or unusual perspective on the story that will provide readers with an emergent or new understanding?

300. "MY PIVOT COMES OUT OF NOWHERE, AND I'M AFRAID IT'LL MAKE READERS FEEL CHEATED. HOW CAN I FIX THAT?"

Focus on developing believability. Look for ways to pivot the story into an unexpected direction *that grows naturally* from what has already occurred. Ask yourself:

1. How does this scene follow logically from the previous one? All pivots have to be built on inevitability and believability. Remove "Why?" moments when readers aren't sure why the events in the story are happening. You want readers to accept each event as it happens and see it as a contingent result of what precedes it. The story's progression should make sense now, not just later, in retrospect, after the pivot has been revealed. Readers need to buy the scenes

when they occur. Make certain that inexplicable events are rare. Let characters act in ways that readers will expect and accept. When a character acts in an unexpected way, make it clear why that has happened and why it's believable after all.

2. What added meaning can I give to this choice or situation? Pivots add new meaning to what has gone before. Readers want to anticipate where the story will go (or how everything will weave together in the end), but they also don't want to be spot on. They want the story to include pivots and turns that they didn't anticipate but, in retrospect, realize they could have.

3. How can I avoid annoying or disappointing readers? Leave the overdone plot gimmicks behind. (For instance, the character was really asleep the whole time! It was all just a dream!) Focus on making everything that happens cause the next thing that happens. Every decision should affect the direction of the story. If events seem to happen for no reason, readers will start to doubt the story's veracity. Include callbacks to earlier scenes when foreshadowed events occurred to make sure readers see that everything that has happened is inevitable.

301. "MY PIVOT IS TOO EASY TO FIGURE OUT. WHAT SHOULD I DO?"

Most likely, there are too many clues pointing to it, that is, too many reasons for readers to believe that it's coming. Redirect their attention by adding red herrings that seem to support the ending of the story *before* the pivot. Alter the clues as needed to hide or obfuscate where the story is actually going.

You're going to want your pivot to delight readers or make their jaws drop as they finally see the story's true direction and each scene's deeper relevance. Take the story into directions that don't seem immediately obvious to readers, given the circumstances, but that will be clear as the story progresses. Insert a new character, complication, or setback that readers wouldn't naturally expect.

Then, go back and confirm that there's enough foreshadowing so that when the pivot occurs, readers will nod and think, *Of course. Yes! That makes total sense.*

Finally, read the book from the beginning, making sure that each scene follows logically (but has surprises in it!), that you've reached the intended effect, and that the clues have served the pivot rather than undermining it.

302. "SHOULD I USE AN UNRELIABLE NARRATOR?"

Maybe, maybe not. In a story with an unreliable narrator, the character who's telling the story might not realize he's deceived and might think he's actually telling readers the truth. For example, he might be the antagonist and not realize it or remember it.

Or, he might *know* he's unreliable. This might be purposeful (to deceive readers) or unintentional (if he's going mad and doesn't know what's real anymore).

Unreliable narrators can create fascinating stories, but they can also leave readers feeling betrayed, lied to, or manipulated. If you do use an unreliable narrator, make sure readers are on his side and that they'll be satisfied rather than let down when the big reveal comes.

303. "IF I INCLUDE ONE BIG PIVOT, DOES IT NEED TO COME AT THE CLIMAX?"

In a sense, every scene will have a pivot—that is, readers won't be able to guess exactly how it'll end or how it'll get to the end, but then it'll conclude in a way that's both logical and surprising.

Most of the time, the biggest (or most significant) pivot will come last (unless it's a way of setting up the world of the story for all that follows, in which case it might come early on). Either way, remember to save the most stunning or satisfying pivot for last, or readers might feel let down by the story's ending.

304. "WHAT NEEDS TO HAPPEN AT THE CLIMAX?"

All of the primary narrative promises converge to find closure, and the main character faces the moment that seems the most hopeless of the entire story. The odds will be stacked against her success to a greater degree than at any other time so far.

The most poignant image, the most significant choice, or the greatest sacrifice will come at the climax. It's the moment before which the solution seems impossible and after which no more escalation of tension would make sense or be believable.

Yes, you might include a closing chapter to wrap up any remaining loose ends, or you might include a teaser to your next book, but after the climax, your story is complete.

305. "WHAT WILL LEAD UP TO THE FINAL CONFRONTATION BETWEEN THE HERO AND THE VILLAIN?"

Before the protagonist faces off against the forces of antagonism, there's usually a scene in which he's suiting up (sharpening his sword, loading his gun, putting on body armor, etc.).

Earlier in the story, you might also include a scene during which a character who knows the destructive power of the forces of antagonism explains how evil or unstoppable those forces are: "This guy, he's like no one you've ever seen before. He's killed over a dozen people—five of them cops." Or, "This breed of genetically-engineered sharks will not turn away until they have found and slaughtered everything in the water that moves—and when I say 'everything,' I mean *everything*."

Make sure the climax follows naturally from what precedes it and also contains at least one surprise.

Remove coincidences through foreshadowing, that is, show the character's special skill or ability earlier. Don't introduce it right when he needs it at the climax: "Good thing I studied karate back in high school and have kept my skills sharp over the years! I'll take these guys out, no problem!"

A villain's pride or cowardice is often responsible for his downfall, especially if, with a touch of poetic justice, his plan boomerangs back and takes him out in the way he thought he was going to vanquish the hero.

306. "DOES MY STORY NEED A MOMENT OF HOPELESSNESS?"

Perhaps not, but most stories do have one.

Take your protagonist to the place where she feels ready to give up or throw in the towel. (Maybe she even does for a moment.) Make her the underdog at the climax. It'll need to be a come-from-behind victory if there's going to be any victory at all. Stack the deck. The odds are against her. Every betting person would wager that she doesn't stand a chance—but yet, she *does* because of her willpower, tenacity, resolve, cleverness, or inner strength.

The most desperate scene for your character is the most important one for your readers. It's that moment when the very thing the character has been fearing will happen does, and it seems like there's no way in the world that she's going to succeed in overcoming the forces of antagonism.

There's no way out.

It's too late.

But wait...

A solution arrives as the character reveals her cleverness or perseverance. It's often a subtle solution, but not so subtle that it now seems to come out of nowhere. It was, however, subtle enough that readers didn't notice when its seed was first planted earlier in the story.

307. "WILL READERS FEEL LET DOWN IF THERE'S NO MOMENT OF HOPELESSNESS OR DESPAIR?"

Readers will feel let down if they think the story's tension should have escalated past the place where it did. In other words, if they think things could've believably gotten worse and they didn't, they won't feel satisfied. They'll also feel dissatisfied if...

1. ...they can guess how the story will end or how it'll get to the end,

2. ...the climax feels inauthentic or inorganic to what preceded it,

3. ...significant promises aren't kept, and the resolution to the story remains unclear,

4. ...the ending isn't the logical culmination of the previous events or trajectory of the story.

308. "WHAT WOULD THE MOMENT OF HOPELESSNESS LOOK LIKE IN A ROMANCE?"

Despite all the efforts of the two lovers, it'll appear to readers that they're going to be separated forever. She's on her way to the airport, and if she boards that flight, he'll never see her again. He's trying to catch up with her, but he's stuck in traffic. What will happen? What will he do? How will he get to her in time to tell her of his undying love?

Make it look like there's no viable solution, but then, by a means that readers didn't see coming but are now glad has arrived, the couple (most likely) ends up living happily ever after.

309. "HOW DO I KNOW WHEN MY STORY IS OVER?"

The story is finished when the promises are fulfilled, and the pursuit is complete.

If the next logical step would be the introduction of a new struggle or pursuit, then the story is over.

If readers still expect more from the story, they'll be frustrated if it suddenly ends. Also, if they think it's over and yet it keeps on going, they'll get annoyed.

At this point, any change in the life of the character has occurred (or is about to), and resolution in the three realms of struggle (internal, external, and interpersonal) has happened.

Until readers see the effect that facing the struggle has had on your protagonist, they'll feel that the story lacks closure or resolution, so let her make a final, revelatory choice that shows the change in her life or the change in her own understanding of who she truly is.

310. "DOES THE PACE NEED TO ESCALATE AS MY STORY REACHES ITS CLIMAX?"

Absolutely. You want smoke to rise from the pages as readers race to finish your book.

311. "WHAT IF READERS CAN GUESS HOW MY STORY WILL END?"

Often, readers can realistically anticipate how a book will end before they even read the first page. For instance, if the book is in a series, readers will expect that the hero will win. If it's a heartwarming romance, readers will anticipate that the two main characters will fall in love.

In fact, sometimes readers are attracted to a specific genre precisely because they *do* know how it will end—the cozy mystery, the rom-com, the master detective story.

In those cases, the curiosity that keeps readers engaged comes not so much from wondering how the story will end but how the characters will get out of the bind they find themselves in at the climax or how the detective will deduce the mystery's solution.

You'll want readers to think, *How on earth are they going to survive this hurricane/find true love/solve the crime/locate the terrorist/vanquish the aliens before time runs out?*

To satisfy readers when they can anticipate the ending, realize that you'll need to make the predicament that precedes the climax incredibly engaging and unforeseeable.

Think in terms of what you haven't seen done in this genre before; accentuate the courage, cleverness, or pluck of the characters when it matters most; or show the ingenious or intrepid choices the characters make when it really counts and that reveal what they're truly made of.

Honor genre conventions without opting for clichés. (Familiarity with the genre will help you to know the difference.)

312. "WHAT DOES THE PROTAGONIST NEED

TO DO AT THE CLIMAX?"

She needs to make a meaningful and difficult choice. Often, that choice is one that she would not have made (or could not have made) at the beginning of the story. This is the moment when the story's moral dilemma finds its resolution. Also, she will be the agent of change rather than the person being rescued.

She'll likely have to make a substantial sacrifice, and since there's always a cost to anything worthwhile, vanquishing evil will likely cost her something precious. She will often make a valiant choice or exhibit a selfless act.

Often, the less the climax costs the characters, the less it will mean to the readers.

Typically, you won't let your character come to a life-altering decision after simply thinking about the issues, mulling them over, or praying about the problem. The agent of change, the impetus that tips him into his irrevocable decision, will usually be something external rather than simply internal reflection.

Sometimes, serendipity will help her make the final connection that threads all the clues together or leads to the unforeseen conclusion, but be careful to avoid coincidence as much as possible at this point in the story.

313. "DO I NEED TO WRAP UP ALL THE STORY THREADS AT THE END OF THE BOOK?"

No, but you need to keep all of your promises. Stories end with fulfilled promises—and usually, that's in the form of a transformation of the protagonist's identity, attitude, situation, or relationships.

Remember, readers are investing significant time and emotional energy into your story, so they deserve an ending that satisfies them. While you consider your current ending, ask yourself if readers will feel...

1. ...let down because they were hoping for more resolution,

2. ...as if nothing has changed and the entire story was for naught,

3. ...that there are promises you've made but haven't kept,

4. ...that the ending is too confusing, convoluted, or contrived,

5. ...frustrated because they're going to have to read the next book in the series to find any sense of true closure.

314. "WHAT SHOULD I REMEMBER REGARDING NARRATIVE PROMISES?"

When you make narrative promises, you make a contract with your readers—that you won't waste their time and that you'll honor their expectations. When fulfilling promises, remember:

1. *Character significance*: Have you introduced intriguing characters and then let them disappear from the story? Will readers wonder why the characters never returned? If so, invite them back into later scenes to satisfy readers.

2. *Desire*: Is there a pursuit that the character has been on that has been abandoned or left unfulfilled in the story? If you've accentuated the characters' goals but not provided closure, readers may feel unfulfilled.

3. *Settings*: Have you described a setting in such a way that readers will expect it to play a significant role in the story but then you've never returned to it again? If so, bring

it back.

315. "DO I NEED TO INCLUDE A HAPPY ENDING?"

Most readers prefer honest endings to happy ones. Rather than bending over backward trying to make *everyone* live "happily ever after" in your story, consider allowing happiness to come at great cost through a deep and meaningful sacrifice.

Ideally, your readers will *like* the ending, but regardless, they should nod their heads and say, "Yes. That's true. That's how this story needed to end."

That being said, for the most part, readers do want hope and redemption held out to them in the stories they consume. There are three exceptions:

> 1. If you're writing a cautionary tale (let's say about teenage drug abuse) and it ends with the character feeling the tug to use once again, you might end without the closure that you'd typically include because the broader appeal of the book comes from whether or not the *reader* will heed the warnings given by the tale of this character.

> 2. Readers in shame/honor cultures are more interested in the character having an honorable ending than a happy one.

> 3. In the horror genre, the story might very well end with a dramatic plunge that shows the monster or the supernatural force has lived to terrorize people once again in a future installment.

316. "CAN MY STORY END BEFORE THERE'S A TRANSFORMATION?"

Until your readers see the effect that the struggle has had on your character, they'll feel that the story is incomplete or that it lacks closure and resolution. Analyze whether your character:

- still has his initial problem, struggle, desire, need, or overriding question.
- has learned a lesson or matured in some way during the story.
- has altered his actions or attitude by the end of the story.

Some writing instructors will say that a story is finished when act three (or act four, or five, or whatever) is completed. Unless you're trying to write formulaic stories, it's helpful to step away from that paradigm. The number of acts isn't nearly as important as the fulfillment of promises. (It isn't the *number* of acts that matters most but the *nature* of acts—that they're causally related, escalate in tension, and continue to surprise and delight readers.)

Regardless of the number of acts, readers expect that the main character's pursuit throughout the story will have some relevance to that character's internal world, relationships, or situation in life at the story's end. If her condition remains unchanged in all three realms, it will probably feel to readers like the story is not yet over.

317. "HOW MUCH CHANGE DO I HAVE TO SHOW AT THE END OF THE STORY?"

As much as your story has explicitly promised or implied.

Let's say your detective has to solve a series of murders—that would be the external struggle. He might also be wrestling with internal questions regarding the bounds of justice—is vengeance ever justified? Or, when it seems like no one else will see that justice is carried out, should we take it into our own hands?

The search for the murderer will reveal the detective's cleverness, persistence, and aptitude. It'll also alter or inform his understanding of justice, which will result in him making a meaningful choice at the end of the story that shows that he truly believes this new insight.

He'll also naturally have relationships in the story—family members, love interests, coworkers, a boss, and so on. His journey through the story will often alter or transform those relationships as well.

The end of the story might offer insights to the protagonist about himself (or other characters) and insights to the reader about the protagonist. He does not, however, need to be changed into someone fundamentally different—especially not if he's a series character. Readers don't flock to series characters because they are fundamentally different at the end of every book but because they remain fundamentally the same. It isn't change readers are looking for, but a deeper understanding of who the character is. Though his relationships and circumstances are in flux, he is not. He is learning and growing, but that does not alter who he is at his core.

318. "MY STORY WANDERS A LITTLE, BUT IT SEEMS TO WORK. DO I NEED TO CHANGE THINGS AROUND?"

Narratives don't need to progress in a straight line. Jagged lines often make for better stories than ones that take a simple, predictable, direct route to the end. As long as readers are entertained and not lost, you can have a bit of a meandering plot.

By the way, it can be quite effective when seemingly random story elements or disparate scenes tie together in a way that readers did not see coming. That can be a very powerful way of concluding a complex story.

319. "WHAT IF I'M WRITING A SERIES—DOES THE TENSION NEED TO INCREASE BOOK BY BOOK TOWARD THE FINALE?"

People sometimes complain that in a series of novels or television seasons, each one keeps getting darker.

It's only natural for that to happen.

Each book or episode becomes part of an overarching story, and if the tension doesn't escalate, readers (or viewers) will often feel disappointed or complain that things were "anticlimactic."

Because of this, the stakes will typically get higher, the challenges greater, and the danger more imminent as the stories progress further into the series.

320. "WHAT ARE SOME COMMON STORYTELLING MISCONCEPTIONS?"

Some of these are elaborated on elsewhere in the book, but all of the following principles relate to misconceptions that authors sometimes have about certain core aspects of story.

CONCEPT	CLARIFICATION
Conflict does not equal tension.	Tension depends on unmet desire; conflict does not. Conflict simply involves things going wrong. Tension depends on the desire for them to go right once again.

Motivation does not equal intention.	Motivation leads to intention; intention leads to action. Motivation asks, "Why am I this way?" Intention asks, "What do I want right now?"
History does not equal backstory.	History is all that has happened to a character, while backstory is the fraction of his history that matters to this specific story. History is what makes your character the way he is; backstory is what makes this story the way it is.
Difficulty does not equal dilemma.	Difficulties test a character; dilemmas bring to light what ultimately matters to him. When difficulties come, choices occur; when dilemmas come, choices reveal deep aspects of characterization.
Structure does not equal story.	The number of acts must bow to the greater demands of this story. Structure is here to serve story, not the other way around. Story trumps structure. Always.

SECTION X

EDITING, REVISIONS, AND THE WRITING LIFE

321. "HOW LONG SHOULD MY BOOK BE?"

As short as possible and as long as necessary.

While there's certainly a point at which length does become an issue, readers are (for the most part) more interested in the contingent connection between the events of the story than in the number of pages it contains. They want things to make sense. So, focus more on logic than on length.

Decide which words it needs, then use those and no others.

322. "WHAT SHOULD I DO IF I NEED TO MAKE MY STORY LONGER?"

If someone asks you to "flesh out" your story, take a careful look at it to make sure you've rendered the scenes in a way that readers can see what's happening, that you've created a protagonist who's sufficiently three-dimensional, and that the story is emotionally engaging enough to retain reader interest.

If it seems to you that "fleshing out the story" just means "increasing the word count to a predetermined number" without improving the narrative, then you'll want to stand your ground and push back against making the story more bloated.

Don't add a subplot just to create a longer story. Only add one if it provides necessary dimensionality to the protagonist or depth to the story. Be concise. Make every word count. If you can make your story shorter, do it. If you need more space to tell it, go for it—but don't do so just to hit a certain word count.

323. "WHY DO WE DELETE SUPERFLUOUS SCENES?"

When you include a scene, you're making a promise to readers that it's significant to the story. If it turns out that the scene wasn't essential (or wasn't entertaining), readers will lose trust in you and draw back from emotionally investing in future scenes because they won't trust that there'll be a payoff in the end. When evaluating if you should include a scene, ask:

- What vital information does this scene reveal?
- What clues does it provide?
- What is altered as a result of it?

If the scene does nothing to develop the characterization, advance the narrative, tighten the tension, or entertain readers, it's probably not necessary.

324. "HOW FLEXIBLE DO I NEED TO BE ABOUT CHANGING WHAT I'VE ALREADY WRITTEN?"

Stay as flexible as possible.

You might think that a character desires one thing when you start writing your story, but through the creative process—as you delve deeper into the narrative—you might eventually discover that it's something else entirely that matters to this character.

Good. Now comes the part most authors try to circumnavigate or avoid: going back and recasting the story to fit in with the authentic desires and pursuit of that character.

Edit while keeping the context in mind. Typically, when you edit a scene out of context, the pace will be off, and the state of mind of the characters won't be cohesive. Instead, enter the character's mindset and remember that he'll be thinking about what just happened, what he wants, and how what just occurred is affecting his purpose and the direction of his pursuit.

325. "WHAT IF I HAVE TO CUT A SCENE THAT I SPENT A LOT OF TIME ON?"

Cut anything that distracts from or undermines the readers' engagement with the story. (And yes, that might mean you have to cut scenes or characters that you really like.)

Question the non-negotiables—those scenes that you're certain must remain, that are the cornerstones of your story. Yeah, question those.

Examine your initial idea, the fulcrum upon which the story hinges, that super-memorable character, that powerful theme, that stirring image, or that incredible climax that you came up with. The bedrock. Crack it open. The tectonic plates. Watch them shift and see how it affects the shoreline of your story.

What scene could your story live without? What scene could your readers live without? What about you? Are there any scenes you're just not willing to abandon? What would it look like if you jettisoned that scene you're so in love with and stopped contorting the rest of the story to try to make it fit?

Be ready to dump anything that doesn't contribute to the immersive experience of your readers.

326. "HOW CAN I TELL WHEN I'M DONE REVISING MY STORY?"

When (1) it's so good that you can't put it down when you read it, (2) you can't find anything wrong with it, and (3) you can't improve it.

If you can put it down, readers will too. You're not telling your story well enough. Rework it.

If you find mistakes, fix them. Don't expect an editor to do it. Take responsibility for your story.

If you can improve the writing, do so. Why would you ever presume to publish a book that's less than your best work?

327. "HOW MANY DRAFTS SHOULD I GO THROUGH?"

Finishing quickly and writing brilliantly don't always go hand in hand.

Sometimes, you might need to revise a scene only once or twice. Other times, it might take dozens of revisions (or more) for the scene or the story to work.

To revise a story is to retell it. As you retell your story, you'll be stitching and re-stitching words into it. Every time you remove or change one, you affect the context and the meaning of the other words around it. Changing one word changes the flavor of that sentence, that paragraph, that page. Here's the goal for editing: to leave no scar tissue behind.

A novel is the result of hundreds of thousands (or millions) of choices, each one creating both more limitations and more possibilities, all brought together to create one unified story. If you're able to make those innumerable decisions well on your first time through the story, be thankful. You're in the rare minority. For most of us, it takes months and months of work.

When going through the final edits for your book, you might find that you need to read through the entire novel in one sitting or in a single day to make sure all of it is fresh in your mind so that you can identify issues of internal inconsistency, weed out echoes, and remove continuity errors. Make the necessary changes. If you don't need a word, why would you include it? If you do need a word, why wouldn't you add it?

As you revise, tighten the language whenever possible. Look for more concise, unique, and memorable descriptions and details. Trim the fat.

Also, ask if there is a moment that the readers could live without. In other words, a moment that was put in there because you wanted it in there and not because they would want it in there. If so, you're not serving them. Cut it. If there is a scene that will entertain them or add to their experience of reading the story, even though that scene might not be essential, you may wish to keep it as a way to serve your readers.

Track with me here (and this isn't meant to be glib or dismissive): How many revisions will you need? As many as it takes until you're done. And how do you know when you're done? You don't have any more revisions to make. That's just the way it is.

To find your true, authentic voice and uncover your very best story, you'll likely have to sift through a daunting mountain of words.

So do it. Spend the time and effort crafting a story that's truly worth reading.

Don't cut corners.

Be as brilliant as this season in your life will allow you to be.

328. "SHOULD I KEEP MY LEFTOVER IDEAS FOR ANOTHER BOOK LATER ON?"

It's true—You'll likely have scrap words, phrases, and scenes left over. If you're like most writers, you'll obsessively copy and paste them into a Special File For The Future, thinking that maybe you'll be able to use them someday, that you'll pick through them and pluck out diamonds from the rough that you can insert into your next project.

While it's true that sometimes those scraps will find a place, more often than not, they won't quite fit in your future story.

Don't strive too hard to fit leftovers from one story into another one. Most of the time, the pace and mood and voice will be slightly off, and it might just save time to rewrite the idea in a way that fits in contextually with this new project rather than trying to find a way to thread the old words in.

329. "WHEN I TRY TO MOVE THE STORY FORWARD, IT'S CAUSING ME TO HAVE TO REWRITE MY OPENING. IS THAT COMMON?"

Avoid over-analyzing and obsessing over your story's opening before moving on to write the next scene. It's a common trap that many writers fall into.

It's quite possible that the beginning you had in mind when you started writing the book is no longer the opening you're going to use. As you write, be ready to jettison whatever doesn't contribute to the story that's unfolding here, now, before you.

When you come to the end of your novel, allow yourself the freedom to ask if it really started in the right place, no matter how hard it is to let go of the scene you started with months or years ago. Then, do whatever's necessary for the good of the story and the benefit of your readers.

330. "SHOULD I USE ALPHA OR BETA READERS?"

The first and most important eyes that you'll have on your manuscript are your own. Catching minor glitches and mistakes is ultimately your job, no matter how many editors or readers you might have look over your work.

Don't rely on anyone else to fact-check or proofread your story. The reading public will (rightly!) blame you rather than your editors if they find mistakes.

Alpha readers (typically other authors) or beta readers (typically readers from your target audience) will often tell you what they think you want them to say, or they might try to show off their knowledge, or they just might not know what to look for.

However, they *can* tell you places where their engagement with the story was disrupted, when they found something confusing or unbelievable, when they couldn't picture a scene, or when the story stopped making sense to them. All of that can be extremely helpful.

Consider being as specific as possible when asking readers or editors for feedback. For example:

1. What was unbelievable?

2. What was unmotivated, unclear, or confusing?

3. What promises have I made that I have not kept?

4. Are there any obvious mistakes that jump off the page to you?

5. Do you have any questions that were left unanswered at the end?

6. Are there continuity or pace issues?

7. What did you really like?

Do your best to take readers' comments and queries to heart, but that doesn't mean you'll make all the changes they suggest. After all, it's quite possible that you've thought about their suggestions months ago and discarded them because of the context or the movement of the story.

331. "AT WHAT POINT IS FEEDBACK FROM BETA READERS THE MOST HELPFUL?"

Get feedback after you've established your premise and perhaps developed an initial draft, but before you've come to the place where you're not going to be willing to make any substantial changes.

If you ask for critiques too early, you can smother the idea before it's had a chance to really breathe. If you ask for input too late, it won't do you any good because the story will be full-grown by then, and you likely won't be changing much at that point anyway. Respect everyone's time. Don't ask for feedback that you already know you won't use.

Through it all, remember that this story is your baby and just like having a baby of your own, you'll get lots of advice about how to raise it. In the end, you have to take all of that advice with a grain of salt and raise your child your own way.

332. "WHAT IF I REALIZE THAT MY STORY ISN'T REALLY ABOUT WHAT I THOUGHT IT WAS ABOUT? HOW CAN I SOLVE THAT?"

There's nothing at all wrong with that. You've discovered the true essence of your story. That's something to celebrate, not solve. Make the necessary tweaks. Trust where the story is now instead of trying to revert it back to where you originally thought it would go or to what you originally thought it would say.

333. "SHOULD I FINISH MY FIRST DRAFT AND THEN GO BACK AND EDIT, OR FIX THINGS AS I GO ALONG?"

Many writing instructors will tell you (quite emphatically) to finish your first draft before going back to edit what you've done. Although they have your best interests in mind, be forewarned that following that process can end up being a colossal waste of time.

If you notice a mistake or a plot flaw as you're writing, fix it before it pervades the rest of the story. Make your course corrections when you realize they're needed. Otherwise, because of the contingent nature of fiction, your first draft will take off in the wrong direction, and your story will need to be rebuilt from the ground up.

Every little thing you know about your story that isn't quite right will itch away at your attention. Also, every one of those narrative snags has an implication that affects the story's trajectory. Why not fix the issues when you notice them rather than ignoring them and letting them grow into bigger problems?

It takes a certain amount of mental energy to keep ignoring something that you know you'll need to fix. Resolve the issues when you come across them and move on. Revise as you go so that when you're done with your first draft, you're basically en route to your final draft.

Save time. Keep yourself on the right track. Edit as you go.

334. "WILL MY EDITS REALLY MAKE A

DIFFERENCE?"

Imagine you're a composer, and you're writing a musical score for a movie. You're almost done, but find that there's one note halfway through that doesn't sound quite right. Any astute listener will notice the musical dissonance.

Do you ignore it, or do you fix it? Do you tell yourself, "Well, it's only one note. Not that many people will be able to tell. I'm under a deadline. I need to get this thing done, so I won't worry about it." Or do you resolve it?

It probably doesn't require changing the entire symphony, but it would require you to take into account the surrounding notes, the melody, and the broader context as you address that issue.

And so it is when you edit.

Excellence is within your reach. Strive for it. The goal of editing is to remove the impression that the writing was anything other than effortless.

Keep the melody alive. Stay open to the flow of the story, true to the characters, and flexible about what you've written, but do your best to make sure the symphony is finished before you invite people to listen to it.

Then go and make some more amazing music.

335. "IS PROOFREADING REALLY THAT IMPORTANT?"

Yes. For instance, look at the difference in meaning in each of these examples:

1. When it's time to leave, my wife, she starts doing the dishes.

2. When it's time to leave my wife, she starts doing the dishes.

The first example refers to when the couple is going to leave, and the second to when he's going to divorce her.

1. "Dying is terrible, any way it happens."

2. "Dying is terrible. Anyway, it happens."

In the first, you're emphasizing that however one dies, it's terrible. The second example treats the terrible nature of death dismissively.
Finally:

1. Most of the time, cops look for motives.

2. Most of the time cops look for motives.

In the first case, you're emphasizing that cops often look for motives. In the second, you're telling readers that "time cops" do.

336. "IS IT SMART TO TAKE A BREAK TO FUEL MY BRAIN?"

Give your ideas time to mature. Let them percolate. It's all part of the creative process. It's not wasted time to set your story aside for a while before coming back to it. In fact, it might be just what you need.

If you want your writing to be more honest, go and live a little between drafts. Stroll through the park. Visit the beach. Climb a mountain. Volunteer at a soup kitchen. Spread your wings. Deepen your roots. These journeys into life will give your writing the depth it deserves.

As Henry David Thoreau once said, "How vain it is to sit down to write when you have not stood up to live."

Sometimes, when writers come up with an amazing idea, they dive right in. There's nothing wrong with striking while the iron is hot, but be wary of how much you trust a "brilliant" idea until you've given it time to germinate. Allow the story some space to breathe between drafts. Time buys you context; context provides you with perspective.

337. "WHAT IF I'M A PERFECTIONIST?"

You'll never write a perfect story, so don't even try to. Strive for excellence instead. Pursuing perfection will lead you to become neurotic. Pursuing excellence will bring out the best you have to offer.

PERFECTIONISTS	EXCEPTIONALISTS
Act from a place of fear.	Act from a place of confidence.
Underlying principle: play it safe.	Underlying principle: take risks.
Mantra: "I have to get it right."	Mantra: "I can do it well."
Easily lose perspective.	Change perspective with evolving circumstances.
Can't stand making a mistake.	Can't stand offering less than their best.
Base self-worth on performance.	Don't depend on accolades or applause to feel confident.

Are you trying to write an exceptional story or a perfect one? Only one of the two will ever be within your reach.

338. "SHOULD I FOLLOW MARKET TRENDS?

Don't follow trends, or you'll always be behind them. Write a brilliant, moving, poignant story. Let the trends follow you.

339. "WHAT ABOUT ADAPTING A NOVEL INTO A SCREENPLAY, OR VICE VERSA? ANY TIPS?"

Since movies are more visual (external) and novels often include internalization in the minds of the characters, not all novels translate well into film. Unless you rely on a voiceover, you'll need to physicalize all internal struggles when translating a novel into a screenplay.

There's always a reductive quality to transferring from one art form to another. In other words, you'll always lose something that the first art form offers when you move it to another one. It'll have to be changed, and in that change, it must conform to the limitations of the second art form.

So, be ready for changes that might be a little uncomfortable at first. Just remember, though, that it's all in the service of more effectively telling your story to your new audience in that new medium.

340. "HOW DO I KNOW THIS STORY WILL KEEP ME INTERESTED UNTIL I FINISH WRITING IT?"

All creative endeavors require a degree of trust. Don't ask yourself which idea you should use; ask yourself, "Where is my passion leading me?" When you examine the questions and deep beliefs you have about the world, your work will be more honest and authentic.

Some people will tell you to "write what you know," and that's good advice—if you're writing a cookbook or a chapter in a medical textbook on how to perform brain surgery. But if you're writing a novel, don't write about what you know. Write about what you question, what you're curious about, what you care about, what you marvel at.

Often there's little tension in what you know, so there's little drama in it. However, if you can identify conflicting beliefs that you have, deep questions that you and others are asking, or if you can delve into moral dilemmas that reveal priorities and blind spots, you have the essence of tension. Which means you have the impetus for a great story. Ask yourself...

- Is my heart really in this project? If not, how can I care more about my readers by caring more about my characters?

- Am I writing this because I believe that the readers will benefit from it, or just because I want them to read it?

- Can readers sense my passion on the pages of this book?

Every story that matters was desperate in some way to be told. Consider why this story is begging you to be told. Where is it leading you? What voices in this story can't keep quiet? What about this story speaks from the true place, the necessary place, the quiet and urgent and vital place in you—the place that's on fire?

Find that place.
Listen to that voice.
And set that story loose on the world.

341. "OKAY, BUT WHAT IF I REALIZE THAT I'M NOT REALLY MOTIVATED ANYMORE ABOUT THE PROJECT I'M WORKING ON. SHOULD I ABANDON IT?"

A few thoughts:

1. In every writing project there are moments (or days or weeks or years) when the work becomes drudgery, when you need to slog forward even though you don't feel inspired or particularly motivated. Don't give up on something just because it has become difficult to continue. Soldier on.

2. There's often a tradeoff between artistic expression and financial gain. Sometimes, the stupidest ideas make loads of money while committed artists toil away for years in obscurity and poverty, trying to be true to their art. If this project can make you enough money to pursue your art without financial pressure, then it's worth considering continuing. Some people write for a paycheck, and others for personal fulfillment. Be careful not to judge but also to strive for excellence, whatever your ultimate motivation might be.

3. Find yourself in the story. What makes you weep? What makes you enraged? What keeps you up at night? What wakes you up in the morning? What would you be willing to sacrifice your life (or your freedom) for? Your passion can often prod you past the difficult hours of work on a project.

4. Through it all, remember that life is short and uncertain. If you're not working in a career that brings you joy or satisfaction, you might be in the wrong one, even if you're good at it.

342. "WHAT IF I'M NOT AN EXPERT ON LITERATURE—CAN I STILL MAKE IT AS AN AUTHOR?"

Of course.

In truth, you already know what to include in your story. Just think about the things that cause you to lose interest when you're reading stories by others: whiny main characters, dull and boring scenes, confusing or convoluted plots, shallow, trite, preachy diatribes, and so on.

Okay. So don't include that stuff.

You're here to give birth to a story, and you don't need to be an expert on story anatomy to do that. Just because a person knows how to dissect something, it doesn't mean that he understands how to bring it to life. As William Wordsworth wrote, "We murder to dissect." You're not here to lay a tale under your knife and pick it apart. Leave the dissecting to others.

343. "I'VE BEEN TOLD TO READ EVERYTHING I CAN—BOTH GOOD AND BAD WRITING. IS THAT HELPFUL ADVICE?"

While it's true that you can learn from bad writing—just like you can learn about football by watching your favorite team get blown out—there's the entertainment value to keep in mind, as well as the prudent use of your time.

If you're reading bad writing, yes, you might be learning, but you won't likely be enjoying the story. And that can, eventually, diminish your interest in reading the good stuff and turn you off from reading.

Give yourself permission to bail from a book if the writer shows you that she can't hold your attention or isn't at the top of her game. Often, writers spend the most time honing the beginning of their books, so if you're reading a story that lags early on and you're hoping it'll get better in the middle, you're probably putting your faith in something that isn't going to pan out all that well.

You don't need to be a literary snob to be offended by poor writing. Opt for excellence instead, both in what you read and in what you write.

Read the good stuff. Life is too short to waste it on stories that should never have been published in the first place.

344. "BUT SHOULDN'T A WRITER READ A LOT?"

There's nothing wrong with reading a lot; just don't expect to become a better writer by doing it.

Expecting to learn writing by reading is like telling an athlete, "If you want to be a great swimmer, you should watch the Olympics. If you want to be a better runner, tune in to watch a marathon." To improve, they need to jump into the water or put in the long hours on the lonely, open road.

Reading and writing are cousins. They're as closely related as riding in an airplane and building one.

Spend more time working at your craft and valuing the precious time you spend reading, but don't expect to become a more proficient writer while doing so. Don't use reading as a means to an end; it's an end in itself. And so is writing. To reiterate once again: Set aside the bad writing and delve into something more worth your while.

345. "SHOULD I JOIN A WRITERS' CRITIQUE

GROUP?"

Not necessarily. Most of the time, the members of these groups aren't experts. Since most professional writers are too busy making a living writing, they don't usually have the time or inclination to join critique groups.

If you do join one, take what other members of the group tell you with some circumspection. It seems like in almost every group, you'll find the same five people:

- The Monday Morning Quarterback: He wants to solve what he perceives to be your story's problems. He's always giving advice on what you should do with your manuscript, which basically means what he would do if it were his story.

- The Comma Queen: She has a checklist of punctuation pet peeves and wants everyone to know what they are. Somehow, she'll find a place on every page to add more commas.

- The Self-Proclaimed Expert: He went to a writing conference last year, blogs about his German Shepherd, and has self-published three books, so he knows it all—or at least he thinks he does.

- The Jaded Criticizer: No matter how good your work is, he'll find something wrong with it. He's the guy with the permanent scowl and the red pen.

- The Kindly Grandma: No matter how bad your work is, she'll always find something good about it. She'll probably bring freshly baked cookies to the group. Almost certainly, she'll own a cat.

Accept that those people are as flawed as you are and will see your work through the lens of their own preconceptions, goals, and attitudes. If you decide to bring your work to a group like this, be aware that you'll get lots of contradictory advice and not necessarily the best guidance.

346. "IF I DO JOIN ONE, HOW CAN WE MAKE IT A MORE POSITIVE EXPERIENCE?"

Instead of regarding the critique group as a place where writers go to get advice, think of it as a place where they go to get feedback. Group members aren't there to share their opinion of the writer's work but rather their reaction to it.

For example, rather than telling the writer, "You need to make the villain scarier" (advice), the person might say, "The villain didn't really scare me that much" (feedback).

Here's the key: Group members aren't there to critique the writing but to encounter it and respond.

Also, their goal isn't to find instances where the writer has broken a "rule." Rather, they'll help pinpoint the places where their engagement with the story was disrupted. It's up to the author to take that input and use it as he wishes, keeping in mind the broader context of his work.

How you frame things matters. Most people thrive on affirmation but get discouraged when they're criticized. So, direct your comments toward the writing, not the writer. Instead, of "I hated how you had the main character insult that homeless man," you might say, "I stopped caring about the main character when he insulted that homeless man," or, "It was hard for me to like the protagonist when he said those things."

347. "HOW CAN I DO A BETTER JOB OF GIVING FEEDBACK TO OTHER WRITERS?"

Avoid giving advice and instead focus on what confused you, what promises you felt were being made, what distracted you from the story, or where your expectations went in the wrong direction.

- Consistency: "I'm confused. I thought the waitress was red-haired. Did she change her hair color?"
- Setting: "I'm having a hard time picturing this scene. I might have missed something—I thought there were four people in the room, not three. What happened to Charlie?"
- Continuity: "Two pages earlier, Francesca picked up the gun. Is she still carrying it? Did she set it down, and I just didn't notice?"
- Escalation: "That dream sequence made me really worried, but then when the guy woke up, everything was solved, and the tension was gone."
- Promises / payoff: "With so many details about the woman's knife collection, I thought it would be vital to the story, but then it never came up again."
- Dialogue: "Both characters used the same idioms. They sounded the same to me when they spoke."
- Polish: "This section at the end seems less fleshed out and detailed than the rest of the scene."

Don't attack, and don't advise. Avoid value judgments (e.g., "This is a piece of crap"), but feel free to offer positive comments:

- "I thought it was cool how that engagement ring became such an important clue in the end."
- "That description of the mist-enshrouded forest seemed really vivid to me."
- "When she was walking alone through the parking garage, I could really feel the suspense. I didn't want her

to get killed."

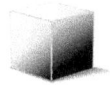

348. "WHAT CAN I, AS AN AUTHOR, DO TO HELP MY CRITIQUE PARTNERS DO A BETTER JOB?"

No clarifying or defending. Here's the key: The point of the critique time isn't to make others understand your narrative choices; it's to help you understand what those choices are communicating to readers.

Don't equate the number of comments or the amount of feedback with how good your work is. The information others provide doesn't necessarily correspond to the *quality* of your writing but rather the *clarity* of your writing.

After people have shared their feedback, you can ask for clarification about any comments you didn't understand. Then, you can ask follow-up questions that will help you better understand your readers' experience with the text. Here are ten key areas you might address:

1. Character Intention: "Based on what you know, what would you say this character wants in this scene?"

2. Inner Logic: "Did the ending seem contrived to you, or did it make sense?"

3. Believability: "Did you feel like this character would really do these things, or were there times he acted in a way that seemed unbelievable?"

4. Causality: "What step do you think he would naturally take next?"

5. Anticipation: "As a reader, what would you be hoping will happen next?"

6. Concern: "What would you be worried about?"

7. Expectation: "What do you expect?"

8. Engagement: "What might disappoint you if it happened in the following pages?"

9. Confusion: "What questions are you left with?"

10. Authorial Intrusion: "Where was your engagement with the story disrupted?"

To conclude the session, if you desire, you can ask for help brainstorming solutions to plot problems. For instance, "I'm looking for a way to show how angry this guy is. Does anybody have any suggestions?" At this point, group members can say, "You could..." However, the phrases "I would..." or "You should..." are off-limits.

Time is a gift, so be appreciative that the people in your group are willing to invest some of their precious time trying to help you become more successful. End by thanking them for their feedback.

349. "ANY FINAL SUGGESTIONS OR REMINDERS FOR CRITIQUING?"

Reminders for those giving feedback: (1) Provide responsive feedback rather than criticism or advice, (2) Help the writer understand how readers are experiencing the text, (3) Target comments toward the writing rather than the writer. If you're giving feedback, you may say:

- "I started to get lost here."
- "I'm having a hard time picturing this."
- "I'm confused by..."

- "Here's what I was hoping for at this moment…"

But you may not say…

- "You could…"
- "You should…"
- "I would…"
- "If I were you, I'd…"

Reminders for the writer: (1) Provide context and specific direction before getting started, (2) Avoid taking anything that's said personally, (3) Don't defend, clarify, or explain your narrative choices. If you're receiving feedback, you may say:

- "Thank you. That's helpful."
- "I understand."
- "I see where you're coming from."
- "That makes sense."

But you may not say…

- "But I was…"
- "I wanted to…"
- "I was trying to…"
- "That'll make sense later when…"
- "But that's true, that part really happened!"

350. "I'M AFRAID PEOPLE WON'T LIKE MY STORY. IS THERE SOMETHING WRONG WITH ME?"

Not at all. Many authors battle with fear and self-doubt.

Wherever you find art, you'll find fear not too far behind, standing, grinning in the shadows. It might be fear of rejection and failure, or fear of embarrassment, or fear that the high school English teacher who told you that you couldn't write to save your life was right.

But it's there.

Fear.

Hungry, hungry fear.

Risk is inherent in creativity. Trust that the fear of the unknown is there to help motivate you, and don't become intimidated by it.

The creation of a work of art is always a foray into the unknown. It requires a choice to throw a shoulder against the dark forces of distraction and defeat that stand sentry at the entrance of the creative path, to muscle past them, and to see the project through to the end.

Don't write to be remembered. Don't write to impress. Don't write to prove something—anything—to anyone. Write to serve your readers.

If you focus your attention in that direction rather than dwelling on yourself and your doubts and fears, you'll have taken the first and most important step a storyteller can take—putting your readers first.

APPENDIX A

THE STORY CUBE

CHARACTER

1. **Status** – Does it vary in different social contexts? Is it sustained when challenged?

2. **Identification** – Will readers care about this character? Will they relate to her struggles?

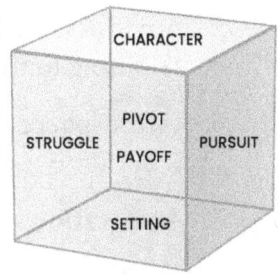

3. **Uniqueness** – Is she someone readers will want to spend time with? What dichotomies or incongruities make her irresistible or remarkable?

4. **Value** – How is she Vulnerable, Admirable, Layered, Unforgettable, and Engaging?

5. **Credulity** – Does she always act in believable ways?

6. **Choices** – Does she exhibit wit, grit, or valor while making high-stakes, meaningful decisions? Is there an

unprecedented sacrifice at the climax?

Remember: The main character will need to be fascinating, intriguing, and have a struggle that readers will care about and, ideally, identify with. She will be vulnerable but not fragile, admirable but not perfect, and unforgettable but not annoying.

Voice comes through more in the distinctive manner in which you tell the story than in what elements the story contains. However, if the character is also the narrator, her voice will come through in her narrative style and word choices. We like to cheer for underdogs. We like characters we can relate to, that are flawed and vulnerable but have the best interests of others at heart.

SETTING

1. **Lucidity** – Is the setting in time and space clear?

2. **Vividness** – Is it evocative? Are details and descriptions contributing to the emotional core of the story?

3. **Atmosphere** – Does the setting enhance the mood of the story (or does it undermine it)?

4. **Integration** – Is the setting vital to this story?

5. **Fusion** – In what ways does the setting hinder or contribute to the character's pursuit?

6. **Subtext** – Does the setting serve to facilitate the truest meaning of this scene?

Remember: The setting is how readers will picture the main character's pursuit. It should enhance the story and provide enough evocative sensory details to draw readers deeper into each scene. Let it be vivid, evocative, and either an asset to the protagonist or a hindrance to him in his pursuit.

STRUGGLE

1. **Initiation** – Does the central struggle originate through a crisis or calling?

2. **Opposition** – Are the forces of antagonism formidable? Do they adequately hinder the character as she tries to obtain her object of desire, avoid danger, overcome challenges, withstand hardship, or avenge a wrong?

3. **Dimensionality** – Are there imperative struggles in each of the three realms (internal, external, and interpersonal)?

4. **Escalation** – Does the tension tighten as the struggle deepens?

5. **Snare** – How do setbacks and dilemmas force the protagonist into a corner?

6. **Forge** – What does the struggle reveal about the character's true nature, priorities, or abilities? Does she change, or does she emerge?

Remember: The stakes will matter, and the struggle/s will deepen as the character faces more and more intimate setbacks and higher-stakes dilemmas that create more tension. If the solution is too easy, too predictable, or too outlandish, readers won't be satisfied.

PURSUIT

1. **Causality** – Are events sufficiently caused—that is, do they have an adequate impetus? Then, do they result in a natural result of their own?

2. **Goals** – Does intention (rather than motivation) influence each choice?

3. **Coherence** – Is the pursuit logical, discernible, and based primarily on the character's unmet desire?

4. **Sacrifice** – Does the character make difficult decisions or suffer meaningful loss?

5. **Ambush** – Could things get believably worse? If so, why don't they?

6. **Closure** – Will the resolution feel honest to readers? Is it the natural and purposeful culmination of all that precedes it?

Remember: A story, at its core, involves a pursuit that readers will care about because the main character cares about it—and they care about her. That concern will evoke emotion and invite more intimate reader engagement.

PIVOT

1. **Surprise** – What will startle readers, stun them, or take them unaware in this scene? What doesn't go according to plan?

2. **Camouflage** – What isn't as it appears to be? Who isn't what they appear to be?

3. **Duality** – What events carry within them the potential for multiple interpretations?

4. **Despair** – Is there a moment at which all seems lost?

(A story can end with the moment at which all seems lost.)

5. **Twists** – Is the ending of this scene (or story) inevitable, unexpected, revelatory, and satisfying?

6. **Cleverness** – How do the character's observational skills or her quick thinking (rather than chance or coincidence) contribute to the pivot?

Remember: The story will pivot past the struggle to the climax, most often through a sacrificial or significant choice of the main character. Avoid *Deus ex Machina*, in which someone else shows up and rescues the protagonist in his time of need. Through dramatic irony, readers might know more than the characters do at certain points in the story, but at the pivot, they'll often be one step behind the characters.

Can readers take everything at face value? If so, you don't have an opportunity to surprise them. Readers want stories in which there is more to the scenes than meets the eye.

PAYOFF

1. **Resonance** – What aspect of this story is desperate to be told or impossible to ignore? Is the story thought-provoking even if it doesn't have a happy ending?

2. **Value** – What makes this story worthwhile? Does it (1) entertain, and (2) do more than simply entertain?

3. **Truth** – Is the story honest about human nature and morality? What is justified? What is condemned? Is there sufficient hope, redemption, or shock at the climax?

4. **Depth** – Does the story mean more than it says? Can we overhear an unforeseen truth? Is action imbued with deeper meaning? Is the takeaway unstated and yet unforgettable?

5. **Fulfillment** – Are all of the relevant and pressing narrative promises kept?

6. **Culmination** – Is there sufficient character revelation or transformation shown (or hinted at) when the story closes?

Remember: Payoff can happen in the same moment as the pivot. (For instance, in a short story with a twist ending.) Payoff will look different depending on the story's shape and genre. (The payoff for a cozy mystery is much different than that of a rom-com or a horror story.) The payoff might include an unstated theme that grows naturally from action and context. It might also contain an ingenious or elegant intersection of multiple, apparently disparate, storylines.

Forget for a moment about theme, symbolism, and imagery. Instead, focus on the overall impact of your story. Write only with the agenda of telling the truth, not of convincing anyone of anything. As long as honesty is your goal, you'll be on track. If you start trying to manipulate people into agreeing with you, then you've opted for propaganda instead of storytelling. Is there a resonant, emotional core at the heart of the story? Will readers be moved by the story, even if they can't explain why?

This is what you're shooting for.

So...introduce us to a memorable and irresistible character who faces a pressing and intimate struggle. Give her choices and sacrifices that matter. Invite us to see the pursuit unfold in an evocative setting. Then, lead us to gasp at the pivot and to nod at the unforgettable payoff.[1]

Delve. Pivot. Propel.

Write stories like this, and you'll have readers knocking at your door, begging for your next book.

---

1 James, Steven, Morrisey, Tom; "THE ART OF THE TALE," 2022

APPENDIX B

100-POINT NOVEL WRITING CHECKLIST

1. **Acts** – Does my story have three easily discernible acts? If so, how will I recast things so the story isn't so formulaic and predictable?

2. **Adjectives** – Am I relying too much on adjectives and adverbs, or am I using nouns and verbs to ground my story?

3. **Antagonism** – If I have external, impersonal forces of antagonism, can I personify them in the eyes of the protagonist so it seems like the tornado is actually targeting him or that the desert is plotting against him?

4. **Apprehension** – Have I revealed enough about any impending peril or threats to create suspense rather than keeping readers in the dark and confusing them?

5. **Attitude** – Will the protagonist's attitude draw readers in or turn them off? Does he have a unique perspective on the events of the story that will make readers smile or nod?

6. **Backstory** – Is the backstory that's included essential to this story, or is it included just for authorial reasons? If it's unnecessary, what do I need to cut?

7. **Barriers** – What's holding my character back from becoming (or embracing) who he truly is? Does the barrier lie mainly inside of him, or is it more external/societal? What would cause him to overcome that obstacle, however resistant he might be at first?

8. **Beliefs** – As a result of this story, what central belief of the main character will be tested or changed? What revelation will occur? What lesson will she learn, or what skill will she acquire?

9. **Believability** – Is everything immediately believable within the story's context? If not, is that pointed out to the readers with a good reason for why things aren't more credible?

10. **Body language** – Have I used a variety of body language references when necessary rather than just "he nodded," or "she shook her head," and so on? Does each movement make sense and contribute to the story, or does it distract from it?

11. **Breaks** – Do my chapter and section endings propel the narrative, or do I include too much closure?

12. **Brevity** – Does brevity serve this genre, and if so, are there any unnecessary words? How can I recast the story to cut them?

13. **Causality** – Have I addressed all glitches in causality or believability (that is, all plot flaws)? What's encroaching on the story's contingency? How will I tackle that?

14. **Choices** – What's on my protagonist's mind? What would his most reasonable next step be? Am I letting his

choices grow from context or from pretext—that is, what he would do or what I want him to do?

15. **Clarity** – Is it clear what the protagonist wants in every scene? Have I allowed him to either tell readers or show them what he wants so they can worry about whether or not he gets it?

16. **Climax** – Does the appropriate amount of story happen after the climax? How can I end the story more quickly while also keeping all of my vital promises in a way that satisfies readers?

17. **Closure** – What do I currently know that readers won't know until the last line of the story? What's the final secret? The final reveal?

18. **Cohesion** – Are all actions completed in appropriate ways? Have I left any action sequences unfinished?

19. **Complications** – How can I add more meaningful and believable complications? What are some ways I can make my protagonist face escalating challenges as the story progresses?

20. **Conflation** – Are there multiple characters who play the same role in this story? How can I shrink the number by conflating them to create a briefer, leaner, and tighter tale?

21. **Context** – Does context determine content? Does every paragraph, every sentence, every word belong and serve the story?

22. **Continuity** – Does the narrative jump around too much, or does it move logically and reasonably forward? Are there any continuity errors that will jar readers or move them out of the story?

23. **Deadlines** – Does a deadline or countdown ratchet up

the tension toward the climax? If not, would it make sense to add one?

24. **Description** – Am I using moving, poignant, succinct descriptions for the characters and the setting? Are the descriptions evocative so readers won't just be able to see the scenes but also feel something about them?

25. **Desire** – Is the overriding desire of the protagonist clear throughout the story—either stated outright or unequivocally shown through action?

26. **Details** – Are the details and descriptions significant, revelatory, and entertaining? Do they make promises in congruence with what's actually important in the story?

27. **Dialogue** – Does the dialogue sound realistic and reveal aspects of each character's personality as well as her history, attitude, and goals toward the other characters?

28. **Disruption** – Is there a clear moment of crisis or calling early in the story that tips the world of the protagonist upside down or initiates his entrance into the story's pursuit in an unambiguous way?

29. **Emotion** – What emotion does this character, event, setting, or struggle evoke in my protagonist? How will he respond to that? What choice will it result in?

30. **Empathy** – Will readers really care about this story? If not, how can I give the characters more of a deep human wound or desire that we all share?

31. **Escalation** – Does the story escalate in tension as the object of desire becomes more difficult to obtain? Do the struggles become more and more pressing, personal, and vitally important as the story progresses? How can I handle sections of de-escalation?

32. **Evocation** – Does my writing both evoke and render?

Are the details meaningful and introduced in ways that add to the story?

33. **Expectation** – Have I anticipated what readers are worrying about, wondering about, hoping for, and expecting in each scene? Have I given them what they want or something better?

34. **Flashbacks** – Are the flashbacks essential, or will readers simply skip past them? What changes do I need to make?

35. **Flow** – Are pace and flow working together as the story progresses? Is the progression too choppy and uneven or appropriate for this genre?

36. **Focus** – Does the prose wander too much? How can I sharpen my story and keep it from going off track?

37. **Foreshadowing** – Have I used foreshadowing to remove coincidences throughout the story? Are my instances of foreshadowing contextually appropriate for the scenes in which they occur, or are they too identifiable?

38. **Goals** – Is it clear to readers what this character wants to achieve, obtain, or avoid, what's stopping him, and how far he will go to reach his goal?

39. **Homecomings** – Does my story circle back on itself at the end (showing a homecoming) or reveal a transformation (a journey)? If it's a circular plot, how can I foreshadow the ending better? If it's a linear plot, how can I more subtly promise how things will change?

40. **Honesty** – Have I told the complex truth about the world, or am I propagating a trite and clichéd axiom like "Follow your heart," "Pursue your dreams," or "Be true to yourself"? What will I change to deepen the story's honesty about life?

41. **Hopelessness** – Have I included a dark moment right

before the climax—one in which all seems lost—and then resolved it through a difficult and unpredictable choice or sacrifice that the main character makes?

42. **Identification** – Does the central struggle of the protagonist portray a universal enough desire that my readers will identify with it? If not, how can I sharpen it or broaden it enough to allow for deeper reader identification?

43. **Identity** – What doesn't the protagonist realize yet about himself? What will it take for him to recognize it? How will he resist that knowledge? How will it change him when he finally comes to accept it?

44. **Impressions** – How does the setting make the characters feel? How can I better show the psychological effect of the environments they encounter?

45. **Individuality** – Do my characters act in consistent ways within the social contexts in which they appear? Do their phrases, habits, and speech patterns serve to solidify their personalities, desires, and attitudes?

46. **Inevitability** – Does the plot escalate inevitably? If there are gaps in logic, how can I address those by foreshadowing, weaving in appropriate motivation, or drawing from backstory?

47. **Intentionality** – Are the characters' intentions clear in each scene, or does action occur without clarity as to what the characters want? How can I more smoothly or effectively let readers in on the intentions of the characters?

48. **Interludes** – During the interludes between scenes, have I made or kept a promise? Are the interludes the right length to allow the characters to process what has happened, but not so long that they detract from or slow down the story too much?

49. **Intersection** – Do the pathways of the protagonist and antagonist intersect at times throughout the book? If not, how can I insert instances of that in a way that isn't clichéd?

50. **Introductions** – Have I paced the introduction of my central characters appropriately? Is the protagonist brought "onstage" early enough?

51. **Intrusion** – Have I resisted the urge to explain, or have I ended up showing off my research? Did I try to be clever or impressive? How can I change those sections so they're no longer intrusive?

52. **Isolation** – If appropriate for my genre, does the protagonist become more and more isolated as the climax approaches? Have I removed his assets and helpers to allow him to face the forces of antagonism alone at the climax?

53. **Logic** – Does this scene require readers to set reason aside? If so, how can I recast it or alter their expectations about this story and what's reasonable within it?

54. **Longing** – Have I written evocatively and honestly enough to create yearning on behalf of my readers toward my protagonist? If not, how can I write with more emotional resonance?

55. **Mentors** – Who is significant in contributing to the main character's pursuit? How will this person serve to motivate or better equip the protagonist to face the forces of antagonism?

56. **Minutia** – Do I focus too much on the minutia of people's body language (furrowing eyebrows, widening eyes, etc.) rather than trusting readers to picture those actions for themselves?

57. **Momentum** – Does the narrative momentum move the

story forward in the right ways at the right times? Does the pace contribute to the story or undermine it?

58. **Moral clarity** – Does my story have a moral footing, or is it sinking into a moral morass?

59. **Moral dilemmas** – Have I developed the story around moral dilemmas rather than stale narrative gimmicks? Will readers feel the tension that the characters face when they have to make difficult and meaningful moral choices?

60. **Narration** – Are the sections of exposition fleshed out enough, and do they move the story forward at an appropriate pace? Are there ways that I can better portray the actions and reactions of the characters in each scene?

61. **Opening** – Does my story begin with a strong enough hook that sets up accurate promises about the direction of the story, its genre, and (if appropriate) the forces of antagonism?

62. **Orientation** – Have I oriented readers to the protagonist, his world, and his pursuit at the appropriate time in the story? Will readers picture him in this setting, care about his condition, and cheer for him?

63. **Peril** – Can I introduce more promises about the peril that the characters will be in or the dangers they'll be facing? What are they at risk of losing? Why would that loss matter?

64. **Perspective** – What's going through the protagonist's mind at the climax? Not just how does he react to the situation, but how does the situation affect his attitude, perspective, or intentions?

65. **Physicality** – Have I trusted readers to picture the

characters while also providing them enough clues about their physicality? Have I used motion and action to help reveal characterization?

66. **Promises** – Have I kept every promise that I've made—both big ones and small ones?

67. **Protagonist** – Is it clear who the protagonist is? Is she someone that readers will be attracted to, despite her flaws? What is she trying to obtain, avoid, overcome, withstand, or avenge? What will happen if she's successful? What will happen if she fails?

68. **Pursuit** – What is my character pursuing? Is she on a journey of self-discovery? Of self-denial in the service of something greater? Of self-revelation as she rises to the challenge?

69. **Relationships** – Is the protagonist enmeshed in a web of meaningful relationships that serve to reveal aspects of his characterization or backstory?

70. **Repetition** – Is there too much repetition undermining the story's escalation?

71. **Research** – Did I fact-check everything?

72. **Resolution** – Is each point-of-view character's storyline complete? If they affect or are affected by the protagonist's pursuit, is it clear how?

73. **Revelation** – Does the story serve to both reveal and alter the characterization of the protagonist? Is the balance right for my genre of story?

74. **Revisions** – Is the story moving? Is there magic on the page? Can I read through the manuscript one more time, looking for ways to advance it from being simply memorable to life-transforming?

75. **Romance** – Have I developed romantic tension? Are

the characters acting in believable ways even as they seek each other's embrace?

76. **Sacrifice** – What will my protagonist give up during his pursuit? Why will it be costly to him? What message does that give to readers?

77. **Scenes** – Did my character achieve what he set out to achieve? If so, was it too easy, or did his success provide too much resolution at this point in the story? If he didn't reach his goal, how does the scene's tension escalate? Was the scene just filler, or did it dial up the tension?

78. **Setbacks** – Have I used setbacks to move things forward?

79. **Setting** – Is the setting integrally woven into the narrative? If not, how can I make it indispensable so I couldn't just pick up the story and plop it into another location?

80. **Showing** – Have I ended up using too much description, that is, telling rather than showing? If so, how can I recast those sections?

81. **Special skills** – Does the protagonist use his special ability or emblem to solve the primary external struggle? If not, would that add to the unity or cohesion of the story? If so, how can I foreshadow the use of the tool or skill so it feels organic to the story and not simply forced in?

82. **Stakes** – Is something vital at stake? If not, where do I need to raise the stakes by clarifying the consequences of the character's failure to achieve what they set out to do?

83. **Status** – Does my protagonist have dimensionality by experiencing different degrees of status in a variety of social contexts? Is the status balanced for each scene so the protagonist exhibits more substantive status by his choices than the antagonist?

84. **Struggles** – When introducing the three central struggles—internal, external, and interpersonal—have I included the initiation of at least one of them on the pages of the novel? If not, how can I recast the story to make that happen?

85. **Subplots** – Do the different subplots (that is, storylines) resolve at times that make sense to the story, retain the story's overall tension, and satisfactorily keep their inherent narrative promises?

86. **Subtext** – Is there appropriate subtext for this genre? In other words, are the scenes about what the scenes appear to be about, or is there some deeper truth or character revelation that's made clear in each scene—especially in romantic encounters?

87. **Suspense** – Does the story develop apprehension born of concern? Are there moments during which readers will worry about the main character? How can I shape those moments to be more poignant?

88. **Sympathy** – Does sympathy for the protagonist exist? Will readers feel an emotional connection to her? If not, can I give her a deeper internal struggle to draw readers in? How can I entice readers to admire her or desire to be like her?

89. **Tension** – Have I made sure that my story is tension-driven rather than trying to make it "plot-driven" or "character-driven"?

90. **Themes** – Are themes and symbols (if they're present) organic to the story, unobtrusive, and in the service of readers rather than just meaningful to me?

91. **Timing** – If I used point-of-view flips, did I use them to the advantage of the story? Have I kept in mind that time passes for everyone in the story at the same rate? If not,

what changes do I need to make?

92. **Tone** – Are the mood and tone appropriate for this genre of story? Did I undermine any scenes by trying to add humor where it didn't belong?

93. **Transitions** – Are the transitions between different settings properly motivated by the events of the story, do they move the story forward, and are they smooth and sensible?

94. **Trust** – Have I trusted the readers to thread together the strands of the story, or did I insult them by explaining too much?

95. **Twists** – Are there twists that reveal deeper meaning to the scenes that precede them, or am I depending on cheap tricks to make the twists work? Does every scene, as well as the story as a whole, end in a way that is both surprising and satisfying?

96. **Unmet desire** – Is the narrative driven forward by the characters' unmet desire? How can I make that desire clearer throughout the story?

97. **Unpredictability** – What would an astute reader anticipate or predict will happen at the climax? What would make sense but also be unexpected? Is there a way I can pivot the scene or the story into a new and more unforeseen direction?

98. **Viewpoint** – Is it clear when the point of view switches? Does each point-of-view character have a unique perspective or voice? If not, how will I address that?

99. **Voice** – Is the narrator's voice appropriate for the story and consistent throughout it?

100. **Vulnerability** – Have I made the protagonist's vulnerabilities and blind spots known to readers? How can

I do a better job of showing those vulnerabilities without undermining the character's status?

ABOUT THE AUTHOR

Steven James is one of the country's premier fiction instructors. He is the critically acclaimed author of twenty novels and dozens of nonfiction books and has served for many years as a contributing editor to *Writer's Digest Magazine*. His previous three books on the craft of writing and storytelling were all recipients of Storytelling World Awards (*Story Trumps Structure, Troubleshooting Your Novel, The Art of the Tale*).

Steven's books have won or been shortlisted for more than a dozen national and international awards, and his articles and stories have appeared in more than eighty publications including *The New York Times*.

Steven earned a master's degree in storytelling from ETSU in 1997. Since then, he has taught writing and storytelling principles at events spanning the globe, appearing more than two thousand times on five continents. He is a regular keynote speaker and workshop teacher at writing conferences and retreats throughout North America.

He lives in Tennessee in the foothills of the Appalachian Mountains. When he's not writing or speaking, you'll find him hiking, playing basketball, or downing bottomless mugs of dark roast coffee.

Visit his official website at www.stevenjames.net
Follow him on social media @readstevenjames.
Subscribe to his weekly podcast The Story Blender.

STORY TRUMPS STRUCTURE

Fiction Key Series Vol. 2

DON'T LIMIT YOUR FICTION – LIBERATE IT

All too often, following the "rules" of writing can constrict rather than inspire you. With Story Trumps Structure, you can shed those rules—about three-act structure, rising action, outlining, and more—to craft your most powerful, emotional, and gripping stories.

When you focus on what lies at the heart of story – tension, desire, crisis, escalation, struggle, discovery – rather than plot templates and formulas, you'll begin to break out of the box and write fiction that resonates with your readers. *Story Trumps Structure* will transform the way you think about stories and the way you write them, forever.

Winner of the 2015 Storytelling World Award

TROUBLESHOOTING YOUR NOVEL

Fiction Key Series Vol. 3

TROUBLESHOOTING YOUR NOVEL WILL TAKE YOUR STORY TO THE NEXT LEVEL OF EXCELLENCE.

Let an award-winning novelist guide you through the process of making your book the best it can be.

By building on the principles and theoretical framework laid out in *Story Trumps Structure*, this book moves to the hands-on level with checklists, timesaving hints and tricks of the trade, and hundreds of questions for manuscript analysis and revision.

Concise, practical, and easy-to-use. Each chapter stands alone so you can flip to the section you need, identify a specific problem, and address it.

Before you publish your novel, make sure you've tackled all of those nagging plot problems, addressed any narrative weaknesses, and developed your characters as deeply as you can. Raise the bar. Troubleshoot your novel.

Winner of the 2018 Storytelling World Award

www.ingramcontent.com/pod-product-compliance
Lightning Source LLC
LaVergne TN
LVHW050738040325
805000LV00016B/101